Inclusive Education in Italy

STUDIES IN INCLUSIVE EDUCATION

Volume no. 10

Scope
This series addresses the many different forms of exclusion that occur in schooling across a range of international contexts and considers strategies for increasing the inclusion and success of all students. In many school jurisdictions the most reliable predictors of educational failure include poverty, Aboriginality and disability. Traditionally schools have not been pressed to deal with exclusion and failure. Failing students were blamed for their lack of attainment and were either placed in segregated educational settings or encouraged to leave and enter the unskilled labour market. The crisis in the labor market and the call by parents for the inclusion of their children in their neighborhood school has made visible the failure of schools to include all children.

Drawing from a range of researchers and educators from around the world, Studies in Inclusive Education will demonstrate the ways in which schools contribute to the failure of different student identities on the basis of gender, race, language, sexuality, disability, socio-economic status and geographic isolation. This series differs from existing work in inclusive education by expanding the focus from a narrow consideration of what has been traditionally referred to as special educational needs to understand school failure and exclusion in all its forms. Moreover, the series will consider exclusion and inclusion across all sectors of education: early years, elementary and secondary schooling, and higher education.

Inclusive Education in Italy

A Critical Analysis of the Policy of Integrazione Scolastica

Simona D'Alessio
Institute of Education, University of London, UK

SENSE PUBLISHERS
ROTTERDAM/BOSTON/TAIPEI

A C.I.P. record for this book is available from the Library of Congress.

ISBN: 978-94-6091-340-2 (paperback)
ISBN: 978-94-6091-341-9 (hardback)
ISBN: 978-94-6091-342-6 (e-book)

Published by: Sense Publishers,
P.O. Box 21858,
3001 AW Rotterdam,
The Netherlands
www.sensepublishers.com

Printed on acid-free paper

DEDICATION

I would like to thank all the teachers, students and head teachers of the schools I visited, whose participation made this research possible and to whom this book is dedicated.

TABLE OF CONTENTS

FOREWORD

Inclusive education is a serious and contentious issue which increasing numbers of societies are attempting to address. The nature of the challenge and the degree of the complexities involved in seeking to gain an informed knowledge and understanding of such developments, is more demanding when set within a cross-cultural dimension. The task includes the exploration of historical, empirical and policy concerns and despite the extent of the work undertaken, we still have very little knowledge and understanding in relation to other societies.

Studies of particular societies are thus an urgent and fundamental necessity particularly if as, D'Alessio maintains we are to:

> ...attempt to shake the conscience from the lethargy of rhetoric and to open up dialogues and possibilities concerning different types of research that presuppose critical engagement and envision radical thinking. (p. 166)

This book, *Inclusive education in Italy: a critical analysis of the policy of integrazione scolastica*, by Simona D'Alessio, represents a new area of research in that it critically examines the historically ground-breaking Italian education policy of *Integrazione Scolastica* through the lens of the social model of disability, and the principles and practices of inclusive education. This policy was introduced in 1977 and led to the dismantling of special schooling in Italy – a policy which has been rightly celebrated in Italy as a liberating educational measure which allowed previously marginalised groups to attend their local community schools and to be members of ordinary classes. Surprisingly, this very radical education policy has received scant attention by researchers and by policy makers in the UK and elsewhere, although those who *do* make reference to it acknowledged that its progressive and historical significance. This book is, therefore, unique and important in critically exploring Italian policy which, for over thirty years, has offered a radical alternative to dominant western approaches in relation to education and disabled children and young people. This is of particular significance in the light of the UN Convention on Disability Rights and Article 24, which envisages the development of inclusive education, and the closing down of segregated schools, internationally.

A particularly innovative feature of this study is the importance given to historical context, and the theorising undertaken in relation to the particular political background against which the policy of *integrazione scolastica* emerged.

Furthermore, the book makes a significant theoretical contribution to the field of disability studies in education in exploring its central topic through the critical application of some key theoretical frameworks. The Social Model of Disability is used as an effective framework for critiquing individual deficit approaches and the Medical Model of Disability with reference to the Italian education context. Theoretical ideas drawn from Foucault and Gramsci are explored to critically examine Italian education policies and practices in ways which reveal the underlying impairment-led assumptions, power relations, and practices of categorisation which underpin the education system which co-exist with the more visible and still radical policies and practices of *integrazione scolastica*.

This book makes an important contribution to our understanding in that it raises questions about the theoretical premises on which the policy of *integrazione scolastica* is founded, rather than examining the policy as an operational or purely technical project. It shows how, in spite of its very radical origins and aspirations, Italian policy in this area is based on a 'special needs' paradigm. A central argument which emerges from the study is that what was once a progressive policy has been transformed into a powerful hegemonic project of normalisation which reproduces micro-exclusions within mainstream settings.

The study is underpinned by qualitative research in which ethnography is the principle methodological paradigm used in the development of case studies. As an insider-researcher, Simona D'Alessio was able to gather rich data of different kinds. A particular strength of the research lies in the high levels of transparency and reflexivity which, she argues (convincingly), contribute to the validity, integrity and reliability of her study. The exposition and discussion of the methodology is one of the great strengths of the book. The principles and processes involved in the analysis of the data are lucidly explained and justified, and the outcomes critically discussed in the light of the research questions and the theoretical frameworks developed in the earlier part of the book. The quality of the data analysis is sensitive and rigorous, and theoretical arguments are developed cogently and convincingly from the data presented.

This study is potentially important in terms of the wealth of ideas and insights it provides for policy-makers, practitioners and other research users. For example: it illustrates the importance of engaging with contextual factors, including the historical and political, in order to understand and probe the rationale, processes and outcomes of education and social policy. It demonstrates a radical alternative to dominant perceptions about 'what is possible' in terms of policy making in relation to disability and education. It provides an original, illuminating and carefully crafted research project which will inspire and challenge other researchers in the field. Finally, it reveals some of the deeply-rooted barriers to developing inclusive policies, even when all children attend the same kind of school.

Inclusive education in Italy: a critical analysis of the policy of integrazione scolastica, is a valuable resource for all those interested in understanding the complexities involved in analysing the often contradictory ways in which values and discourses permeate policies in social life. It is a particularly important piece of work in relation to the study of disability and education, and makes a unique contribution to our understanding of the nature of cross-cultural research. This book is essential reading for all those interested in the question of the nature and purpose of education and its contribution to the realisation and maintenance of an inclusive, non-discriminatory society. We have found the book both a pleasure to read and a challenging educative experience.

Professor Felicity Armstrong
Professor Len Barton

INTRODUCTION

This book gathers the reflections emerging from a research study concerned with the nature and development of inclusive education in Italy. Drawing on the data collected during my doctoral study between the years 2004 and 2008, this book brings to the fore how well-established educational mechanisms may contribute to the perpetuation of forms of micro-exclusion in ordinary school settings despite official purposes of doing otherwise.

The book explores the extent to which the Italian policy of *integrazione scolastica* can be considered an inclusive policy. Its main purpose is to provide a critical analysis of a policy which has been in place for more than thirty years and which has been decisive in counteracting the exclusion of disabled students from mainstream settings. Anti-discriminatory legislation has been very prolific in Italy. This is particularly evident when considering that countries are currently ratifying the Convention on the Rights of Persons with Disabilities (2006) to end segregation of disabled students from mainstream settings whilst Italy had already made such a choice in 1977. Nevertheless, the book makes a case that the passing of legislation may not be sufficient to fully guarantee the participation of all pupils in the process of learning in ordinary classrooms. To address this issue, the book raises questions concerning the theoretical premises on which a policy is based and it challenges dominant interpretations of the notion of integration, its taken-for-granted principles, discourses and practices.

In the light of these considerations, and in order to investigate contradictions and complexities enmeshed within language and notions, I have chosen to maintain the Italian definition of *integrazione scolastica* throughout the book because I wanted to respect the definition used by original documents and research participants. Also, because words and their meanings change across time and place and it is difficult to translate a definition from one language into another without falling into the traps of personal interpretations or ambiguity. It is important, moreover, to reflect as much as possible, on the constraints and the national contexts in which words originate so that their fundamental meaning is not lost when it is transferred into another context with its own historical, social and cultural background.

Similarly, the meaning of inclusive education varies conspicuously across countries - even within countries themselves - and these differences in interpretation are derived from the complex interplay of historical, cultural, political and economic factors. For this reason, this book provides its own interpretation of the notion of inclusion. In most Western countries, many practitioners and academics that support inclusive education celebrate it as one of the most important educational imperatives of current education systems. Indeed it is usually considered, by those committed to equality, to be fundamental in the development of a human rights approach to education.

In the context of this book, inclusive education is interpreted as a process of transformation of education systems and cultures in order to allow all students to participate fully and equitably in the process of learning in regular schools. Inclusive education is not concerned with one specific group of people - such as disabled students - but it engages with, and addresses obstacles that all learners, including disabled people, may encounter, in pursuing their right to education. However, exclusionary and discriminatory practices are more visible and more deeply rooted in relation to, for example, disability, gender, sexuality, race and the effects of poverty and social deprivation. For this reason, the focus of this book is on disabled people and on their struggle for a more inclusive education system. Nevertheless, it is important to underline that the study of inclusive education, as interpreted within this book, has got nothing to do with the 'inclusion of disabled pupils' in ordinary settings, rather it is concerned with the study of how contexts, settings, policy and practice could be made 'inclusive' by removing institutionalised and deeply embedded forms of discrimination that shape our society and education systems.

In order to investigate the extent to which the policy of *integrazione scolastica* can be considered an inclusive policy, the book draws on the application of the social model of disability as the main theoretical framework. Through the application of this model, the book argues that an educational policy should not be evaluated solely from an operational level, such as the articulation of political purposes (for example allocation of resources for disabled students) and their application at a school level, but it should also engage with issues of power relations, especially those operating within the process of policy making. Moreover, a sociological approach, as the one utilised in this book, brings to the fore the theoretical standpoints upon which policies and practices are embedded, thus portraying how different ideologies may impact upon practices and determine the availability of alternative solutions to existing barriers. Although different theoretical frameworks – such as medical/individual model versus social model or inclusion paradigm versus special needs education paradigm - may, arguably, be equally valid, they nevertheless focus on different aspects, providing different explanations and related solutions for similar phenomena, such as disability. The adoption of a sociological lens for the analysis of the policy of *integrazione scolastica* therefore contributed to the development of different understandings in relation to the education of disabled students in regular settings. It also influenced the modality of gathering data, and the type of data collected, suggesting alternative views to dominant ways of conducting research. Clearly, the social model of disability is also an attempt to draw on the experiences and perspectives of disabled people.

The social model used within this book also provides an effective framework to critique individual deficit approaches to disability. Under an individual/medical model in fact, the research focus usually leans towards an examination of individual deficiencies, and the modifications required to favour the 'integration' of a disabled child in ordinary settings. Consequently, observations do not focus on the individual experiences of disabled pupils, their development, the work of specialised teachers or the interaction between specialised teachers and the pupil with a Record of Needs, rather:

Sociological analyses focus on the institutions that treat, house, and manage disabled people – including families, schools, hospitals, and rehabilitation clinics – and above all, they examine disability as a stigmatized social status, exploring the means by which stigma is created, maintained, and resisted. (Stone, 1984:3)

This book draws attention to the structural, cultural and educational constraints that require a disabled child to be certified and classified with a statement of special educational needs in order for him or her to be provided with the same learning opportunity as other non-disabled pupils. Observations are concerned with the organisation and structures of mainstream schools, general teachers and the consequences of adopting traditional forms of curriculum, pedagogy and assessment for all pupils. Finally, a sociological approach looks for explanations that do not only concern the provision of special support for disabled children and the allocation of extra resources to schools. In contrast, they seek to understand why some children are considered less equal than others as they are required to adopt a 'special' identity in order to exert their rights to education.

Along with the social model of disability, the works of Gramsci and Foucault are fundamental to understand the intrinsic nature of mainstream schools beyond the enlightened vision of teaching and learning. Their works are relevant as both authors interrogated the conditions under which education systems operate and power is exercised. In particular, Gramsci suggests ways of looking at the sociological implications of education for the wider society. He also provides inputs to conceptualise the hegemonic quality of *integrazione scolastica*, a policy which misunderstood the means (such as integrating disabled pupils into regular classrooms), for its end (such as changing the education system). Foucault, on the other hand, suggests ways of questioning the reasons why societies need to adopt particular regulatory systems – for example naming, categorisation, classification and labelling – as a means of understanding and of controlling particular social groups. His works identify discourses that perpetuate exclusionary attitudes and practices in the school setting. Drawing on these thinkers, this book invites researchers, teachers, educators and policy makers to critically interrogate their assumptions and practices by detaching their actions and behaviours from their immediate contexts – classrooms, local education authorities and schools – and to consider their consequences.

Unless the structure of mainstream schools is made problematic, pedagogical and organisational innovations linked to *integrazione* are destined to fail or to remain at a very superficial level. What is crucial is to develop an understanding of the different theoretical premises supporting inclusive education on the one hand and *integrazione scolastica* on the other hand. This book is an attempt to do so especially by drawing particular attention to the historical and political contexts in which the policy of *integrazione scolastica* emerged.

THE BOOK RATIONALE

When I first set out to conduct the main study, a traditional way of interpreting *integrazione scolastica* and of conducting research concerning this policy inevitably influenced my work. I did not want to deny or undermine the achievements made by *integrazione scolastica*, nor did I want to underestimate the importance of the 'good practices' that paved the way to the social integration of disabled people in universities and work places. Therefore, my original purpose was to understand how this policy could lead to the development of inclusive education within the Italian education system. Most particularly, I wanted to observe how *integrazione scolastica* operated in two schools perceived as being good exemplars of 'good practices' and potentially situated in an 'inclusive' context. Yet, despite the passing of *integrazione*, some students, in particular disabled students, were still facing some forms of discrimination and marginalisation in the schools in which I worked as a support teacher. Therefore, I was strongly motivated to understand the possible reasons for the perpetuation of these forms of discrimination. Put simply, I wanted to understand why some contradictions and tensions were still in place within a major liberating policy initiative, which had allowed previously marginalised sections of the population to be educated in ordinary settings. Although the policy of *integrazione scolastica* is considered a fundamental standpoint in the development of inclusive education in Italy (Canevaro, 2002; Ianes, 2005), and is often perceived as a synonym for inclusion (Canevaro, 2001; 2002; 2006), many contradictions arise that need to be analysed and explored. This book also results from the efforts made to address such issues and provide them with an explanation.

At the end of 2004 I began the process of seeking permission to conduct research in two schools located in the north-eastern part of Italy, a region that most Italian commentators identified as one implementing 'inclusive' policies. Among the different provinces I decided to conduct my research in a small town, which for ethical reasons I will not identify by its real name but by the pseudonym of *Adriazzurra*. The choice of site for my study was not due to convenience or proximity but it was determined by my study objectives (Walford, 2001). I soon concentrated on the analysis of this policy initiative and of the school practices that could be considered conducive to inclusion.

After a few weeks of fieldwork, I realised that I was conducting my research with the assumptions that the policy of *integrazione scolastica* was not only an unproblematic anti-discriminatory policy, but also that it was an 'inclusive policy', although under a different name. Gradually, by engaging with the works of social model activists (Oliver, 1990), social theorists (Gramsci, 1971; Foucault, 1977) as well as policy analysts (Fulcher, 1989; Ball, 1990; Ozga, 1990; Armstrong, 2003), I became aware of the complexity of the notions of policy, disability and policy making and I started challenging my own presuppositions, and context-embedded assumptions alike.

Consequently, I decided to disentangle my study from traditional research modalities that have characterised the analysis of the policy of *integrazione scolastica* so far. A review of the Italian literature regarding *integrazione scolastica*, shows that despite the passing and the application of this groundbreaking policy, very little research has been conducted in the field of *integrazione* at a national level (Maviglia, 2008). Indeed, some Italian scholars (Canevaro & Ianes, 2001; D'Alonso & Ianes, 2007) have conducted studies concerning this policy, but they have primarily focused on a description of local practice of *integrazione scolastica*, without providing any relevant empirical findings concerning the outcomes of this major policy decision for society, schools and most importantly for the life of disabled pupils. What emerges instead is that most Italian research investigated whether the policy of *integrazione scolastica* – mainstreaming of disabled pupils in regular settings - was being applied or not. Yet, researchers did not seem to question the rationale that drove forward the passing of *integrazione scolastica*, beyond the humanitarian idea of 'doing good' to 'vulnerable' groups. Furthermore, there did not seem to be any attempt to question this policy, especially in the light of new social, economic and political challenges, such as the application of neo-liberal theories to education and the pressure on raising the standards of schools that modern education systems face today.

Interestingly enough, research in the field of *integrazione scolastica* in Italy seems to have focused primarily on issues concerning the legal application of this policy at a school level by safeguarding the allocation of an adequate quantity of resources and specialist support. A relevant example of this type of research can be found in the questionnaire developed by the National Institute for the Evaluation of Education, Training and Teaching known as *INVaISi* to measure the level of implementation of the policy of *integrazione* scolastica in state schools (InValSi, 2005–2006). What emerges therefore is that, firstly, traditional research has essentially aimed to provide evidence of how *integrazione scolastica* has had a positive impact on the learning of disabled people in ordinary settings, especially when compared to the education taking place in segregated settings (Cornoldi and Vianello, 1995; Vianello, 1999; Nocera and Gherardini, 2000). Secondly, it has produced indicators necessary for the evaluation of the quality of technical and administrative arrangements – such as the number of support teachers - that foster the implementation of 'good practices' of integration (Canevaro, Cocever and Weis, 1996; Nocera and Gherardini, 2000; Canevaro and Ianes, 2001; CDH Bologna and CDH Modena, 2003; Ianes and Canevaro, 2008). Thirdly, it has examined processes of diagnostic assessment based on new categorisation procedures as a basis for a re-distribution of resources (Ianes, 2004; 2005). Fourthly, it has suggested ways of developing special didactics and pedagogy to facilitate differentiation of teaching and individualisation of learning (de Anna, 1997; 2003; Canevaro, 2006; 2007). Recently, an attempt to break from a research tradition that measures the quality of *integrazione* based on the numbers of disabled people enrolled in regular schools has been made by two national research projects. The first project is a national survey for families with disabled children (D'Alonso and Ianes, 2007). It investigates further the consequences of the policy of *integrazione scolastica* for the families of disabled people thirty years on from its enactment. Yet it fails to investigate the policy of *integrazione scolastica* beyond the framework of the old debate which measures 'inclusion' by opposing segregated education to integration and it still focuses on the experiences of disabled students, without questioning educational contexts and systems or examining the theoretical underpinning in which the policy is still rooted. The second project consists of a ministerial programme, known as I CARE (*Imparare, Comunicare, Agire in una Rete Educativa*), which seeks to strenghten the process of integration of disabled pupils in regular schools by focussing on the work of teachers and local stakeholders. The preliminary empirical findings of this national survey provides an extremely valuable picture of the current situation regarding the application of the policy in Italy and of the attempts to bring innovation and action research within the school setting.

During my fieldwork, therefore I was faced with the following dilemma:

> While inclusive practices were to be found…it was easy sometimes to lose sight of these amid the exclusive practices and cultures. It is the latter that we inevitably see more of, but the former that we really need to address. (Nind et al., 2005:202)

Thus, although inclusive features were to be identified, my focus gradually sharpened to become an analysis of those barriers that could prevent the development of inclusive education in the schools under investigation. This shift of focus was due to the fact that the study of inclusion inevitably encapsulates the study of exclusion and how the latter is materialised in policies and practices (Booth, 2000). My study was not concerned with measuring the effectiveness of its application according to predetermined categories and standards, rather it interrogates why this particular policy initiative was being enacted rather than a segregating one and what were the theoretical underpinnings of such a policy when compared to those of special needs education.

THE STRUCTURE OF THE BOOK

In order to investigate the level of 'inclusiveness' of the policy of *integrazione scolastica*, the book interrogates the nature and the development of this major policy initiative using three strands of analysis. Firstly, a historical analysis of the conditions that led to the enactment of this policy. This strand of analysis provides an alternative reading of the policy of *integrazione scolastica* by examining the theoretical premises in which the policy is embedded. Secondly, a policy analysis that investigates milestone documents, legislative measures and the discourses deployed within them. Such an analysis provides relevant information about how the notion of disability has been constructed and how such a construction may determine the perpetuation of mechanisms of micro-exclusion. Thirdly, an empirical data analysis based on the accounts (e.g. interviews, observations) of how this policy is implemented in schools.

The following chapters therefore engage with discourses and practices as they emerge from documents, empirical data, and the use of a specific language that is concerned with the social construction of the notion of disability. Chapter One provides an overview of the uniqueness of the Italian context and it examines the historical development of the policy of *integrazione scolastica*. The focus is upon the conditions that led to the enactment of this policy and on the analysis of alternative accounts of how the policy came into place. This chapter also seeks to shed light on potential links with the notion of special needs education that have gone unnoticed for many years. Chapter Two provides a general description of the concept, and of the policy of inclusive education and of how a different concept-ualisation of inclusion has influenced both the theoretical underpinning and data collection of the study. Much of the discussion concerning inclusive education is about an international interpretation of the concept of inclusion and its current interpretation within the Italian literature investigated for this study. Chapter Three questions the reasons for adopting a social model of disability as the main theoretical underpinning used to investigate dominant assumptions and perceptions concerning the education of disabled people. The social model of disability is discussed as an alternative to the individual/medical model. A critique of the use of the International Classification of Functioning, Disability and Health (WHO, 2001) as the current model of understanding disability in Italy is also provided. Chapter Four is concerned with a critical analysis of the process of policy making and its consequences for the development of inclusive education. This chapter provides an overview of the main interpretations of the policy of *integrazione scolastica* and how such interpretations may impact upon school practice. An alternative reading of how national and statistical data can be interpreted is discussed. Chapter Five provides a description of the struggles being fought at the level of schooling for the implementation of the policy of *integrazione scolastica* and how the latter may impede or contribute to the development of inclusive education.

By investigating its dominant discourses, Chapter Six deconstructs the policy of *integrazione scolastica* and constructs it as a hegemonic discourse of normalisation of disability. Finally Chapter Seven draws together some recommendations concerning possible ways of developing inclusive education further. The last chapter re-capitulates the main issues addressed within the book, including the limitations of a single researcher's study and it offers recommendations of how to develop inclusive education.

STRUGGLES FOR *INTEGRAZIONE SCOLASTICA*

Historical and Legislative Analyses

This chapter is concerned with a description of the historical context and the struggles that led to the enactment of the policy of *integrazione scolastica* in Italy. This chapter however does not simply describe the history of integration but it seeks to understand why 'at a given time, out of all the possible things that could be said, only certain things were said' (Ball, 1990:3). To put simply, this chapter seeks to understand why whilst the majority of European countries chose to segregate disabled students, Italy began the process of mainstreaming disabled pupils into regular schools and classrooms. The aim is 'to analyse particular ideas or models of humanity which have developed as the result of very precise historical changes, and the ways in which these ideas have become normative or universal' (Ball, 1990:1).

Following a brief introduction concerning the Italian policy context and education system, I will provide a critical analysis of the main policy measures with a focus on the possibilities of infiltration and transmutation of special needs education paradigm into the policy of *integrazione scolastica*. In the third section, I will display the interplay of different forces that brought this policy into existence and the factors that paved the way to the passing of this policy. By bearing in mind the context in which the policy is rooted, my attempt is to trace the origin of current discourses and practices and to understand why out of all possibilities available, Italy chose to develop an integrative policy rather than a segregating one.

QUESTIONING THE POLICY OF *INTEGRAZIONE SCOLASTICA*

Amongst the many challenges that inclusive education has to face is the struggle against discrimination and exclusion, in particular, the macro-exclusions which are inherent in special education in segregated settings and the various forms of micro-exclusion perpetuated in both 'special' and ordinary settings. Many education systems still place some groups of students outside the mainstream system (EADSNE, 2008). Decisions about placement are often made on the basis of students' physical and intellectual impairments or cultural and social differences, and they deny some students their right to education with their peers. Similarly, many education systems have tended to rank and stream students into levels of attainment and according to their performances and achievements, thus negatively affecting students' life chances. As the following sections will describe, Italy took a different pathway. In 1977, despite the difficulties arising from systemic constraints and the lack of research and resources, the country passed a piece of anti-discriminatory legislation known as *integrazione scolastica.* As a consequence of the application of this policy, all students are welcomed into their neighbourhood schools regardless of socio-economic background, physical and intellectual impairments, or of any other selective categorisation designed to segregate and exclude. At the same time, special schools have dramatically decreased in number and have been almost completely dismantled. Moreover, since the passing of this policy, teaching and learning procedures in ordinary schools have sought to respond to all students' requirements, in particular by drawing upon specialised forms of pedagogy and teaching methods.

Given these considerations, the Italian policy of *integrazione scolastica* appears to create an ideal context – legislative, educational, pedagogical and social – for the development of inclusive education. This is particularly evident whenever *integrazione scolastica* is compared to other policy contexts in Europe, in which segregated education is sometimes the only available option for disabled students. Therefore, why should *integrazione scolastica*, which led to the full integration of disabled students in regular schools, be questioned as a policy that could hamper the development of inclusive education? During my personal experience first as a support teacher and then as a class teacher in ordinary secondary schools I became aware that, despite the passing of this 'progressive' policy, some students were still experiencing certain forms of exclusions. Some families, especially those with disabled children, often reported their children were being discriminated against whilst attempting to avail themselves of their right to education in regular schools. Evidence for this can be found in the increased number of tribunal hearings. Similarly, some disabled people' organisations have reported the maintenance of segregated institutions despite the passing of the *integrazione scolastica* legislation which was intended to ensure mainstream education for all (Barbieri, 2007).

On the one hand, Italy's decision to adopt the policy of *integrazione scolastica* was part of a wider educational policy of 'comprehensiveness' whose purpose was to break the reproduction of inequalities through a selective education system (such as the Fascist education system). At the same time, this policy was part of the post-war reconstruction, which aimed to maintain the political unification of the newly re-formed state. One view is that during the 1970s, the education system was not 'ready' to embrace the broad diversity of students because of the limited amount of research available and the lack of resources and of opportunities for professional development for teachers. It is not surprising that, when the legislation on *integrazione scolastica* was passed in 1977, situations arose in which some disabled students were placed in unprepared school settings. On the other hand, all students attended their local schools, while the education system was, arguably, seeking to develop structural and organisational modifications. However, the choice to integrate did not arise from research on education, but as a part of a wider political and social discourse that requires further investigation. This is particularly important, following Oliver's observations (1996a; 1996b) that, until recently, many sociologists have engaged with issues of segregation and the concomitant development of special education as a means of social control and as a way of increasing or maintaining the power of professional experts (Barton and Tomlinson, 1981; Armstrong, 2003), but they have only peripherally investigated the theory and the practice of integration.

In line with the above consideration, the research sought to question a traditional notion of the policy of *integrazione scolastica* as an essentially un-problematic, and perfectly designed top-down initiative that led to the development of inclusive education. I fully concur with Oliver (1996b) who argues:

> It is important to emphasise that I am not claiming that the struggle for integration is over except in an ideological sense. There is almost universal agreement that integration is a good thing given the right level of resources, the appropriate training of teachers and so on. The point that I am making is that the success of integration at an ideological level has made it almost impossible for it to be examined critically. (Oliver, 1996b:85)

An attempt to critically examine the policy envisages the need to disentangle some key issues from a conservative research tradition which considers *integrazione scolastica* merely as a technical 'debate about the quality of educational provision' (Oliver, 1996b:82) and 'divorced from the views of disabled people themselves' (Oliver, 1996b:83) as such a tradition leaves education systems and mainstream schools unquestioned. For example, there has been very little attempt to investigate the original principles of *integrazione* undoubtedly considered as the crucial standpoint for the development of inclusion. In contrast, such an awareness seems to have limited the possibility of undertaking alternative forms of research which could question the 'naturalness' of this policy and could suggest ways of ameliorating practices and, consequently, of developing mainstream education systems. Evidently, this policy partly modified culturally negative attitudes towards disabled people, but, as things currently stand, its impact upon mainstream education has been fairly limited.

The Italian Education System at the Time in Which the Research was Conducted

The Italian education system consists of four main stages of state schooling:
- Infant education for pupils between the ages of 3 and 6
- Primary education (five years of schooling) for ages 6 to 11
- Lower secondary education (three years of schooling) for ages 11 to 14
- Upper secondary education (five years of schooling) for students between the ages of 14 and 19

Unlike England, Italy does not have SATs (Standardised Attainment Tests) and OFSTED (The Office for Standards in Education) inspections. Neither are there league tables. Moreover, with the passing of the Autonomy Law in 1999, the compulsory national curriculum (also known as national programs), has been slowly replaced by National Guidelines (i.e. *Indicazioni Nazionali*). However, by looking closely, these differences are less radical than they appear, and similarities become more evident when investigating current political trends (for example decentralisation, standardisation and marketisation) and the language used (for example quality, excellence and efficiency) in national policy documents. Under the international pressure of the PISA studies, Italy developed a National Institute for the Evaluation of Education, Training and Teaching known as *INValSi* (*Istituto Nazionale per la Valutazione del Sistema Educativo di Istruzione e di Formazione*) which is officially aiming to evaluate the national education system by measuring school performances starting from the year 2009/2010 (Commission of the European Communities, 2008).

Despite the many attempted school reforms of past governments, education is primarily state run. This is also reflected in the sway of policy documents, circulars that are periodically sent to schools by ministerial departments. Although these documents are mostly interpreted as recommendations and guidelines, they provide evidence of the existing asymmetrical power relations between state and schools, notwithstanding recent reforms supporting school autonomy and decentralisation. At the same time, private education, usually provided by religious orders, plays a marginal role. However, regarding the education of disabled students in private schools, also known as '*paritarie*' (private schools that follow the same curriculum as state schools), it would be interesting to investigate why the state had to legislate (Law n. 62/2000) to ensure that the process of *integrazione scolastica* was made compulsory in private schools too. Nevertheless, state schools – corresponding to the maintained schools in England - are the dominant venues for the transmission of what is seen as relevant knowledge and the propagation of social attitudes and values. It seems as if parents gave their children to the state so that 'the State may form them according to certain norms' (Foucault, 2003:256).

As will emerge in the following sections, a sense of community and solidarity has traditionally played an important role in the Italian school system. Arguably, the original purpose of the Italian education system was to create a public system capable of merging and homogenising the new school population – such as peasants migrating from the southern regions into the northern cities and poor children leaving the countryside to live in rich urban areas – with the children of the new bourgeoisie and old aristocracy. This view of the role of schooling is a legacy of the Fascist school whose purpose was to transmit a particular type of knowledge. The passing of the Law known as the *scuola media unica* (comprehensive lower secondary education) in 1962, sought to change the school as established during the Mussolini dictatorship, for example by putting an end to the previous division between grammar and vocational schooling for students aged between 11 and 14 (originally passed under the Fascist Government in 1923). The heritage of the selective and traditional system of Gentile (Mussolini's minister of instruction), however, remains visible today through the role played by the national guidelines on curricula and programmes of study in upper secondary schools.

With this in mind, it is not surprising that the first policies concerned with the 'mainstreaming' of disabled people into regular schools, were not primarily concerned with the dismantling of special schooling but with how to modify the rigidity of the newly formed education system in order to enable it to welcome the increasing diversity within the student population. It is interesting, however, to consider whether such 'comprehensiveness' was meant to provide all citizens with the same opportunities and rights, or whether is was also a way of maintaining state control and power through non-coercive apparatuses (Althusser, 1971). Not unrelatedly, drawing on Foucault (1970; 1977; 2003), schools have always been hierarchical institutions where students were supposed to be disciplined into becoming good, productive and docile subjects.

Consequently, as the following sections will show, it seems that the formation of a national compulsory education system in Italy was more than an enlightened project to educate all. Arguably, a compulsory education system in Italy was, in its initial conception after the country's unification in 1861, a cultural and political means to create a sense of nation, and secondly, after World War Two, a social tool to reconstruct a poverty stricken and politically divided country.

Regarding the national curriculum, schools have a certain degree of autonomy to decide what to teach (20% of the curriculum can be locally established) depending on specific requirements and geographical locations. This is particularly true after the passing of the Autonomy Law 1999 (*Legge Delega* n. 59/1997) and its enactment through the Presidential Decree n. 275 in 1999, an educational reform which affected the education system as a whole. This reform known as *Autonomia Scolastica* made an effort to innovate the school system, through a 'decentralisation' of state power to local government bodies (such as the Reform of the Article 5 of the Constitution) and schools. With the passing of this reform, schools became autonomous bodies as they gained didactical, pedagogical and organisational freedom, as well as the possibility to carry out projects and conduct research, as indicated in the school development plan also known as *Piano dell'Offerta Formativa* (POF henceforward). At the same time, schools are still required to comply with a list of goals and to teach 'core' subjects and knowledge that will allow students to attend upper secondary schools. This is particularly evident in the use of textbooks whose content is more or less the same notwithstanding the publishing company and the region in which they are used. Thus, educational targets and aims, both in terms of curricular contents and competences, remained centrally defined and against pre-determined national standards. The latter are also in line with the objectives stated within the European Council of Lisbon (2000), to be achieved by 2010. Although, apparently, schools are given the possibility to choose what to teach and how to teach, they exercise their freedom according to certain norms (such as the *Indicazioni Nazionali* or National Guidelines) and within set boundaries (for example the International European Standards, the PISA studies and the European Council of Lisbon benchmarks).

In line with the *Autonomia Scolastica*, the government in place during my data collection laid down another relevant school reform, known as the Moratti Reform (Law n. 53/2003). It aimed at modifying the original stages of schooling by creating two main cycles of instruction. The first cycle (eight years) would have included primary and lower secondary education, while the second cycle (five years) would have included upper secondary education in grammar schools or, alternatively, in vocational centres (four years). While the grammar schools were to be run by the state, vocational schools were to be administered by regional education bodies. Due to the collapse of the Berlusconi Government in 2006, only some of the modifications envisaged for the first cycle of schooling came into force. Nevertheless, the possibility of this reform coming into force had an impact upon schools in which the research was conducted and it was often the object of debate among school practitioners.

Although, the Moratti reform did not directly oppose the process of *integrazione scolastica*, it put an emphasis on standardised student performance and accountability of educational sites, which inevitably reduced the possibilities for fostering optimal conditions for the development of inclusive principles. For example, when the *INValSI* tests were first carried out, disabled students were basically excluded from assessment procedures. Students who were perceived as unsuitable to qualify for the national tests, essentially pupils with intellectual impairments (for example autistic spectrum disorders and learning disorders) were provided with a different test paper, created by support teachers rather than by ministerial experts and identified with a 'code' (know as *codice di particolarità*) attached to test papers. When collected, coded test papers were not sent to the ministerial department for evaluation along with the other students' papers, but they remained within school buildings. In this way, the tests taken by disabled children were not counted and they could not influence the overall outcomes in terms of school performance. Although, policy makers officially reported that they attempted to safeguard students from failing and experiencing frustration, they ended up discriminating against them. Disabled students were not only discriminated against, but they were also cheated by a system that pretended to 'include' them, by having them sit for the tests along with their peers whilst at the same time, excluding them as learners. The then disability rights movement, supported by the National Observatory for the Integration of Disabled People, was working to produce national tests that could be adapted to meet the requirements of disabled students. This body is still attempting to bring about an end the discrimination experienced by disabled students. In 2007, the *INValSI* required that the tests prepared by support teachers in 2005 were sent to the Institute. This was an attempt to share those tests among the teaching community and to have materials to administer depending on the type of impairment. At the same time, the assessment of disabled students' performance remained embedded within a framework that considers assessment of disabled students as an additional and separate aspect of the education system, and often of an 'inferior' type, rather than an integral component of Italian schooling.

THE LEGISLATIVE MEASURES THAT PAVED THE WAY TO THE POLICY OF *INTEGRAZIONE SCOLASTICA*

Historically speaking, the origin of an 'integrationist mentality' in Italy could be traced back to the promulgation of the Italian Constitution in 1948 (articles 3, 33, 34, 38), the enactment of which represented a turning point in anti-discrimination legislation. Soon after World War Two a democratic Constitution was passed (1948) and it triggered the enactment of social integration policies, which inevitably contributed to the development of *integrazione scolastica*. Women voted for the first time in Italy and different conflicting forces (Catholic, liberal and communist) were united against Fascism. Since the Fascist dictatorship had denied individual freedom, one of the first targets of the democratic Constitution was to put the dignity of the person and the rights of minorities at the centre of the constitutional charter. For example, participation was to be guaranteed by the State, which now had a duty to remove all social, economic and cultural obstacles (article 3) to citizen participation. All citizens had the right to education, including disabled people (articles 34 and 38).

Thus, although traditional accounts of the policy of *integrazione scolastica* claim that the first legislative act that favoured the placement of disabled students into regular classrooms was Law n.118 in 1971, the spirit and ethos for integration was already encapsulated in the Constitution charter. Nevertheless, Law n. 118 entitled civil invalids and physically impaired people to education alongside their 'normal' peers. Despite the innovative content of this legislative measure, however, Law n. 118/1971, was still inscribed within what Armstrong defines as a 'functionalist' approach to disability (Armstrong, 2007). This law in fact focussed on the benefit payments, assistance and protection, and humanitarian concerns of social welfare, to be guaranteed to those who were perceived as different from the norm. Law n. 118 was not particularly concerned with pedagogical and organisational issues but with the provision of special services and financing such as free transport to schools for a particular 'category' of students and the removal of architectural barriers – pending the availability of funding. Furthermore, the word 'invalid' suggests a link between the role of financial compensation played by the national welfare system in relation to war veterans, and the role of the education system whose duty was to assist civil invalids also as learners.

Although Law n. 118/1971 was an important legislative measure which started off the process of mainstreaming (de Anna, 1997), yet the word *integrazione* does not appear in the text of the legislation. Moreover, the legislative measure fails to address issues related to the closing down of special schools. Conversely, it leaves room for manoeuvre for those supporting the maintenance of special education (see Nocera, 1988). This is evident in section 28 of the Law, which states that:

> Compulsory education must take place in regular schools, in public schools except in those cases in which the subject suffers from severe intellectual deficiency or from physical handicaps so great as to impede or render very difficult the learning processes in the regular classroom. (Booth, 1982:15)

In this extract, a translation of the original Law by Booth (1982), the education of impaired people must take place in normal state schools, unless there are severe physical or intellectual impairments that prevent students' placement into normal classrooms. This clause, therefore, indicates that Law n. 118 only envisaged ways of 'facilitating' the process of integration, rather than struggling to make it compulsory. Similarly, special schools and classes were not abolished but rather reinforced (Nocera, 1988), and school officials could have easily evaded the enrolment of disabled children whenever they could not (or rather, did not want to) integrate them. In 1975, senator Franca Falcucci coordinated a national enquiry to provide research data, which would support the process of integration of disabled students into ordinary settings. It was the first attempt to conduct research to provide findings to support the principles of *integrazione scolastica* and also the first time when the definition of *integrazione scolastica* was officially used. The *Falcucci* document (Ministero della Pubblica Istruzione, 1975) was a milestone in the process of *integrazione scolastica* as it contained some inclusive features that later legislative measures did not contain (for example Law n. 517/1977, Law n. 104/1992). In this document, for example, the barriers to the process of *integrazione scolastica* were cultural and social prejudices and not only the biological conditions of the child. Moreover it suggested that *integrazione scolastica* should start with a transformation of the entire education system, its methodology and its conceptualisation. Clearly, this was a more 'inclusive' legislative measure when compared to recent legislative measures that focus on individual impairments (for example Law n. 104/1992, Presidential Decree, 1994). At the same time, the language used in the document is evidence enough of the central role still played by the medical model of disability, in particular when it positioned the experience of disability as a personal tragedy to which society was to provide a remedy. This is also visible in the role of the expert, who is considered essential for the process of *integrazione scolastica*, and in the need to rely on a medical diagnosis to take action concerning disabled pupils. The *Falcucci* document had its impact on legislation that began to investigate ways of reviewing traditional teaching. However, the challenging ideas incorporated in this document lost their original power and were hardly to be found again in later legislative measures.

Officially, the policy of *integrazione scolastica* is linked to the enactment of Law n. 517 in 1977, which demanded the closing down all differentiated classes and schools. In this Law, the term *inserimento* (placement) is finally replaced with the term *integrazione specialistica* (specialist integration). However, the term *integrazione scolastica* still does not appear from the text, since this terminology was only formalised in 1992, with the passing of the Law n. 104 also known as *Legge Quadro* (*Framework Law* henceforward). Not only did the Law n. 517/1977 officially abolished differentiated classes and special schools, but it also provided additional resources by which ordinary schools could be improved, such as support teachers and local specialised personnel. Thus the schools were provided with a series of technical and pedagogical instructions as to how to implement *integrazione* into practice, such as special training required by the support teacher (section 7), the organisation of interdisciplinary activities to support the learning of disabled students (section 7) and the principle of individualisation of learning (section 2). Although this Law amended the terms *invalido* (invalid) and *minorato* (impaired), usually interpreted as synonyms of subnormal and abnormal people with handicap (handicapped) or *portatore di handicap* (carrier of handicap), it failed to address issues concerning structural factors that might have impacted upon the learning of disabled people causing them difficulties. Conversely, despite Law n. 517/1977 having usually been considered as the milestone of *integrazione* (Canevaro, 2007), I argue that it has, paradoxically, contributed to the reproduction of special education dis-courses inside the mainstream – as the term *integrazione specialistica*, used through-out the text, also suggests. Consequently, although discourses in relation to the policy of *integrazione scolastica* began to change from an earlier discourse of segregation to a discourse of special expertise (section 2, Law n. 517/1977), disability was constructed as individual impairment that required the assistance of specialist personnel and the protection of the state.

In the 1980s the policy of *integrazione scolastica* was implemented in infant schools (1982) and in upper secondary schools (1987). The implementation of the policy of *integrazione scolastica* in other grades of schooling did not necessarily correspond to an increase in the participation of disabled people in society. On the contrary, with national financial problems accompanied by the increasing individualistic mentality dominating the newly born Italian capitalistic society, the state reinforced the welfare state through the passing of incapacity benefits for disabled people, to the detriment of their actual participation in society. Thus, society guaranteed marginalised sections of the population basic economic support, but the cultural and psychological distance between disabled and non disabled people grew wider (Selleri, 1987). For example, many disabled people had to renounce their employment in order to obtain incapacity benefits. Segregation was not taking place through physical separation, but through the lack of debate with disabled people and the reduction of social participation.

Framework Law n. 104/1992: The Milestone of Integrazione Scolastica

Despite the economic and cultural barriers, the process of integrating disabled students into ordinary classes was considered as something of a 'natural phenomenon' of the Italian education system. As Canevaro (2001) argues, however, such 'naturalness' represented a double-edged sword. Whilst it promoted the placement of disabled people in ordinary schools by opposing segregationist forces, it also prevented the undertaking of a 'scientific' study of this policy on a large scale. Put simply, some commentators (Adams, 1990; Meijer and Abbring, 1994; Mittler, 2000; Johnson, 1993 in Thomas and Loxley, 2001) claimed that Italy not only was implementing *inserimento selvaggio* ('wild' integration - placing disabled students in common settings without changing the conditions in which their education took place), but also that it did not provide any satisfactory empirical evidence that showed how disabled students' achievements improved once they were educated in integrated settings. Although very little information is available at an international level and in English language, some research was indeed conducted (Cornoldi and Vianello, 1989; 1990; 1995; Vianello, 1999; Nocera and Gherardini, 2000, Vianello and Lanfranchi, 2009). To define the first steps of integration only in terms of 'wild integration' would not do any justice to the work that, despite the numerous difficulties, was done in Italy in those early days. Instead, some Italian research showed how *integrazione* could positively influence the learning experience of disabled people when compared with the experience of other disabled students placed in special settings, and how the education system could take advantage from the adaptations – curricular and organisational – required for the 'mainstreaming' of disabled students in ordinary settings. The underlying principle was that what benefited disabled students could benefit all students and that such awareness would have an impact on the rigidity of school settings (Fiorin, 2007). At the same time, however, many policy makers often interpreted *integrazione scolastica* primarily in terms of locational integration without placing sufficient emphasis on the changes required in the nature of schooling.

In order to clear *integrazione scolastica* from assumptions and doubts concerning procedures, roles and competences, in 1992 the Framework Law n. 104 was finally laid down. This law provided a detailed description of how disabled people were to be integrated into society, since it encompassed all social sectors – employment, housing, services – and, of course, education. The Framework Law underlined the importance of networking among institutional bodies (local education authorities, local health units) and schools, paving the way for the experimentation of new approaches to teaching and learning (such as team teaching and cooperative learning) with actions to be taken in all grades of schools (from infant schools to universities) and all sectors of society (from training centres to employment settings).

With the benefit of hindsight, the Framework Law was a revolutionary legislative measure as it envisaged the removal of social barriers that could hinder the participation of disabled people in society (section 14). This Framework Law adopted a change of emphasis, from focussing on the individual deficit to the settings in which people were situated. Today, it can be considered as the bridging legislative measure between previous policy documents entirely embedded in a special education framework, and which focussed only on the individual deficit - to policies which began to take into consideration societal and environmental factors. On the one hand, this law was characterised by sections concerning specialist assistance, medical rehabilitation (section 7), eugenic discourses on pre-natal screening and medical diagnosis (section 6), provisions allocated according to the severity of impairment (section 3), and the creation of special institutions for severely impaired people (section 8). On the other hand, it seemed to anticipate the notion of disability as something that should be reduced by removing environmental factors (sections 1, 5, 13, and 14). Yet, from an inclusive perspective, the Framework Law remains enshrined in a construction of the notion of disability in terms of deficit, thus sharing continuity with the special education paradigm. This is evident because although it argues for the need to remove societal barriers, it fails to focus on which social obstacles may impact on participation and even determine the very limitations individuals encounter and how they could be removed. Moreover, when it does mention societal barriers, they are always identified in relation to a specific impairment that needs to be adequately provided for, either with professional and/ or economic support (section 5). This position is also reinforced by the use of a discriminatory and outdated language that does not distinguish between disability and impairment, the former still considered as the direct consequence of personal deficiencies (section 3). The Framework Law certainly sanctioned legal entitlement for many disabled people in all sectors of society, along with the provision of services and educational facilities, but perhaps, to the detriment of full active citizenship (Selleri, 1987). In particular, in the Framework Law, issues such as self-representation and self-advocacy are not introduced and disabled people were still deprived of their chance (and power) to self-determination.

The limitations embedded in the Framework Law 1992, such as the predominance of a medical model of disability, the lack of self-representation by disabled people, and the fact that it was not a coercive measure, resulted in the passing of further legislative measures that are clearly stepping back from an environmental perception of the notion of disability. In particular the Presidential Decree passed in 1994, known as the *Atto di Indirizzo* which was concerned with the coordination of rights and duties of local health units to provide disabled students with adequate responses to their 'special' needs. This Presidential Decree sanctioned the dominant role of physicians and psychologists in the implementation of *integrazione scolastica* in schools and reinforced the lack of self-regulation by disabled people. Along with the use of outdated language, such as *portatore di handicap* (carrier of handicap), the decree not only constructed disability as a personal problem, but also reinforced the hierarchical position of medical professionals in the issue of *certificazione di handicap* (statement of 'special educational needs'). For this reason, while the Framework Law n. 104 set out to undermine fixed categories of 'handicap' by focusing, when possible, on exhisting environmental barriers, the Presidential Decree in 1994 clearly re-established them. For this reason the Italian Ministry of Public Instruction is officially planning to substitute the Presidential Decree 1994 with a new diagnostic assessment procedure based on the International Classification of Functioning, Disability and Health (WHO, 2001) which requires the participation of a committee of experts for the issuing of a statement of 'special educational needs' rather than of a single medical expert. Such a new procedure is an attempt to reinforce the role of non-medical personnel in the process of issuing a statement of special educational needs and to emphasise the role that environmental barriers may play in the process of learning of pupils with impairments. At the same time however, some commentators (Iosa, 2008; Nocera, 2008) have argued that this new procedure could be another administrative device to reduce the number of certifications (Ministerial Decree n. 185/2006) and financial support allocated to schools and students. Clearly, as I will explain in more details in Chapter three, the problem with the adoption of the International Classification of Functioning, Disability and Health (ICF henceforward) as the new diagnostic assessment procedure lies in the fact that there is no real attempt to question the procedure of categorisation as the standpoint of the process of *integrazione*.

AN ALTERNATIVE HISTORY OF *INTEGRAZIONE SCOLASTICA*

Traditional accounts of the policy of *integrazione scolastica* claim that this policy resulted from a sudden political decision encouraged by the civil rights movement along with disability associations and their lobbying (Canevaro, 2001; Mura, 2007). At the same time, however, it is necessary to investigate the wider historical and political scenario of those years, in order to interrogate other possible sources of knowledge that could provide alternative accounts of the reasons why the policy of *integrazione scolastica* was enacted.

The enactment of the policy of *integrazione scolastica* has usually been associated with the socio-medical movement led by the Italian psychiatrist Franco Basaglia. This psychiatrist campaigned for the dismantling of mental asylums and contributed to the passing of a Law in 1978 that bears his name: the Basaglia Law, which shut down all mental hospitals (Segal, Maigne and Gautier, 2003). As Canevaro (2001) argues, however, although there may be links between the process of *integrazione scolastica* and the dismantling of mental asylums, these relations are only secondary. This position is due to the fact that the process of *integrazione* not only began before the actual dismantlement of mental asylums (in 1971) but was the result of a broader social campaign and lobbying and not simply the advanced idea of a single person or of a small group of 'forward thinking' scholars (Canevaro, 1999). Nevertheless, the closing of mental asylums, along with special schools, are clear indications of political priorities in those years. In particular, the de-institutionalisation process was a way of responding not only to general demands to safeguard constitutional rights and social justice (as social upheavals led by students and workers required), but also to provide economic and political responses to unemployment and recession after the international oil crisis of 1973. It is important to keep in mind that, as Foucault (1977) also observes, a process of de-institutionalisation does not necessarily correspond to the termination of state surveillance and control. On the contrary, it may represent a 'swarming of disciplinary mechanisms' (1977:211) that function in an invisible and widespread way of maintaining order and it is necessary to explore who benefited from the closing of special institutions. This view, therefore, entails taking into account that the process of de-institutionalisation may cost less than maintaining such institutions and that it also produced job opportunities within the new disability-related professions which proliferated (Wolfensberger, 1989).

The years in which *integrazione scolastica* became compulsory (1970s) are also known as the *anni di piombo* (the leaden years). These years were characterised by political upheavals, which saw opposing forces - new fascist movements and radical communist forces - fighting against the state. Italy has always been characterised by many internal divisions and apart from Catholicism, there has never been much internal national cohesion (see Boggs, 1976). A civic effort to contribute to the development of an ideological cohesion capable of awakening the conscience of those involved in fighting against fascist reactionary anti-democratic forces was represented by the Constitutional Charter. Nonetheless, during the 1970s police and other military forces were often the object of bombing raids. Consequently, the political and social climate was tense and the state needed to provide an adequate response to this situation. The response was two-fold: firstly the state sought to control opposing social forces by incorporating them into institutionalised bodies – such as trade unions. Secondly, it conceded many of the social demands – for example by creating employment opportunities and by passing welfare assistance policies. Therefore, the policy of *integrazione scolastica* could also be interpreted as a state managerial effort to answer to pressure groups. This is also evident by the fact that the policy of *integrazione* at school did not, at first, concern disabled students, but migrant students who were abandoning the southern agricultural regions for the northern industrial towns. In those years, therefore, the lobbying of disabled people's associations in favour of mainstreaming was not a separate voice but part of a broader social movement which saw workers and university students campaigning together for justice and democracy for all social minorities.

In the 1970s, the disability rights movements, in particular represented by parents associations, joined the global intellectual movements for democracy and justice and fought for the passing of anti-discriminatory legislative measures. Thanks to their lobbying, segregation in education was practically banished. At the same time, it is important to note that the disabled people's associations were mainly comprised of parents and voluntary organisations lobbying on behalf of disabled people; at that time, only a few associations were run by disabled people themselves, such as the *Fronte Radicale Invalidi* - Invalids Radical Front - (Tescari, 2004), while the majority of disabled people were not considered capable of representing themselves in court or in Parliament. These associations campaigning for disabled people's rights were known as the *associazioni storiche*. Although such associations helped many disabled people emerge from a condition of total marginalisation and poverty, they also inevitably contributed to the spreading of discourses of assistance and care, which possibly contributed to the construction of disability in terms of dependence.

The politics of lobbying and campaigning by organisations, families and unions played a central role in the passing of anti-discriminatory policies and their subsequent implementation. The pressure applied upon governmental bodies and decision makers allowed voices to be heard and preliminary changes to occur. As Gramsci (1971) also indicates, it is only by organising themselves into pressure groups that marginalised social groups and their own intellectuals may lead the process of change. Thus, the policy of *integrazione scolastica* may have provided a fertile terrain for the voices of previously marginalised groups of the population to be heard and listened to. At the same time, it seems that historical descriptions of the policy of *integrazione scolastica* as a humanitarian policy which fought for the civil rights of disabled people should also be complemented with other accounts which are not only concerned with education but which engage with issues around state control and management of difference/deviance, as the following sections will attempt to describe.

Social and Economic Factors

The post-war years witnessed a wider movement of reform across Europe both from a social and economic perspective (Armstrong, 2003). After the destruction of the war period, modern societies aimed to (re)constitute social order, civic unity and economic prosperity. They began to organise themselves in such a way that anything that threatened to destroy the new order was necessarily deemed in need of identification and designation, and consequently, destined to be excluded or, alternatively, incorporated. Arguably, societies were more prone to incorporate diversity – assimilating difference into the norm – rather than allowing the existence of diverging forces, which could challenge the structure of the social system (Stiker, 1999). As Stiker argues, in the Western world, 'integration is more of a constant in human society than exclusion' (1999:15). Consequently, an inclusive trend was privileged over an exclusionary one (Armstrong, 2003). This rationale could be traced back in social and economic policies which were passed in the aftermath of World War Two. One example of this were the paternalistic policies enacted by the state which aimed to rehabilitate and re-integrate veterans into society. Stiker (1999) asserts that it was only a question of time before similar treatment was reserved for disabled people and other disadvantaged groups (for example migrants from southern Italy). This attitude, in particular, is evident in the Italian Law n. 118/1971 which establishes benefits and services for civil invalids and impaired people. However, the benevolence of the state cannot be read only in humanitarian terms. There are instead other reasons that originated in social and economic rationales that promoted the passing of integrative policies over segregating ones.

From an economic perspective, for example, integration policies could be seen as a way of promoting the development of capitalism. They not only maximised the potential of labour forces by providing education for all citizens (see the Constitution Charter), and hence motivated the workforce as well as making it more skilled, but they also helped the state to keep public spending upon poor people to a minimum (Armstrong, 2003). The new order required new citizens. Thus, the education system was considered as a crucial tool to create social cohesion and, most importantly, a productive working force to boost the economic revival (Armstrong, 2003). Unlike Britain, however, Italy prioritised integrative policies, over segregating ones as it attempted to re-create a new society by sweeping away the legacy of Fascism. This choice resulted in the closing of special schools (Law n. 517/1977) and the dismantling of mental asylums (Basaglia Law 1978). At the same time, the resilience of a regulatory framework of identification, assessment and categorisation of difference/deviance was maintained within society and mainstream schools.

When *integrazione scolastica* was implemented, the welfare state played a central role in the redistribution of wealth in a post-war poverty-stricken Italy. As Stone (1984) also argues, people were entitled to economic support on the basis of two presuppositions. Compensation was to be given for a loss (for example of a limb during the war) or for incapacity (for example civil invalids). What was important though, was that individuals were not 'found guilty or responsible' for their loss or incapacity. In order to identify and ascertain such a condition, the role of the medical professionals as arbiters of the re-distribution of wealth became central. Possibly, a similar rationale of compensation and remediation was transferred into the education system which enacted integrative policies towards those students who were identified as lacking a social or economic background [see Don Milani (Scuola di Barbiana, 1996)] or were perceived as being defective in their body/mind.

The welfare system became a tool for re-distributing wealth according to the severity of 'needs' and it represented the rationale for the allocation of resources within the policy of *integrazione scolastica*. At the same time, it is necessary to remember that Italy should be identified as a 'welfare society' rather than a welfare state (Rodger, 2004). As Rodger (2004) argues, unlike the British welfare state system, the Italian welfare system is characterised by the presence of intermediate bodies between the state and its subjects. These bodies, which are responsible for the re-distribution of wealth, contribute to the creation of a supporting network in the management of financial resources. The former is based on the principle of subsidiarity and suggests that although the state remains the main welfare provider, local bodies are responsible for wealth re-distribution policies. The welfare society differs from the welfare state since the former is based on the principle of 'horizontal subsidiarity' rather than 'vertical subsidiarity' (the state and its local bodies). Horizontal subsidiarity in fact, allows the participation of private bodies (the so-called third sector) in the redistribution of resources and services along with the state ones. This is particularly true for the province of *Adriazzurra*, where the research was conducted. The local policy maker reported that the province of *Adriazzurra* was renowned for cooperating with private associations and bodies whose contributions were crucial in the implementation of *integrazione scolastica*:

> Law n. 328/2000 establishes the criteria of vertical and horizontal subsidiarity. The vertical one, which has now been substituted by the article V of the Constitution, consisted of a separation of competences among different institutional bodies, from the region down to the province and the municipality. Instruction remains centrally and state regulated in terms of national indications and educational objectives to be achieved. Horizontal subsidiarity instead consists of a partnership among different local bodies which work in the area and that can make decisions concerning education and schools. The novelty is the participation of the third sector in this decision making process. Whilst the state and provincial bodies have an institutional responsibility, the third sector instead, which is to say the non-governmental organisations and associations, they bring the surplus, they are another important resource ... they do not substitute the institutional bodies but they add to them. (Interview 19, policy maker, Provincial Education Authority)

As this statement shows, the principle of horizontal subsidiarity was perceived as a value added factor. Thus the participation of non-governmental organisations in the field of education was favoured and promoted. Although such a principle could be viewed as an example of a strong social fabric in the province in which the study was conducted, it took for granted that third sector organisations are 'people with good-heart'. Clearly it is not possible to question intentions, but such a principle can be negative since it endorses voluntary sector and non-governmental organisations whose purposes may not always align with the process of empowerment and independence of disabled people. Furthermore, as Mura (2007) also argues, these associations may risk transforming their original voluntary mission into a more entrepreneurial one, thus serving their own needs, rather than addressing the requirements of the people they ought to represent. The principle of horizontal subsidiarity therefore needs to be carefully analysed in particular in those regions where there is a limited civic tradition and where the state is often absent, allowing the maintenance of criminal organisations (such as the Mafia), often disguised as third sector associations.

The development of a welfare society based on the collaboration among different local bodies and state schools is still a crucial ingredient of the policy of *integrazione scolastica* as it contributes to the development of a social approach to disability and education which is based upon solidarity, community assistance and networking among local bodies (see Law n. 328/2000 and Policy Guidelines, 2009). However, unlike the social model of disability, this *solidarity and community approach* to disability does not focus on the need to differentiate between impairment (individual) and disability (social), and on the active political role disabled people should play in the process of change, but rather on the need to ensure social and economic resources and public assistance to those people who needed additional state support.

The role of this sympathetic and civic approach to disability and education is also corroborated by the study of Putnam (1993). He argued that 'social capital' - strong social fabric, a sense of community, solidarity, civic traditions - was the relevant factor that contributed to the making of democracy in Italy (Putnam, 1993). The growing societal links enabled collaboration among local forces to implement the democratic policies formulated at the top. Following Putnam's analysis, some Italian policy makers claimed that 'social capital' was to be identified as a fundamental factor for the development of integration (Stellacci, 2003). At the same time, however, this position fails to examine possible economic explanations as the basis of this civic collaboration. Putnam's study actually fails to mention the possible links between the development of a community care system for dependent social groups and the fight against unemployment. As Oliver (1985) and Wolfensberger (1989) argue, it is evident that segregated provision provided a limited amount of work placements compared to community care provision and, consequently, the latter was also a way of creating extra employment at a local level. Providing care within the community ameliorated the lives of former asylum patients and promoted *integrazione*, but it was also a way of increasing the opportunities for social and assistance workers of the third sector. Many professionals who were originally working in segregated institutions moved into community services. This could also corroborate the idea, as shown in the following chapter, that a special education paradigm was exported along with the expertise of the personnel from special schools within the new mainstream setting.

The third sector contributed to the increasing employability of disabled people and therefore, to the reduction of public expenses. Disabled people who become independent and autonomous, thanks to community services, require less assistance in the long term, and, from an economic perspective, less funding than those disabled people who are dependent and live in segregated institutions for their entire lives. Evidently, this consideration motivated policy makers to increase the financial resources allocated to education and in particular to the education and training of disabled people. On the other hand, though, the role of the third sector, and the professionals working for disabled people, very rarely challenge the relation of power between disabled 'clients/users' and non-disabled 'providers' of services, leaving in place the hierarchical relation of those who define the needs of others and those who are in need (Armstrong, 2003). Such situation contributed to the production of discourses of dependency that construct disability as an individual deficit.

Pedagogical Factors

Unlike the English setting, the Italian context possesses a strong pedagogical tradition which identifies pedagogy as a 'scientific basis to the theory and practice of education' (Simon, 1999:38). The importance of pedagogical studies in the country was a crucial factor that paved the way to *integrazione scolastica*. The impact of international pedagogues and psychologists, in particular from France and the USA, contributed to the development of special pedagogy, a specialist branch of pedagogy dedicated to the study of learning of pupils with impairments (Canevaro, 1999).

Among the French scholars, the research of Séguin and Itard with the young boy Victor was a fundamental pedagogical underpinning that confronted the discourse of 'ineducability' in relation to disabled students. At the same time other theorists such as Maria Montessori (1870–1952), Sante de Sanctis (1862–1935), Giuseppe Ferruccio Montesano (1868–1961), Oury (1920–1998), Freinet (1896–1966), Decroly (1871–1932), Claparéde (1873–1940), Dewey (1859–1952), Piaget (1896–1980), Vygoskij (1896–1934) and Bruner (1915–) contributed and still contribute, to the development of educational theories supporting the process of *integrazione* of disabled people in ordinary settings. Furthermore, the work of Don Milani (1923–1967), a priest and an educator, had a strong influence upon Italian teachers. He founded the school of S. Andrea of Barbiana where he argued against a selective and rigid education system, which reproduces social class division between the rich and the poor. He challenged traditional teaching methods by introducing new tools and procedures that could meet the requirements of under-privileged students, especially those migrating from the south of Italy and/or the countryside.

Indeed, a crucial pedagogical factor that paved the way for the enactment of the policy of *integrazione scolastica* was the psychological study of learning exploring how it takes place and how it can be improved. Many Italian scholars (see Rugiu, 1979; Canevaro and Gaudreau, 1993; Cambi, 2005) emphasised that learning needs a stimulating setting for its development to take place and that, as in the work of Vygotskij (1987), it gains from the interaction between two or more individuals. Moreover, the pedagogical studies in Italy focussed on the *process* of learning of pupils rather than on the idea of fixed and inherited learning capacity. With this in mind, learning could be improved depending on pedagogical means and the development of research studies in cognition (Bruner, 1972). These studies challenged the traditional idea of learning as a one-way transmission of knowledge and underlined the importance of the central role played by the learner and the interaction with peers. Consequently, to promote significant learning, the school context needed to be modified both in terms of its structures (Oury and Vasquez 1982) and also in terms of cultural assumptions and practices (Bruner, 1996). Clearly, special school settings did not provide such encouraging conditions in relation to the development of learning as outlined by pedagogues and psychologists. Such considerations presented a fertile terrain to those opposing segregated schooling and aiming at creating an education system capable of ameliorating society.

Subsequently, the 'active school movement' developed by Decroly, Claparéde, Bovet and Piaget as well as the 'progressive pedagogy' of Dewey, paved the way for a vision of schools that could modify society into a democratic arena (Borghi, 1984). The influence of Dewey was incorporated into the development of CEMEA (*Centri di esercitazione ai metodi dell'educazione attiva* – active education training centres), and of MCE (*Movimento Cooperazione Educativa* – movement for educational cooperation) and, in the pioneering experience offered at the CEIS (*Centro Educativo Italo Svizzero* – Swiss-Italian Educational Centre) in Rimini. Such experiences were all attempts to break with the rigidity of the Italian education system and they anticipated some of the changes that *integrazione scolastica* attempted to introduce in regular school settings such as the process of individualisation of learning and the principle of learning through experience (active learning).

Clearly, pedagogy, and more specifically special pedagogy, has always played a crucial role in the development of teaching and learning. This position has been particularly relevant for developing ways of promoting learning for disabled students, as it has reinforced the idea that disabled students, in particular those with intellectual impairments, can improve their learning depending on the modalities within which they are taught and where they are taught. As in the work of Corbett and Norwich (1999) on connective pedagogy, Canevaro (1986) developed the concept of '*sfondo integratore*' (integrative framework) in order to underline how the quality of teaching and of the school support are crucial elements to promote the link between individualised teaching and classroom curricular objectives. However, what was crucial for special education pedagogues (Cornoldi and Vianello, 1995; Canevaro, 1999; Neri, 1999; Vianello, 1999; Canevaro, 2002) was that the principles behind teaching and learning for disabled students were not fundamentally different from those of students without impairments. What needed changing was the degree and the intensity of teaching and learning modalities (such as adaptation) for students with impairments compared to students without impairments (Ainscow, 1994). Special pedagogues argued that teaching and learning modalities specifically adapted for learners with intellectual impairments could become significant levers of change to enhance education for all students (Canevaro, 1999). Put simply, the experience of schooling of disabled students was conceived as the 'tip of the iceberg' of an education system that needed to be renovated and improved, by starting with testing out new teaching approaches and materials deriving from special education. Much in agreement with the work of Corbett and Norwich (1999), special pedagogy in Italy attempted to find models of pedagogy that could suit the common, specific and unique individual needs of each pupil and at the same time, that could be transferred from the special to the mainstream sector. However, as this book illustrates, distinct pedagogies were difficult to implement in the schools I visited for my research. Furthermore, theoretical studies about school change were rarely formalised into school practice and the processes of systematisation of adapted teaching procedures remained at a local level. With hindsight, what seemed to emerge was that special education was transplanted into the mainstream settings by means of focusing on individual adjustments and personalised responses for disabled pupils, without any formalised attempt to plan for a re-organisation of the mainstream setting nor for the identification of learning goals and teaching skills that could be shared by all students, as inclusion should do (Ainscow, 1997; 2000). Consequently, specific pedagogic approaches often led to separate learning pathways, either in segregated or in mainstream settings, rather than improving the quality of education for all students.

Nevertheless, the predominance of psychological and educational theories, contributed to the production of discourses about 'learning' constructed in cognitive, developmental and constructivist terms as well as to the construction of a specific type of educated subject (Fendler, 1998). Learning began to be interpreted in normative forms and in relation to average population referents. Consequently, although these pedagogical developments might have facilitated the dismantling of special institutions as places for learning, they also contributed to the construction of current assumptions of what is 'normal' learning and what counts as knowledge. For instance, they might have reinforced misconceptions about learning that determined the production of discourses and new labels such as 'special educational needs' (Corbett, 1996), 'learning difficulties' (Nind et al., 2005; Rix et al., 2005) and most recently 'attention deficit hyperactivity' and 'behavioural disorders'.

Religious Factors

Although Italy is a Republican State, the Church has always played, and still plays, a crucial cultural role, with the Catholic religion representing the dominant ideology. This was evident in the political role played by the Christian Democratic Party which ruled the country for more than 40 years and in the teaching of Roman Catholic religion in all state schools following the *Concordato* – a document signed between the Pope and Mussolini in 1929. As Foucault (2003) also indicates in most Western countries, ecclesiastical power has always sought the support from disciplinary and educational systems to establish its role. In order to understand the ideological role played by the Church in Italy I shall draw on the work of Gramsci (1971) who distinguished between political society - the State, bureaucratic and clerical bodies - and civil society - private sector and other voluntary and religious associations. My argument is that possibly, as a consequence of the signing of the Concordat between the State and the Church, there was a unification of political society (State) with civil society – mainly represented by the Roman Catholic Church. Somehow the Church was incorporated by the State so that they could both maintain their hegemonic power against opposing forces (such as communism). As Boggs (1976) indicates:

> Church in Italy was not merely part of the institutional status quo, a privileged bastion of economic wealth and social status; nor was Catholicism strictly a metaphysical set of beliefs. Religious ideology performed a concrete political function in containing and distorting popular rebellion, for example by stressing the natural (God-given) character of existing structures such as private property and the family, the importance of transcendental commitment over everyday ('earthly') collective action to change the world, the supposed moral virtues of poverty and weakness, and the sacrosanct nature of all forms of established authority. (Boggs, 1976:43)

This statement suggests that Catholicism permeated all social ranks and contributed to the development of discursive formations that complied with Church values. The influence of the Catholic Church impacted upon the construction of the notion of dis-ability, and consequently, on the formulation and implementation of the policy of *integrazione scolastica*. In particular, the role of the Church seems to have been central for the construction of disability as something inevitable, or a 'personal tragedy' where the disabled person is perceived as someone in 'need' of cure and assistance. This is particularly true when reading the Gospels (see for example the Gospel of St. Matthew) where Jesus Christ restores health to the poor and the deformed. This incident is often mentioned in public speeches and is exemplary of the role of the Church in the conceptualisation of the notion of disability. For instance, in the speech delivered by John Paul II during the Jubilee of Disabled People, the Pope referred to disability as a 'ruin for the world in which we live today but a joy for the other world' and to disabled people 'as the blessed creatures who will be compensated in Heaven' (Giovanni Paolo II, 2000). These statements, not only circulated discourses of charity and assistance in society, but also had a negative impact on the lives of disabled people, as they promulgated passivity and acceptance rather than political action, participation and possibly rebellion. Clearly, with hindsight, the Church might have contributed to the replacement of eighteenth and nineteenth century assumptions of sin and guilt, usually associated with disability, and might have substituted these misconceptions with alternative notions of accept-ance and human dignity (Onger and Robazzi, 2008). Nevertheless, I argue that the Church articulated discourses of charity and pity that negatively influenced the development of an independent and empowering disabled people's movement, deceived by a discourse of a better life after death.

In addition, the role of the Church and its alliance with the State can be considered as an example of 'pastoral power' (Foucault, 1982), and 'bio-power' (Foucault, 1978) and how the state manages to perpetuate its power through mechanisms of control. This pastoral power is not only concerned with the salvation of each single individual, but also with the modalities in which the shepherd keeps watch over, and manages to control, his flock individually. As Foucault indicates in the interview on 'Politics and Reason' (Foucault, 1988), this pastoral technology is a matter of constant attention that individualises, normalises and governs individuals. To put it simply the Roman Catholic Church has always played a central role in Italy and its influence is still visible in the organisation of the welfare state and in the reinforcing of discursive practices of dependence, vulnerability and assistance concerning disability and the management of disabled people in society. As Gramsci (1971) pertinently writes, the alliance between the Church and the State to achieve, maintain and sustain the unification of the country was an exemplar of hegemonic bloc.

This alternative account of religious factors is an attempt to increase social awareness regarding taken-for-granted discourses of 'benevolent acceptance' and 'voluntary assistance' and to start questioning the limits embedded in religious-based constructs and organisations.

CONCLUSION

In this chapter I have provided an account of the context relating to the reasons that led to the passing of this historically 'progressive policy'. As this chapter has shown, the policy of *integrazione* did not arise from a research-based decision about education. Although some research was conducted to demonstrate the validity of the policy from a pedagogical, social and economic perspective, the policy of *integrazione scolastica* appears to be the result of the fusion – or the hegemonic bloc - of different social groups. They were used to support the ruling group's major interests and to maintain the status quo of the newly born state against possible perils (Armstrong, 1999) as exemplified by the social upheavals of the 70s. The interests of ruling groups – for example state and Church - were transferred and shared by different lobbies – teachers, psychologists, educationalists, parents, and disabled people – and it was only through such a social consensus that *integrazione scolastica* was conceived as the only possible alternative to segregated education. Subsequent legislative measures therefore, attempted to add educational value and quality to decisions taken under the pressure of political, economic and social contingencies. By acting as a hegemonic bloc, the policy of *integrazione scolastica* managed to concretely disseminate a philosophy of integration and to put an end to segregated education throughout a divided country. Despite the existence of a few exemplars of special schools (which should be further investigated), nowadays almost all students attend local schools and this is certainly one of the most important legacies brought about by the policy of *integrazione scolastica* that needs to be acknowledged. At the same time, this chapter indicates that this policy shares continuities with the special needs education paradigm. In the following chapters, evidence to substantiate such an argument will be presented.

INCLUSIVE EDUCATION AND SPECIAL NEEDS EDUCATION

Much in agreement with a radical interpretation of the notion of inclusion, this chapter exemplifies the differences among the concepts of inclusion, special needs education and integration and their being embedded in different theoretical frameworks. The argument presented in this chapter will seek to break out of the traditional 'special education' rationale which immediately locates the issues of inclusion and exclusion with the identification and remediation of students categorised as 'different' on the basis of an individual impairment, social and economic disadvantage and/or ethnic origin (Ainscow & Booth, 1998). The chapter will be divided into four main sections beginning with an analysis of why inclusive education is usually associated with disability and an investigation into inclusive education as an international educational imperative. Then a section will address the issue of inclusive education as a theoretical and sociological concept with its own critical approaches to education and educational goals. The chapter then looks at the notion of inclusive education in Italy and how different contexts and histories may determine different interpretations of such a concept. Finally, after a brief historical description of the development of special education in Italy, the chapter will focus on the resilience of special education language and how such a language may represent a barrier for the development of inclusive education.

INCLUSIVE EDUCATION AND DISABILITY

An increasing number of supra-national and governmental bodies suggest that inclusion is the key educational principle through which to address issues of equality and diversity in education and to improve the overall quality of the education systems (Department for Education and Employment, 1997; Department for Education and Skills, 2004; Kyriazopoulou & Weber, 2009; OECD, 2004; UNESCO, 1994, 2003b). Under the banner of inclusion, many struggles, concerned with the removal of all discriminatory barriers, are being fought for the construction of a more just and equitable society. It is not surprising that the inclusion principle becomes morally and ethically shared by those who believe in the development of a more democratic education as the basis and requirement for wider social reforms. Although this principle is widely shared among theorists and policy makers, there is still, arguably, a lack of consensus about what inclusion means and, most importantly, what its implications are at the level of policy and practice (Ainscow & Booth, 1998; Ainscow, Booth, & Dyson, 2006; Felicity Armstrong & Barton, 2001; Campbell, 2002). Slee and Allan (2001) argue, that the notion of inclusive education is often misinterpreted and considered as a progressive continuum stemming from a special education needs standpoint. This latter misconception inevitably results in many people, in particular disabled people, still experiencing exclusion in modern societies (DPI, 2005; EDF, 2004) despite the passing of anti-discriminatory legislative measures.

A common aspect of the policy of inclusion is that although there are different interpretations, they usually focus on the learning experience of disabled people and of those students defined as having 'special educational needs'. The interpretation of inclusion used within this book makes a case that inclusive education does not concern only disabled people and students perceived as having 'special educational needs'. The focus on the experience of disabled people is due to the fact that firstly, disabled people continue to experience discrimination at school, as exclusionary practices become more visible 'along the lines of class, 'race', ethnicity and language, disability, gender and sexuality and geographic location' (Slee, 2001:116)' and secondly, because their experience of political and social struggle may be relevant in understanding how exclusion manifests itself in society today (Armstrong and Barton, 2001). As Armstrong et al. (2000) state, disabled people have taken the lead in exploring political aspects of education and they have embraced the principle of inclusion as their underpinning value (DPI, 2005). For this reason the issue of how disability is conceptualised suggests a useful and important starting-point in understanding how different actors make sense of inclusive education both in terms of theory and of practice. At the same time, the focus on disability issues does not preclude the incorporation of issues of discrimination and exclusion concerning the wider society; nor does it confine its focus to legal entitlements and particular requirements for an identified and 'categorised' minority (F. Armstrong, 2003b).

In addition, the disability movement is relevant as an emerging new social movement at the forefront of the struggle for a more inclusive society and education (Barnes, Mercer, & Shakespeare, 1999; Barnes, Oliver, & Barton, 2002; Charlton, 1998; Mike Oliver, 1990). Much in line with a Gramscian vision of the potentially transformative effects of action of new social groups (1971), the role of the disabled people's movement can be conceived as a new social movement capable of triggering radical changes that can influence politics and promote action for change by 'presenting old issues in new forms' (Oliver, 1990:130). Moreover, it is necessary to underline that disabled people have for a long time been on the sideline of the social fight for civil rights in the history of disability and education. Therefore it is necessary to provide a space for their voices and perspectives to be heard (Armstrong, 2007; Barnes, et al., 1999).

As argued elsewhere (D'Alessio, 2009), inclusive education therefore, has got nothing to do with the inclusion of disabled pupils into regular classrooms but it is concerned with the making of inclusive education systems. Inclusive education goes beyond issues of access and equality related to pupils identified as having special educational needs in order to encompass issues of systemic educational change – radical changes of the education systems for all students. How changes are to occur, and what types of changes are required are the main questions confronted by those who are involved in the struggle for inclusion (Barton & Armstrong, 2007).

INCLUSIVE EDUCATION FROM AN INTERNATIONAL PERSPECTIVE

Soon after the international Salamanca World Conference on Special Needs Education (UNESCO, 1994), the word inclusion appeared in almost all major international documents and reports of most supra-national bodies (Meijer, Soriano and Watkins, 2003b; OECD, 1997, 1999; UNESCO, 2003b). In these reports, the education of children at risk of being excluded and marginalised is promoted as one of the main points on the international agenda. Following the demands of the Convention on the Rights of the Child (United Nations, 1989) and the subsequent United Nations Standard Rules on the Equalizations of Opportunities for Persons with Disabilities (United Nations, 1993), all children, youth and adults 'with disabilities', are, in principle, entitled to the same educational opportunities in an integrated setting (UN Standard Rule n. 6). Similarly, the UN Convention on the Rights of Persons with Disabilities (2006) has reasserted the principle of inclusion as a way of fighting all forms of discrimination (including segregated education) as an issue of human rights. This international commitment to inclusion, however, has not resulted in a common interpretation of the concept of inclusive education, which still means different things to different researchers, reflecting contrasting theoretical and ideological contexts in which inclusion is considered (D'Alessio and Watkins, 2009).

As is evident from cross cultural studies conducted by different international bodies such as UNESCO (2003b, 2008), European Agency for Development in Special Needs Education (EADSNE, 2008; Meijer, Soriano and Watkins, 2003a) in some countries, inclusive education is mainly concerned with the dismantling of segregated education, whereas in other countries it is concerned with the attempt to increase the number of pupils accessing basic education. In particular, in the European context, we may identify two main conceptualisations of the notion of inclusive education: the first one concerning the provision for children identified with 'special educational needs' - either in regular or special settings – and how these settings can respond to pupils' different needs (Meijer, Soriano and Watkins, 2003; 2003b), and the second one concerning the 'education for all' (EFA) project and how to guarantee basic education to all pupils (UNESCO, 1990, 2000, 2003b). As a consequence of these two international priorities - the 'mainstreaming' imperatives and the 'education for all' - some countries have enacted anti-discrimination policies which have been mainly concerned with the entitlement of disabled students to attend local schools – for example the Special Needs Education and Disability Act 2001 (HMSO, 2001) in the UK and the Law 12/2/2005 in France.

Different interpretations of the concept of inclusive education, however, determine the enactment and the implementation of different and often diverging educational policies and practices in different contexts. An example of this problem emerges from the report of the European Agency for Development in Special Needs Education (Meijer, Soriano and Watkins, 2003a) in which inclusive education seemed to be interpreted, by some country members, as a new terminology for special needs education, thus allowing the maintenance of forms of segregated settings within the education system despite the passing of 'inclusive policies'. Recently, however, the interpretation of inclusive education in Agency member countries has undergone relevant changes to include issues that go beyond the study of a 'category' of pupils, such as those identified as having special educational needs to incorporate the study of how contexts and schools are attempting to undergo changes in order to welcome the diversity of the student population.

As far as the notion of 'Education for All' is concerned (UNESCO, 1990, 2000), inclusive education is often interpreted as a way of ensuring access to basic education to all children, notwithstanding the type of context in which education is taking place particularly in those countries in which people are fighting with issues such as poverty, famine, diseases and war. This target is to be achieved by developing policy guidelines that fight against all forms of discrimination and improve the quality of schooling for all, taking into account social, political and economic constraints that may impact upon the localised meaning and the making of inclusion. This view is also supported by the Disabled Peoples' International (DPI henceforward) an international organisation of disabled people that understands and promotes inclusive education as an 'Education for All' policy (DPI, 2005). It has been suggested that this interpretation of the notion of inclusive education could contribute to the passing of legislation necessary to improve students' access to curricula and their participation in learning (UNESCO, 2003a, 2003b, 2008).

Lately, however, international organisations such as UNESCO and the European Agency for Development in Special Needs Education, have discussed inclusion in terms of participation, equality and quality of the general education system, thus supporting the current interpretation of inclusion as a human rights issue (UNESCO, 2009; D'Alessio, Watkins and Donnelly, in press).

Defining the Concept of Inclusive Education

Inclusive education is a controversial field because there are almost as many definitions as there are people who study it and who rely on differing theoretical frameworks. Dyson (1999) for example, talks of 'inclusions' rather than 'inclusion'. This view is also supported by scholars who argue that there exists, from a synchronic perspective, different types of inclusion which overlap with one another, such as 'full', 'responsible' and 'cautious' inclusion (Vaughn and Schumm, 1995; Hornby 1999 in Evans & Lunt, 2002). Likewise, Peter Clough and Jenny Corbett (2000) emphasise that there are many different diachronic interpretations of inclusive education depending on the dominant historical paradigms of the time. They distinguish between five key theories of inclusive education, each one characterised by a specific ideological approach to education as follows: the psycho-medical legacy, the sociological response, the curricular approach, the school improvement strategies and the disability studies (Clough & Corbett, 2000). Similarly, Cigman (2007) distinguishes among three different types of inclusion: radical, moderate and the UNESCO positions. She argues that the first position can be identified with the works of the Centre for Studies on Inclusive Education (CSIE) and Parents for Inclusion, who strongly support the dismantling of special schools and the education of all pupils within regular school settings. The moderate position is the one supported by Mary Warnock and her followers who argue that for some pupils with profound learning difficulties and impairments (for example pupils with autism), ordinary schools are 'potentially catastrophic' (2007:XIX). Consequently, their interpretation of inclusion offers space for sustaining some special schools. The last position, which Cigman identifies with the UNESCO position is not concerned with the old debate which opposes special to mainstream schools, but focuses instead on the need to reform schools so that they can meet all students' requirements. This vision, Cigman (2007) claims, takes into account the possibility of maintaining special schools, as some 'needs' may, it is argued, only be addressed in special settings. Inclusion, she argues is not about where you educate students, but how you address the 'dilemma of difference' (2007:XXII), hence to provide the adequate number of resources and distribute them equally according to peoples' needs (Nussbaum, 2000; Sen, 1992). The conceptualisation and the response to difference are very complex educational issues, especially for those pupils who have been identified as 'more vulnerable' (Terzi, 2005). Two opposing perspectives seem to emerge within the education sector. On the one hand there is an approach that supports the use of classification systems necessary to ensure adequate provision of resources depending on pupils' needs (Warnock, 2005:11). On the other hand, there is an approach that argues for the need of eliminating these systems of classification as they may end up discriminating some pupils through a labelling procedure. The human right approach to education, as theorised by inclusive education theorists (Armstrong & Barton, 1999; Barton, 2008) is an attempt to address such a contradiction.

As a consequence of the different ways of defining inclusive education, each study concerning inclusion must have as its point of departure its own definition of inclusion. In this book, inclusive education is defined as the educational principle that aims at transforming education systems and creating more equal and just societies. It is concerned with all of us and suggests possible routes to make radical educational and social changes. It fights against political, social, economic and cultural barriers that hinder the participation of all students in the process of learning regardless of their biological condition, social and economic background and ethnic origin. As Barton puts it:

> Inclusive education is not merely about providing access into mainstream school for pupils who have previously been excluded. It is not about closing down an unacceptable system of segregated provision and dumping those pupils in an unchanged mainstream system. Existing school systems in terms of physical factors, curriculum aspects, teaching expectations and styles, leadership roles, will have to change. (Barton, 1998:84)

This statement challenges current dominant interpretations and actions concerning schooling and education, stresses the way in which inclusive education demands a variety of efforts both at the level of theory and practice. Inclusive education does not only concern itself with the technicalities of teaching and learning (for example didactics) and how students with difficulties may access the curriculum. It must also explore the theory and ideology which informs teachers' actions, and equally importantly, take account of issues related to what education is and what its fundamental purposes are (Ainscow, et al., 2006; F. Armstrong, 2003a, 2003b; Giroux, 2001; Slee, 1998, 2007).

Inclusive education is a contentious issue that requires continuous conceptual re-definition depending on the context and the actors under discussion and analysis. However, as Barton (2001b) argues, the struggle for inclusive education is neither utopian nor inconclusive and despite the attacks in Mary Warnock's pamphlet (2005), there is enough evidence that research has been conducted in the field of inclusive education to support its further development (Ainscow, 2005, 2007; Ainscow & Booth, 1998; Ainscow, et al., 2006; Allan, 1999, 2003; D. Armstrong, 2003; F. Armstrong, 2003b; Barton & Armstrong, 2007; Booth & Ainscow, 2000; UNESCO, 2003b). The possibility of creating an inclusive society through an inclusive education system increases with the number of people who share that hope. That is why the experience of disabled people becomes central to the struggle for change. As Barton has argued, inclusive education is not an individual or a fragile aspiration, but a 'collective hope' (Barton, 2001a:4).

Exclusion Processes

Some commentators have argued that in order to overcome the issues of inter-pretations and policy implementation in different contexts, inclusion could be better understood in relation to exclusion (Ainscow & Booth, 1998; Booth, 1995). This view entails responding to questions such as: who is excluded, from where, for what reasons and which mechanisms determine exclusion.

Not only can exclusion take many forms (for example curricular, organisational and institutional), but it is often, also, invisible (Armstrong, et al., 2000). Like the issue of inclusion, exclusion is not as straightforward as it may seem. Exclusion may take different forms ranging from segregation in special institutions and classrooms to the process of effacing diversity by 'fusing the abnormality with the normality' (Stiker, 1999:136). As Stiker (1999) argues, exclusion is very often disguised in Western countries as a form of integration. Thus, integrative policies may paradoxically contribute to the disappearance of difference, rather than to its celebration (Stiker, 1999). Unmasking all different forms of exclusion is not only a matter of dismantling segregated systems of education, but may also include dealing with covert forms of exclusion inside the mainstream. In line with this consideration, Booth has introduced the issue of 'coded' forms of exclusion which may be found embedded in a system (Booth, 2000:91). Similarly, Ainscow, Booth and Dyson (2006) have described exclusion not only as a state of being banned from a local school but also as the perpetuation of discriminatory processes in place within schools (and society). In order to be discovered, such forms of exclusion require a thorough analysis of those practices and policies already in place, which are often taken for granted (hence their invisibility) and that can be discriminatory despite ostensible good intentions to be otherwise. An example of this is the process of statementing students with 'special educational needs' in the UK. This procedure allows the allocation of fundamental resources to promote the inclusion of some students into the mainstream, whilst nevertheless contributing to the construction of some students' identities as 'others' in relation to the majority of peers without a statement of special educational needs or a Record of Needs.

The process of analysis of visible and invisible forms of exclusion requires a changing lens through which things have traditionally been seen and understood. Charlton (1998) for example, argues that when investigating the oppression of disabled people, we can be faced with the analysis of internalised paradigms – structures with which people have lived for so long that they consider them as natural. Educational changes from an inclusive perspective imply, of course, a change of these internalised paradigms, based on an understanding that things are not natural but instead result from decisions taken by specific actors, with particular aims and in particular historical and contextual settings (Apple, 2008). All these elements, including issues of power relation (such as who is making the decision, where and how), need to be further explored if we want to fundamentally challenge all forms of marginalisation and exclusion. Most importantly, in order to fight against exclusion in all its different forms it is necessary to listen to the voices of those who have been excluded. This view necessitates 'listening to unfamiliar voices, being open and empowering all members' (Barton, 1998:85) such as students, whose ideas and wishes are too often neglected by policy makers, as well as disabled people, migrants and travellers' children, whose rights have often been put aside.

As Barton suggests, inclusive education should fundamentally be a 'celebration of difference' in which human diversity is valued and each individual's dignity is respected (Barton, 1998:80) - not a system reinforcing existing inequalities. Consequently, discourses of valuing diversity and difference as educational resources must be detected and transformed in order to shift from a mere process of acceptance and tolerance into a real process of celebration of difference. In order to concretely develop the process of inclusion, a celebration of difference should include debates about how diversity can be valued within and outside schools and should also take into account the crucial changes that curriculum, pedagogy and assessment procedures should undergo in the mainstream settings. Taking full account of different forms of exclusion, the study that informs this book analysed those policies and practice that have been in place long enough to be considered as 'natural'.

INCLUSIVE EDUCATION: A PROCESS OF TRANSFORMATION OF THE EDUCATION SYSTEM

Inclusive education has been described as a continuum rather than as a static condition (Jordan & Goodey, 1996). Often defined as an ongoing process (Ainscow & Booth, 1998; 2000; Rustemier & Booth, 2005), inclusive education may be understood as requiring a continual effort to improve the level of responsiveness of schools to all of their students' requirements, keeping at the forefront inclusive values and ethos (Corbett & Slee, 2000). It would be impossible, of course, to ensure universal inclusive education by devising a uniform model – not least, because a school cannot be 'made' inclusive by following a recipe for policy and practice. What can be implemented and disseminated is, rather, an attitude towards change in relation to all those conditions that hamper inclusion and foster exclusion (Booth & Ainscow, 2000). Fundamental to such an undertaking is an understanding that schools are embedded in different contexts which produce different constraints (D'Alessio & Watkins, 2009).

For this reason, inclusive education does not encompass only schooling and the way schooling is organised and provided, but must also be concerned with the radical and broader changes necessary to improve the living conditions of all citizens in which education plays a major role. As Armstrong et al. (2000) argue:

> ....inclusive education is not an end in itself. Nor ultimately is the fundamental issue that of disabled people. In educational terms it is about the value and well-being of all pupils. Thus, the key concern is about how, where and with what consequences do we educate all children and young people. This inevitably involves both a desire for, and engagement with, the issue of change. (Felicity Armstrong, et al., 2000:1)

These authors underline how inclusive education relates to the consequences of educating all children and to improvements in their life prospects and does not constrain itself to the process of mainstreaming disabled students into regular settings. For them, inclusive education concerns the wider society, in which education is conceived of as being an agent of change rather than being a reproducer of social inequality (Armstrong & Barton, 1999).

Developing inclusive education in any one school necessitates careful consideration of the school's starting point and its specific cultural, historical and social contexts. Such an approach suggests that inclusion involves two processes:

> ...the process of increasing participation of pupils within the cultures and curricula of mainstream schools and the process of decreasing exclusionary pressures. (Booth, 1996:34)

The clear implication here is that the development of inclusion requires action inside and outside schools. Changes at the level of curriculum delivery inside the school, for example, would not result in any real change, if teachers were not relieved from external pressures that society and, most particularly, assessment procedures and standardised attainment of traditional knowledge, placed upon them [see the insights of teachers constrained by a highly selective and exclusionary education system (Armstrong & Moore, 2004)]. As a consequence of this view, interpretations of inclusive education entail a sociological analysis of education and pedagogy that explores the forces that may oppress schools and teachers along with the attitudes and behaviours that perpetuate exclusion.

As Mittler (2000) argues, inclusive education can also be defined as a process of reform. In this regard, inclusive education is not concerned with a particular group of students but with the restructuring of the education system in general; a system capable of responding effectively to the totality of children. Taking account of the limited amount of resources available and current curricular and assessment constraints in Western world systems of education, it may prove difficult in the immediate future to implement a change of the education system. Consequently, some authors indeed (Campbell, 2002; Ianes, 2005; Terzi, 2007) argue for the implementation and development of special schools, or of systems of classification, such as the International Classification of Functioning Disability and Health (WHO 2001) for an equal (re)distribution of resources, in order to establish priorities whilst a more thorough transformation of the education system is developed. This view may be seen as part of the wider debate about how to tackle immediate problems. Nevertheless, it ends up reinforcing ill-founded claims (Barton, 2005) that deflect the attention from a necessary debate about how to improve schooling for all and how to *transform* and not only reform existing education systems. In fact, while a 'transformation' implies a re-conceptualisation of education systems by taking into account new challenges and educational objectives for the school of the twenty first century, a reform implies a process of adaptation of already existing systems. Thus, when we are concerned with the redistribution of resources and the increasing of funding to manage diversity we are probably addressing inclusion as a process of reforming education systems, and therefore may risk reducing the issues regarding inclusive education to one of making a call on more public funds (Slee, 2007):

> This often has little to do with establishing an inclusive curriculum, pedagogic practices or classroom organisation to reconstruct schools. More typically it is a systematic approach to acquiring human resources to mind the disabled student. (Slee, 2007:181)

In addition Slee observes that:

> Authentic inclusive school reform is costly as it does imply the need for reforms to workforce preparation, pedagogic practice, curriculum orientations and materials, evaluative frameworks and the physical design of many existing school structures. The redeployment of existing structures and incremental increases to special educational resources is regarded as an easier option for government and is industrially more palatable. Such conditions place different students at continuing risk of exclusion in and out of regular schools. (Slee, 2007:181)

Much in agreement with the previous statements, inclusive education is not about meeting the needs of a 'vulnerable' minority in a mainstream setting, but should rather be concerned with answering fundamental questions about what type of school is needed to meet the requirements of all students and, most importantly, what the goals of education should be:

> A movement towards inclusion is not about making marginal adjustments but rather about asking the fundamental questions concerning the way in which the organisation is currently structured. (Ainscow, 1997:5)

It is within this radical position of inclusive education and the issues around change that this book has chosen to align with.

INCLUSIVE EDUCATION: ITALIAN STYLE

The use of terminology such as inclusive education is rather new in the Italian context (Caldin, 2004; Canevaro, 2006b, 2007; Canevaro & Mandato, 2004; Dovigo & Ianes, 2008; Ianes, 2005; Ianes & Tortello, 1999; Medeghini, 2006, 2008). Historically speaking, the term inclusion in Italy has always been used to refer to 'social inclusion' without any clear reference to education. Documents from the Ministry of Labour and Social Security and the Ministry of Social Solidarity report that *inclusione* consists of a social policy which aims to foster equal opportunities to access education, training, employment, housing, services and health, particularly for disadvantaged groups within the population such as migrants, prisoners, drug users, disabled people and in general all those who are at risk of being excluded from society. Lately, however, a clear reference to the concept of inclusive education has been made by the Ministry of Public Instruction with the carrying out of a national action-research project named 'I CARE' (Ministero della Pubblica Istruzione, 2007).

Until recently there has been a general tendency of rejecting the term inclusive education considered as inappropriate for the Italian context (Canevaro, 2001; Vianello, 2008). Yet, there is the need to create a new terminology which encapsulates the new international trend of inclusion and to maintain, at the same time, the legacy of *integrazione scolastica* (de Anna, 2007). With this in mind, the new expression '*integrazione da una prospettiva inclusiva* – integration from an inclusive perspective – was coined (Canevaro & Mandato, 2004). Evidence of this general tendency can be found in the following extract:

> Let's take into consideration the possibility of adopting, as required, the Anglo-Saxon terminology, and change the word *integrazione* to that of inclusion. According to the Anglo-Saxons, inclusion indicates, without any ambiguity, a person who is born in an inclusive environment, such as an environment which includes him since the very moment in which he is born and does not need to integrate the newly born in the future (as also said elsewhere). Nevertheless, the Italian language does not refer to inclusion with the same positive connotations of the English language. Perhaps, under the constraints to conform with international trends, we might end up adopting this terminology [such as inclusion] - although, in the past, we have argued that it was inadequate for the Italian context; at the same time, however, we do not want that the strength, which is implicit in the word *integrazione*, intended as a continuous process which has never been taken for granted, may be lost forever. (Canevaro and Mandato, 2004:168)

From a linguistic perspective, the word inclusion does not seem to possess positive connotations when translated into Italian as it may echo the idea of being 'enclosed' (put inside or alternatively segregated). At the same time, in the statement above, inclusive education is not always used interchangeably with that of *integrazione scolastica*, as the latter is considered to possess a legacy of cultural, political and social struggles that the concept of inclusion does not express and encapsulate. The Italian scholar provides a possible interpretation of inclusion that is interpreted in terms of 'environmental' adaptations which foster universal access. Arguably, inclusive education is mainly perceived as a new mainstreaming policy that focuses on school settings rather than focussing only on pupils' deficits. Nevertheless, such an interpretation failed to make sense of the complex paradigmatic shift that the appropriation of the term inclusion should entail.

Clearly, there seems to be a pressure to adopt a new terminology. Yet, this is a very difficult situation as different theories can reclaim the appropriation of inclusion without taking into account the theoretical principles supporting it. The concept of inclusive education could be easily usurped by forms of argument that pretend to support inclusion, but which are instead only a reproduction of previous discriminatory mindsets (Slee, 2007).

At the moment, it is possible to identify two main definitions of inclusive education in the Italian context. The first definition suggests that *integrazione* and inclusion are considered as synonyms. This is particularly visible in the recent Ministerial Policy Guidelines for the Integration of Pupils with Disabilities (Ministero dell' Istruzione Università e Ricerca, 2009) in which the term integration is used together with that of inclusion. Inclusion is also used in connection with the following words: 'inclusion of pupils with disabilities' and 'scholastic inclusion of disabled pupils', thus suggesting a link with the process of mainstreaming disabled students into regular schools (as integration does) rather than with a process of transformation of school cultures and contexts (as inclusion implies). The second definition interprets inclusive education as a broader type of *integrazione*. Such a definition associates inclusive education specifically with the experience of those students at risk of being excluded from the process of learning, such as those students identified as having 'special educational needs' but without a statement (Canevaro, 2006a; Ianes, 2005).

In relation to the second tendency, which links inclusive education with the education of students perceived as having 'special educational needs' without statements, Ianes argues that:

> ...it is important to distinguish between the practice of *integrazione* and those of inclusion. *Integrazione* concerns disabled students, such as those students who have statements of SEN, whereas, inclusion refers to the praxis of individualisation. The latter tackles all educational needs of all students with special educational needs [such as those without a statement]. By taking into account all special educational needs, we are inevitably responding in an inclusive way, such as taking on board all students' requirements and respecting their dignity. A true inclusive intervention consists in providing the necessary individualised formative response. (Ianes, 2005:70).

Although Ianes seems to be genuinely concerned with the learning processes of all students, he appears to envisage meeting their requirements through a special needs education approach. As this statement indicates, inclusive education is perceived as the type of education that caters for all students individually, and in particular for those students who have difficulties at school but are not provided with a statement of special educational needs. Thus inclusive education is interpreted as a way of tackling the limits of a re-distribution policy that does not take into account those students who fall outside the medically constructed eligibility criteria, but who still need extra support and resources. The focus, therefore, is still on the pupils and their deficiencies rather than on the structures of the education system.

Recently Canevaro (2007) takes into account the possibility of changing the theoretical perspective from which scholars and practitioners alike should consider inclusion:

> Inclusion is a fundamental right and it is in relation with the concept of 'belonging'. People with or without disabilities can interact as peers. An inclusive education allows the ordinary school to improve its quality: a school in which all children are welcomed, where they can learn according to their own pace and, most importantly where they can participate, a school where children manage to understand all diversities and that these diversities are enriching. Thus diversity becomes normal. The same for the work place, for transportation, for social and cultural life. The purpose of inclusion is to allow each individual to access 'normal' life in order to grow and develop as a complete human being. (Canevaro, 2007:12)

This definition seems to officially set the date that records the Italian turn for the approval of the new terminology of 'inclusion'. Eventually, it could also sow the seeds of a new conceptualisation of inclusion in terms of participation and belonging within the theoretical framework of human rights. However, this interpretation retains the dichotomy between normality and disability that shares continuity with that which is found in special needs education. In particular, some interpretations of the concept of inclusion still do not question a dominant abilist view of normalcy (Oliver, 1999). In contrast they seem to argue for facilitating the access of disabled people into normal life by accepting diversity as a common human feature and by reducing its 'specialness'.

Lately, a small group of researchers (Fornasa & Medeghini, 2003; Medeghini, 2006, 2007, 2008; 2009; Medeghini & Valtellina, 2006) including myself (D'Alessio, 2004; 2005; 2007a; 2007b; 2008; 2009; 2010) have sought to address the issue of inclusive education through the application of new premises, such as the social model of disability (Oliver, 1990; 1996). They support the need to adopt inclusion not as a linguistic and semantic exercise, but as an attempt to challenge current school organisation and routines as the starting point for a discussion regarding inclusive education. They argue that the terms *integrazione* and inclusion are not synonyms, rather they are based on different conceptual standpoints:

> The approach used by integration currently refers to the special education needs principle and the forms of rationalisation of the school system (resources, procedures and structures); the approach of inclusion, based on a non-deficitarian notion of difference, focuses on all people that take part in social and institutional life, on social and educational relations, and on the barriers to learning and participation that may determine exclusion or marginalisation from education and training pathways (Medeghini, et al., 2009:51)

This statement indicates that there are different interpretations of the concept of inclusive education, and that whilst integration is usually interpreted in relation to pupils with statements and the way to respond to their 'needs', inclusion is interpreted in terms of exclusion mechanisms that need to be identified and dismantled in order to allow the full participation of all pupils in the process of learning. Such an interpretation, however, still constitutes a small academic niche in the debate concerning the development of inclusive education in Italy.

As a result of the Italian translation of the English *Index for Inclusion* (Dovigo & Ianes, 2008) the term *inclusione* has been used as a substitute of *integrazione* or in association with the latter. Nevertheless, the dominant Italian definition of inclusive education remains ontologically different from the definition used within this book that is derived from and influenced by usages from British social modellist theorists and literature sources. Put simply, in Italy, when adopted, the term inclusive education is generally interpreted as a new definition of *integrazione scolastica* and it usually refers to pupils at risk of being excluded from the process of learning in the mainstream setting. Therefore, it refers to the pedagogical attempts (such as processes of adaptation, differentiation and individualisation of teaching and learning) made by specialised personnel to respond to the 'needs' of 'vulnerable' minorities (such as migrant students, disabled pupils or pupils with 'special educational needs' without a statement) and with the allocation and re-distribution of extra resources to ordinary schools.

SPECIAL EDUCATION IN ITALY: A HISTORY OF CARE AND COMPENSATION

The issue of special education and schooling – either private or state – is an underdebated topic in the Italian literature. This is clearly a limitation as, when looking at the history of special needs education in Italy through the lens of the social model of disability and the works of Foucault, it is possible to find enough evidence of how the special needs education paradigm might have influenced the development of integration policy and consequently limited the development of inclusion. For example, most Italian literature concerning the policy of *integrazione scolastica* takes for granted that special schools and institutions have completely disappeared (de Anna, 1997). On the contrary, national statistical data available on the international database of the European Agency for Development in Special Needs Education (EADSNE, 2006; 2008), for example, illustrates that special schools are still part of the education system in Italy. Although they occupy a very peripheral position, they clearly have not been completely dismantled. These schools include special schools for blind and deaf students (9 in total in 2008). Similarly, the president of the national federation for disabled people (known as FISH - Federazione Italiana Superamento Handicap), Pietro Barbieri (2007) recently argued that institutionalisation is still a reality in this country and that it squanders the financial resources that could be better used to promote integration.

It is important to emphasise that unlike Britain (Tomlinson, 1982), the history of special education in Italy paid very little attention to the study of possible social motives that might have contributed to the implementation of segregated education. It focussed instead on the need to provide special education facilities for those children with impairments who were usually hidden at home, victims of ignorance, superstition and religious fears. For this reason, segregated settings and primitive forms of special education in Italy were inevitably positively accepted, especially when comparison was made with previous forms of marginalisation of disabled pupils who were usually kept at home (Meijer & Abbring, 1994). Thus, although Italy was the exception to the big growth of special needs institutions throughout Europe (Stiker, 1999), and state special education was introduced very late as a consequence of the economic boom of the early 1960s (Meijer & Abbring, 1994), it was clearly welcomed as a valid and widely accepted alternative for the education of disabled people within the national education system.

From a historical perspective, the first legislation to explicitly engage with the education and assistance of disabled people was Law n. 753 enacted in 1862, when charitable institutions began to cater for 'the poor and the sick'. A clear reference to the education of *idioti* – people with intellectual impairments – was made in 1884 when the first mental asylum was opened in Rome (Zappaterra, 2003). Subsequently, in 1890, the State promulgated a series of legislative measures to create and administer new public charitable institutions (known as IPAB, *Istituzioni Pubbliche di Assistenza e Beneficienza* – Charity and Public Assistance Institutions) that were in charge of educating and guiding marginalised groups of the population. Gradually, other institutions were opened and people, first considered as 'uneducable', were provided with some sort of education, yet in segregated settings. The underlying assumption, which justified their segregation, was that these individuals were 'dangerous, both for the community and for themselves' (de Anna, 2000:138). That is to say 'the individual who is not exactly ill and who is not strictly speaking criminal' (Foucault, 2003:34) but who requires medico-legal intervention to control their *dangerousness*. Consequently, as Gelati (2004) has also argued, since the nineteenth century, the role played by medico-judicial officers has continued to be crucial, and it has influenced the conceptualisation of disability as an individual condition caused by functional deficits.

Depending on geographical proximity, philosophical heritage and linguistic similarities, the pedagogical experimentations held in France at the beginning of the nineteenth century, strongly influenced the development of special education in Italy. In their study on the history of special education in Italy, some scholars (Canevaro & Gaudreau, 1993; Gelati, 2004) locate the theoretical underpinnings of *integrazione scolastica* in the works of two French doctors, Jean Marc Gaspard Itard and Edouard Séguin. The historical and pedagogical 'myth' (Canevaro, 2007:14) within which the policy of *integrazione scolastica* is originated is the account of how Itard (and Séguin) managed to educate a young 'wild boy' found in the French forests of Aveyron, and subsequently 'named' by his educational tutors as Victor. On the one hand, this episode clearly contributed to the understanding that all students could be educated regardless of their physical and mental conditions, if they were provided with adequate support and assistance. On the other hand, it inevitably suggested continuities between the special education framework and the *integrazione* epistemological paradigm, both intended specifically as the academic subjects concerned with the education and rehabilitation of disabled pupils. As Foucault remarked in his works on the three major figures of abnormality in Western society (Foucault, 2003), it was in the nineteenth century that the discourse of *rectifiability*, promoted by the French medical establishment, substitutes that of the *incorrigibility* of abnormal individuals:

> Disability may well be something that upsets the natural order, but disability is not monstrosity because it has a place in civil and canon law. The disabled

person may not conform to nature, but the law in some way provides for him. (Foucault, 2003:64)

The 'wild boy' Victor could be seen as an example of what Foucault (2003) identifies as the individual to be corrected and who falls under the technologies of particular types of knowledge (for example medicine, psychiatry, eugenics). This subject becomes the centre of an apparatus for correction, and it runs counter to an interpretation of *integrazione scolastica* as an inclusive policy. In contrast, this narrative contributes to the re-production of misconceptions of disability as something 'wrong' located within the person that must be 'rectified' and 'corrected' by professionals. Consequently, by linking the roots of *integrazione scolastica* to the works of Itard and Séguin, Italian and French scholars (Canevaro, 1999; Canevaro & Gaudreau, 1993; Gelati, 2004) reinforce the link between special education and what Armstrong (2007) defines as a 'functionalist' history of disability:

> The 'functionalist' perspective is based on the premise that disabled children have particular needs as a result of their impairments which require specialist provision, often including separate structures and the involvement of specialist professionals. The response to impairment is understood in terms of the policies and adaptations put in place that are seen as being necessitated by the impairments and difficulties of the individual child. (Armstrong, 2007:563)

This statement is illuminating in understanding how particular assumptions about disability were socialised into the education system, until they were transformed into discursive formations. In particular, the narrative of Victor might have brought into existence dominant discourses of 'educability' and 'doing good' to disabled children, which are still regularly deployed in policy documents. Finally, disabled children could learn as 'normal' children do, with the only difference that disabled pupils required particular kinds of specialist treatment, based on the identified characteristics of their needs, first in special institutions and subsequently in ordinary settings.

Following the example of Itard and Séguin, a group of Italian researchers and educationalists, Montessori, Montesano and De Sanctis, began to open many institutions for 'mentally' and sensory impaired pupils. Maria Montessori, in particular, was one of the first Italian scholars who struggled for the education of 'disadvantaged' children. She argued that 'disadvantaged' children did not need to be treated or catered for, but only educated. Although Maria Montessori was a physician with a strong orientation towards remediation and care, she understood that economically and socially disadvantaged children were not uneducable because they were 'mentally retarded' but because they had been deprived, throughout all their life, of all necessary inputs and supports to learn (Montessori, 1991). This pedagogical standpoint strongly influenced the development of primary education in Italy and the development of student-oriented teaching theories and practices in ordinary schools.

Education for disabled students was generally a matter dealt with by private and/or charitable initiatives. Prior to the Fascist Royal Decree, the only legislative measure that referred to special education was the Daneo Credaro Act in 1911 that established the *patronati* - private boarding schools assisting disabled students. It was only in 1923 that Gentile, Mussolini's minister of education, passed a series of legislative measures to guarantee state education for the illiterate masses. There followed a strong division of school careers between poor and wealthy pupils, the first attending vocational schools and the latter attending grammar schools. During the Fascist period state special education for blind and deaf students became compulsory in Italy (Royal Decree n. 577/1928). In the 1930s and 1940s there existed three main types of segregated education: differentiated classes in ordinary schools for 'difficult' students, special schools for 'sensory and mentally' impaired students, and special boarding schools for severely impaired students. Later on, in 1952, education for blind children up until the age of 16 became compulsory in state special schools and in the 1960s local health units were accountable for the education of people 'outside the norm', either in differentiated classes in ordinary schools or in separate special schools (Circular n. 4525, July 1962 and Circular n. 934/6 2nd February 1963).

Drawing on Zelioli's historical account of the development of special education in Italy (in Canevaro, 2002), differentiated classes reached their peak during the 1960s and 1970s (after the economic boom), with the number of schools increasing from 3,394 in 1965 to 6,692 in 1974 when, suddenly, the rate of special schools along with that of differentiated classes began to decrease (see Nocera, 1988). This decrease can be accredited to many different factors, as I shall illustrate later on in this chapter, but certainly a central role was played by negative economic conditions. Moreover, the cultural climate of the 60s and the 70s, which was dominated by an ideology of social justice, democracy and participation, clearly opposed the maintenance of segregated provisions. Nevertheless, in the 1960s special education was still a valid option in Italy as many acts, which were concerned with the organisation and maintenance of special institutions, (Law n. 1073 - 24th of July 1962; and Law n. 942 - 31st of October 1966) were passed during that decade. Even the groundbreaking Law n. 1859 for the *scuola media unica* in 1962 included indications for the development of differentiated classes within the ordinary settings for *alunni disadattati scolastici* – 'maladjusted' students (section 12). Similarly, in 1968, the legislation envisaged the creation of special schools, classrooms and institutions for young children with intellectual, sensory and physical impairments attending kindergarten schools (Law n. 444/1968).

It is not surprising, therefore, as Nocera (1988) also illustrates in his historical account of special education in Italy, that special schooling was never really dismantled. His study, dating back to the 1980s, made a strong case that special education remained a real menace and that policies should not leave room for manoeuvre for those people supporting the re-opening of special education systems. Nocera's analytic study of pro-integration legislative measures pinpointed the way in which integration policies often included clauses that, on the one hand seemed to oppose segregation, but on the other hand, seemed to ensure the very maintenance of special schooling for specific categories of people (Nocera, 1988). For example, the Delegate Decrees enacted in 1974, sanctioned the legal validity of special schooling by legislating for the presence of professional health practitioners in 'normal and special schools' (Decree n. 416/74). This is evident in article 9 of the Decree n. 970/75 which speaks about the maintenance of special schools by acknowledging that support teachers could qualify as specialised teachers for ordinary schools by 'training in special schools'. It is possible that the state had to face the problem of unemployed specialised teachers who were forced to leave special schools caused by the dramatic decrease in enrolments of pupils at the end of the 1970s. As a consequence of this, the Supreme Court of Cassation ruled that 'severely handicapped students had to be educated in special schools' (Sentence n. 478, 1981). Soon afterwards the state issued two ministerial circulars (n.185/1982 and n. 258/1983) by which the minimum quota of disabled students per class in special schools was established and which also underlined the practice of educating 'severely handicapped' students in segregated settings either in special schools or in special classes.

Although accurate and indicative of the contradictions arising within the education system, Nocera's account of special education is still embedded in an interpretation of special education as concerned only with segregation and special institutions. This account fails to investigate other forms and mechanisms of special education that can be reproduced within ordinary settings. Special education instead is a resilient form of social organisation that utilizes different mechanisms to maintain its role in place. Some of these mechanisms can be identified with the macro-mechanisms of segregation and exclusion in separate settings, but there also exist other micro-mechanisms that can be reproduced within the mainstream settings. Although under different names and labels, the outcomes of these mechanisms are equally discriminatory and excluding. As Derrick Armstrong (2003) argues, special needs education is an expression of modern societies which struggle to maintain social cohesion:

...the 'defective', in ever increasing numbers, were to be controlled, not merely excluded, and the mechanisms of control were to be but one aspect of the application of broader technologies of differentiation and control that normalised the regulatory power of reason. (2003:14)

In alignment with the above considerations, therefore, this book has attempted to identify those technologies of power that have been in place for more than thirty years and that still share a legacy with special education thinking and framework in the Italian setting.

The Resilience of Special Education: Why Language Matters

Inclusive education is usually discussed and described in relation to, or in conjunction with, special education and with pupils identified as having special educational needs. Although, there is a general agreement that there has been a considerable shift from special to inclusive education, at least at the level of principle and policy making (Clough & Corbett, 2000), the boundaries between these two concepts remain blurred. Special education still plays a major role in education (Ainscow & Booth, 1998), especially whenever inclusive education is discussed only in relation to students with Records of Needs (Allan, 1999). One example of the role played by special education, which is particularly relevant is when professionals and practitioners claim that they are working for the benefits of disabled students whilst at the same time disabled people are deprived of the chance to speak for themselves.

In order to combat the resilience of the dominant concept of special education, it is important to approach the issue of language (Slee, 2001). The terminology we use is not neutral but reflects attitudes and influences our practices. Problems do not necessarily reside within the linguistic structures of discourses, but rather in the legacy that some terminology can bequeath. The issue of language is therefore central because it relates not only to the domain of communication, but to the way researchers, practitioners, and teachers - as well as disabled people - interpret and shape reality through a series of discourses. Moreover, from a definitional perspective, the need to challenge current linguistic usage and conventions, in relation to discourses around special education derives from the attempt to identify inclusive education by virtue of such confrontations. This might include for example, considerations of ideas of integration in relation to inclusion.

In 1986 Barton began to question the use of 'special educational needs' which he defines as an 'euphemism for failure' (Barton, 1986:273). Corbett (1996) insists on the need to replace the language of 'special' with a new language that is not weighed down with assumptions and biases. The language of 'special' that is used by practitioners today, she argues (1996), belongs to the medical domain. Consequently, this language supports an individual/medical model of disability, and an idea that disability is a personal tragedy (Oliver, 1990). Thus, disability and its language become a 'stigma' that marks the boundaries of normality ('we') from the abnormality ('they'), by focusing on the impairment rather than on the person. Much in agreement with Corbett and Barton's critiques, Slee argues that:

> Special educational needs became an all-embracing metaphor for the defective child. In turn, the functional label of 'special educational needs child' has metaphorically become a refugee camp for the casualties of schooling. (Slee, 1998:102)

From an educational perspective, the use of the language of special, hence the labelling process, does not speak of a discourse that encourages students to develop their potentialities. By defining a pupil as being 'with special educational needs', schools run the risk of influencing both the way people will perceive that pupil and the way those pupils will perceive themselves. As Stiker (1999) argues, language matters and the language of 'special' in education may be dangerous for the development of inclusive education:

> To name, designate, point out, is to make exist. Our natural assumption is to believe that language expresses the real, that it duplicates reality so that we can think about ...and manipulate it, in our minds and in our conversations! But quite the contrary, language operates, transforms, creates. In one sense, there is no other reality than the language... (language) is an institution, in the double sense that is socially established and that it arranges the social fact. (Stiker, 1999:153)

In this analysis, Stiker (1999) indicates how language may maintain existing assumptions and influence actions. The process of naming and, at the same time, marginalising through naming, is a dilemma over which researchers working in the field of inclusive education often stumble 'by positioning some groups as being naturally the subject of marginalisation' (F. Armstrong, 2003b:2) and analysis in the studies of inclusive education.

Language is the most effective channel through which a dominant ideology can be acted out and reproduced, not only by behaviours, attitudes and deeds, but also by the way we speak about things (Stiker, 1999; Armstrong, F., 2003b). Thus, the phenomenon of labelling people via the language of special education reinforces the medical practice of classifying them into specific categories and of justifying the work of social workers and other intermediary figures who can deal with 'that knowledge' behind a label. The process of labelling, although sometimes 'born of the best intentions' and aimed at benefiting students at risk of being further marginalised, is often used as an administrative procedure to obtain additional provision or assistance. Stiker states that such a procedure is paradoxical since it is likely to provide somebody with 'an alien passport to be like the others' (Stiker, 1999:151) - to possess a label in order to become 'normal' citizens. Disabled people simply ask for rights (in education, employment, access to transport and information) that other people have always possessed without the need to be stigmatised.

Following on from this analysis, we should seek to understand what it is about societies that produce the need to categorise and label some citizens and not others:

> Labels and categorisation originate in social structures much more than in simple fact of physical and psychological affliction. In our Western society the desire to integrate rises out of the incapacity of the social fabric to permit the disabled person to live there. (Stiker, 1999:159)

It seems that the main problem lies in society's incapacity to deal with the diversity of its populace and the need to manage such diversity, by diluting it to the norm (Stiker, 1999). Stiker (ibid.) underlines the ways in which society may construct 'disability' as a social, economic and administrative category arguing that Western societies, in particular, are historically obsessed by social conformity, and homogeneity. His analysis, however, does not specifically address the issues of conformity and homogeneity in terms of political and economic oppression and social control as the social model of disability does. Nevertheless the issue of language and how it develops across centuries offers an important illustration of how the greatest challenge is not simply about avoiding the use of the language of 'special' but about challenging the language of the 'norm' by exploring where it originates and why.

Evidence of the reminiscence of a special needs education tradition in Italy is visible in the language used to refer to disabled students. In the two schools invest-igated as my case study sites, the following terms were often articulated (in Italian):

- *studente in situazione di handicap* (student in a situation of handicap)
- *studente con certificazione di handicap* (student with a statement of needs)
- *studente con handicap* (student with a handicap)
- *studente con disabilità* (student with a disability)
- *portatore di disabilità* (carrier of a disability)
- *portatore di handicap* (carrier of a handicap)

- *handicappato* (handicapped)
- *studente con deficit* (student with deficit)
- *diversamente abile* (differently able)

Despite the differences, a common element can be found in these definitions; a tendency to construct disability as something related to the biological conditions of pupils with impairments. Nonetheless, the need to disentangle the concept of disability from a notion of disease and adopt a terminology that differentiates between 'deficit and handicap' is not new in Italy. Drawing on the ICIDH (1980), some Italian scholars argued for the need to introduce a new definition for disabled pupils, namely 'student in a situation of handicap' (Canevaro, 1999; de Anna, 1998; WHO, 1980). Such definition was meant to differentiate between impairment (functional limitation) and handicap (social problem), the latter being a form of disadvantage in which the person with deficits finds him/herself as a consequence of the way in which society is structured. As my research will show, however, teachers still use the notions of 'handicap' interchangeably with that of 'individual deficit' or 'disability', thus failing to acknowledge the complexity of the notion of disability and disablement.

Considering the centrality of language and the need to use language to facilitate a cultural change, Ainscow and Booth (2000) suggest that we should substitute the word 'needs' with that of 'barriers to learning and participation'. While the former locates the learning difficulties within the child, thus reinforcing a deficit model, the latter suggests that barriers can be, and often are, at the level of the system rather than at the level of the individual.

CONCLUSION

This chapter has provided some insights into current debates concerning the nature and the development of inclusive education both at an international and national level. By acknowledging and valuing opposing and diverging voices, I have positioned the discussion about inclusion used in this book within the radical position of the on-going debate around inclusive education. The history of special education and the perpetuation of the language of 'special' addressed in this chapter have also given examples of the way in which exclusion may occur in mainstream settings disguised as integration. This chapter has clearly indicated that inclusive education is a complex process and that there should be a differentiation of the theoretical premises in which special needs education, integration and inclusion are originated. Put briefly, in this chapter I have tried to indicate that inclusive education:

'[…] is a time consuming, demanding and disturbing task and there are no easy short-cut recipes and therefore there is no room for complacency' (Barton, 2005:319).

CHAPTER 3

A SOCIOLOGICAL APPROACH TO THE STUDY OF
INTEGRAZIONE SCOLASTICA

> As far as disability is concerned, if it is seen as a tragedy, then disabled people will be treated as if they are the victims of some tragic happening or circumstance [....] Alternatively, it logically follows that if disability is defined as social oppression, then disabled people will be seen as the collective victims of an uncaring or unknowing society rather than as individual victims of circumstance. Such a view will be translated into social policies geared towards alleviating oppression rather than compensating individuals (Oliver, 1990:3)

This book is situated in a research paradigm that can be broadly defined as the social model of disability. So much has been written about the social model of disability in the UK (Oliver, 1990, Barton and Oliver, 1992, Skakespeare and Watson, 1997, Barnes, Oliver and Barton, 2002), that it is sometimes more difficult to find examples of how such an approach to disability may be used to study education policy. The purpose of this chapter is therefore to discuss how this model has been adopted as the main conceptual framework for a sociological analysis of the policy of *integrazione scolastica*. I have chosen to define the approach used as a sociological one as I bring to the fore the strengths of the social model of disability, as theorised by Mike Oliver (1990) and I attempt to overcome some of its limitations with the theories and the works of other scholars.

Considering the uniqueness of the Italian history, its social and political setting, the sociological approach used within the book has drawn on, among others, the works of Gramsci and Foucault. Their works have been extremely illuminating for understanding issues around power relations and change, both relevant standpoints in a critical engagement with the struggles and contradictions relating to the investigation of *integrazione scolastica* from an inclusive perspective.

Nevertheless, the analysis provided in this book looks at the social model of disability not as a the only possible way of looking at disability and study education policy, but one possible modality that 'has encouraged us to change the focus of interrogation from the disabled person to the social context that disables or enables people ...' (Slee, 1998:105). It is with this in mind that my enquiry has used the social model as a 'lens' through which people make sense of schooling and education in a way that may help them to discover elements that they may have not seen and considered before.

In this chapter, I will, firstly, introduce the historical development of the social model of disability as a possible new approach to the theorisation of disability and how it can contribute to the development of inclusion. Secondly, I will discuss how the medical model and its variations, such as the psychological model of disability

(Shakespeare and Watson, 1997), have provided a functional definition of disability (Pfeiffer, 2000) and have been particularly dominant in the Italian context. Thirdly, I will present a general framework concerning the current critiques of the social model of disability. Fourthly, I will provide a brief analysis of the International Classification of Functioning, Disability and Health (WHO, 2001). During the present period in which I am writing there is an on-going discussion at a national level concerning the adoption of this international classification manual as the new model to study disability in Italy. Finally, I will look at some relevant works of Foucault (1972; 1977; 1978) and Gramsci (1970; 1971) as innovative theoretical underpinnings in analysing educational policies and practices.

THE SOCIAL MODEL OF DISABILITY

The ideas underpinning the social model of disability were first conceptualised by Paul Hunt (1966) in the 1960s and subsequently developed by Vic Finkelstein and other disabled activists associated with the 'Union of the Physically Impaired Against Segregation' (UPIAS henceforward) movement in the 1970s (Flood, 2005). Gradually, the model was developed and supported by the works of academics such as Oliver (1990), Barnes (1991), Barton (Barton and Oliver, 1992), Shakespeare and Watson (1997) and Thomas (1999). The model consists of a new way of approaching disability which involves a sociological theorisation of the phenomenon and aims at changing society rather than helping an unfortunate minority of disabled people to adjust to society (Thomas, 1999). The social model of disability promotes the active participation of disabled people in the theorization and conceptualisation of their own condition and the creation of an organisation of disabled people rather than for disabled people. The British disability movement, in particular, represents the ideological foundation of the new model, as it produced the first version of the Fundamental Principles of Disability (UPIAS, 1976), a political manifesto in which disabled people defined themselves as an oppressed group of society.

The social model of disability, as it has been named by the field of Disability Studies (Barton and Oliver, 1997; Barnes, Oliver and Barton, 2002) is characterised by three key elements that can be summarised as follows: first, the difference between impairment (biological condition) and disability (social condition); second, a distancing from the medical model of disability, which locates limits within the person's 'deficits'; third, the condition of oppression experienced by disabled people in society. Those who advocate the social model of disability claim that:

> In our view, it is society which disables physically impaired people. Disability is something imposed on top of our impairments by the way we are unnecessarily isolated and excluded from full participation in society. Disabled people are therefore an oppressed group in society. To understand this, it is necessary to grasp the distinction between the physical impairment and the social situation, called 'disability', of people with such impairment. (Oliver, 1996b:22)

The scholars writing from a social model stance break with the traditional idea that disability consists of individual impairment enshrined within a medical approach to disability. Conversely, they argue for a model with strong political roots which supports a political programme, and envisages the direct participation of disabled activists (Thomas, 1999). This model allows researchers (and disabled people themselves) to distinguish between those aspects of the disabled person's experience that are amenable to medical and therapeutic intervention and those aspects that require social response and require political action (McKenzie, 2009)

Put briefly, within this approach, disability is understood as a social construction. Such an understanding allows education policy analysts to look beyond the impairment of the pupils and the 'special' responses required by it, and to look at the disabling conditions of society (and of schooling) that may affect the lives of disabled people (and students).

The social model is fundamental for the conceptualisation of the notion of disability as its conceptualisation informs the underpinning theoretical framework required for a new understanding of societal barriers and, therefore, for the development of inclusive thinking.

> From a social model, disability is not a personal tragedy, an abnormality or a disease needing a cure. It is a form of discrimination and oppression in which patronising, sentimental, disenfranchising and overly protective attitudes and values legitimate and maintain the sorts of individualised pathologising that we previously referred to. (Barton, 1998:79)

Following this approach and perspective, it is possible to look at disability in terms of the oppression and marginalisation experienced by a particular social group in society. The experiences of discrimination and oppression became exemplars of catalysts for shifts in understanding and the development of inclusive thinking and the removal of disabling barriers. Specifically, the social model of disability allowed me to study the policy of *integrazione scolastica* a problematic policy that required further investigation.

THE INDIVIDUAL/MEDICAL MODEL OF DISABILITY

Disability is an ongoing concept whose meaning changes according to the historical period in which it is located and depending on the perspective from which it is analysed (Stiker, 1999). Thomas argues that disability is located spatially, temporally and economically (Thomas, 2002). At the same time, despite differences in the interpretation, disability has usually been analysed from a medical model (Scull, 1979; Stone, 1984; Stiker, 1999). The medical perspective has been dominant for over a hundred years and, especially so, after the International Classification of Impairments, Disabilities and Handicaps schema (ICIDH henceforward) was produced in 1980. This was particularly true for the Italian context in which the ICIDH was used to prepare the diagnosis of disabled pupils. Not surprisingly, in the schools investigated in this book, the traditional categorisation provided by the ICIDH was still considered the dominant way of perceiving and identifying impairment, disability and handicap.

The ICIDH provides a three-level conceptualisation of disability:

> Impairment refers to 'any loss or abnormality of psychological, physiological or anatomical structure or function'. 'Disability' denotes 'any restriction or lack

(resulting from an impairment) of ability to perform an activity in the manner or within the range considered normal for a human being'. 'Handicap', is the 'disadvantage for a given individual, resulting from an impairment or disability, that limits or prevents the fulfilment of a role that is normal (depending on age, sex and social and cultural factors) for that individual'. (Barnes, 2003:11)

As the above quotation indicates, the ICIDH focuses on the division between impairment, disability and handicap (WHO, 1980). Impairment is related to the biological condition of the person as deviating from a norm, disability is a consequence of this impairment which results in the person's inability to engage with everyday life activities, and the term handicap is used to indicate the social disadvantage that derives from disability (Drake, 1999). The ICIDH definitional framework clearly encapsulates all the characteristics of the medical model of disability, as the 'solution' to disability is still located in medical interventions rather than in societal change (Barnes, Mercer and Shakespeare, 1999).

This classification tool was an attempt to identify a 'working' definition of a complex phenomenon and to use it across countries. The schema provided within the ICIDH allowed researchers and practitioners to rely on a 'scientific' tool to identify a phenomenon. It also provided indications about how to 'measure' disability for research and how to implement related policies. However, the schema failed to acknowledge that disability is not only an individual condition and that its concept-ualisation varies enormously across cultures, countries and historical periods (Pfeiffer, 1998). Moreover, the ICIDH reinforced an abstract construction of a normal functioning of the average human being, with inevitable labelling consequences for those who, in one way or another, found themselves 'deviating' from an established norm.

A prevalent medical model conceptualised disability as the:

Outcome of impairment: it is a form of biological determinism, because it focuses on physical difference. Disabled people are defined as that group of people whose bodies do not work; or look different or act differently; or who cannot do productive work. (Shakespeare, 1996:95)

In the medical model, therefore, there is no distinction between impairment and disability: disability is the impairment (Thomas, 2002). In time, the medical model came to develop two different strategies to deal with disability: on the one hand the eradication of impairment, subsequently developed through eugenics and genetics (Armstrong, 2003); on the other hand, the normalisation of impaired conditions, in particular through the rehabilitation process (Stiker, 1999; Thomas, 2002).

Barnes (1997) has identified the roots of the medical model of disability in the work of Parsons in the 1950s. Drawing on Parson's work, Barnes argues that 'the normal state of being in Western developed societies is 'good health', and that conse-quently 'sickness', and by implication, impairments, are deviations from normality' (Barnes, 1997:5). This statement brings to the fore the current link between 'normality' and 'disability', the latter considered as a deviance from the former and often asso-ciated with something that needs to be controlled and compensated for. This medical legacy, in fact, has contributed to the conceptualisation of disability as a disease, to which medical intervention was to find a solution through cure, rehabilitation and therapy (Oliver, 1996b). Such an intervention was initially in segregated settings and then arguably, in mainstream settings, through covert forms of exclusion and marginalisation.

As Oliver puts it, social model activists do not oppose medical intervention per se, but the individualisation and medicalisation of disability (Oliver, 1990; 1996a; 1996b). Unpacking Oliver's (1996b) observations, I argue that the social model of disability should be considered in contrast to an individual model of disability which ties together medical and psychological individualistic perspectives of disability. The individual model of disability, Oliver argues, is associated with the idea of disability as a 'personal tragedy that suggests that disability is some terrible chance event which occurs at random to unfortunate individuals' (1990:32). Thus, disability is theorised as something 'which does not work' inside the person (Oliver, 1996b). As a consequence of this perspective, disabled people often blame themselves and feel responsible for their social and personal condition (Oliver, 1996a; 1996b). This view implies that disabled people contribute to the construction of their own condition as passive citizens – mere receptions of humanitarian, caring and welfare policies. There is little evidence of an attempt to question whether there are other reasons, other than their biological conditions, that may have determined, or alternatively, that could have improved their actual conditions beyond a medical intervention – the latter being often useless for chronic diseases. Moreover, as theorised by Oliver (1990; 1996a), the individual model of disability, and the concomitant view of disability as a personal tragedy, may be seen as inevitable consequences of capitalism in the way that it reflects the spread of new individualistic and materialistic values following the industrial revolution in Western societies (Oliver, 1999). Some scholars suggest that the process of industrialisation modified the mode of production and inevitably excluded those sections of society who could not keep up with the new pace of production (Scull, 1979; Oliver, 1990). It was then that the first large institutions developed, which – in some respects - mirrored the scale and organisation of the new factories, and fulfilled the dual roles of controlling an increasing the number of potentially deviant unemployed people and, at the same time, of responding to the enlightened spirit of care and assistance of newly constituted humanitarian and charity organisations (Oliver, 1990).

Furthermore, the international classification frameworks (for example the International Classification of Functioning Disability and Health, 2001) indicate that the medical model is embedded in a vision of reality based on underlying assumptions – abstract human being – and dichotomies - normal/abnormal, disabled/ non-disabled, sick/healthy. Moreover, the medical model and its classification tools, are clearly based on values that belong to the Western world and do not acknowledge that disability is also a cultural construction (Pfeiffer, 1998). Yet, as Oliver argues (1990; 1996b) medical intervention and suggestions are important allies of disabled people and the social model has not been developed in order to deny such a position. What the social model of disability seeks to underline is that the medical sector should not interfere with spheres of disabled people's lives that are not strictly linked to the treatment of impairment or its painful effects. This view is particularly true when professional and medical advice govern educational sectors wherein a pupil with impairments is always considered as a pupil with 'special educational need' regardless of what the pupil may require. Medical doctors and experts must address illnesses and not disability, since they may not be the people best fitted to make decisions in relation to recruitment, education, transportation and housing. Furthermore, disabled people should play a central role in the process of decision making, especially regarding their own lives.

In conclusion, the critique of the medical model and the work of Oliver (1990; 1996b; 1997) amongst others, have opened up new insights into the conceptualisation of the notion of disability in different countries. In addition, this critique has also suggested new trajectories for research and policy making that may underpin inclusive thinking. All different models of disability, such as the medical and the psychological models discussed above can be grouped together under the aegis of the individual/medical model of disability, considered as the 'core ideology' (Oliver, 1990) to overthrow. This ideology not only locates the problem within the person, but also constitutes a hindrance or barrier to societal change. My argument is that this individual/medical model of disability is still dominant in Italy and that although I do not deny the contribution that medical doctors and medical sociologists and psychiatrists have made to the cause of disabled people, to the stabilisation of their medical conditions or to the fact that impairment and disability can be related, it nevertheless encapsulates some limitations for the development of inclusion that need to be addressed. Along with Oliver, Barnes and Barton (2002), I argue that disability has less to do with impairment and is not caused by functional limitations, but has instead, more to do with society's failure to meet all people's requirements, including those of people with impairments.

An example of the predominant role played by the medical model can be found in the way class and support teachers referred to disabled students in the schools investigated in this book:

The school should be in charge of the problematic kid, not only the classroom. The entire school should be in charge of this *problematic case*. We have this problem and, the question is, how are we all going to face it all together? (Interview 18, support teacher, *Fellini* School, my emphasis)

In the second grade we have the *case* of Valeria. If the support teacher is not in the classroom you have to switch on the computer for her and prepare big font papers. That is why when the support teacher is not around I go mad! (Interview 15, Mathematics teacher, *Don Milani* School, my emphasis)

There are *cases* and *cases*. For example with my kids, I have two girls with mental retardation, I do a lot of things that do not appear on the individualised education plan, these activities are submerged, but I do it on purpose to privilege their relation with the mainstream teachers. (Interview 06, support teacher *Fellini* School, my emphasis)

When a new *case* arrives at school I usually listen. I listen to the head teacher during the staff meetings, and I anticipate what it could be like with those *cases* at school without any biased idea in favour or against these students.

Then when the head teacher decides which support teacher should follow a particular *case* I start doing things. (Interview 09, support teacher, *Don Milani* School, my emphasis)

By referring to disabled pupils as cases, the student is seen as an individual that must be identified and assessed, someone whose needs should be measured and quantified by a team of experts who can make decisions regarding what type of provision is required. Although, in the Italian context this identification procedure does not entail the transfer to special school settings (as may happen in other countries), it nevertheless adds to the creation, maintenance and resistance of a stigmatised social status. I am not arguing that disabled students should not be adequately catered for, as any other child should be, but I believe that we should investigate disability not only in terms of impairment and of how the state could compensate for it (for example by providing adequate resources), but we should also explore which restrictions hamper participation, which students are facing those obstacles, and why.

In Foucault's work (1977) the notion of 'case' is particularly relevant for what I shall be arguing in this book:

The examination surrounded by all its documentary techniques, makes each individual a 'case': a case which at one and the same time constitutes an object for a branch of knowledge and a hold for a branch of power. The case is no longer, as in casuistry or jurisprudence, a set of circumstances defining an act and capable of modifying the application of a rule; it is the individual as he may be described, judged, measured, compared with others, in his individuality; and it is also the individual who has to be trained or corrected, classified, normalised. (Foucault, 1977:191)

This extract is central to the regimes of surveillance and control over disruptive individuals and it is reminiscent of the concept of 'normative judgement' that transforms all students, including disabled children, into subjected individuals and docile bodies (Foucault, 1977). What is critical is how schooling remains the 'critical agent in defining, labelling and treating disability' (Slee, 1993:353) and that the type of control exercised over disabled children is of a different type when compared to other children without a statement of 'special educational needs' (Allan, 1999).

CRITIQUES OF THE SOCIAL MODEL OF DISABILITY

When arguing in favour of a social model of disability to investigate the extent to which the policy of *integrazione scolastica* is an inclusive policy I do not necessarily imply that the social model is devoid of any limitation. Conversely, I am aware of some of the existing critiques of this model, some of which will be presented below. Nevertheless, despite the limitations, the social model of disability has provided this research with a completely new insight into the study of the Italian situation and policy. Firstly because, a social model allowed a shift of paradigm through which I have looked at disability and, consequently schooling, both at the origin of the issue of transformation required by inclusion. Secondly, because the social model of disability has been conceptualised by disabled people themselves, thus suggesting the need to address the issue of power relation when investigating the process of policy making and its implementation at a school level.

Current critiques of the social model of disability engage with issues concerning the nature of the social model and its application. For example it is possible to identify two main critiques, one arising 'inside' and another one coming from the 'outside' the social model of disability analytical framework. The external critiques encompass the following concerns: the incorporation of personal and experiential matters, lessons drawn from feminist writers, and, the capability approach. The internal critiques arise from an awareness that the social model of disability is not a 'theory' but a model and that it must not be used as a social theory (Oliver, 1996b). Yet, it should be used to increase the understanding around disability. The latter critique seeks to look beyond the social model of disability by providing alternatives to it that may overcome its limitations.

External Critique of the Social Model of Disability

One of the first critiques of the social model of disability was generated by Liz Crow (1996). Her critique reflects the need to take into consideration personal and experiential matters when discussing what disability means to disabled people in order to overcome barriers to participation. She reappraises the value of the term impairment and suggests that the social model of disability fails to acknowledge the disabling implications of impairment. She states that impairment has also 'caused disadvantage as well as disability' (Crow, 1996:59) and that disabled people should not be afraid to express the negative consequences deriving from their functional or intellectual impairments. In so doing, she insists on the need to renew the social model of disability by integrating impairment into the politics of disability. She supports her critique by showing how, even if all social barriers were dismantled, some people would still experience some limitations due to their individual impairments. In similar vein, French (1993) points out the peculiarity of her condition as a visually impaired person, who will always experience certain barriers, such as the lack of visual clues when greeting a neighbour, even when all social barriers have been removed. Although these critiques provide disabled activists with reflections and strategies to develop and improve the theorisation of disability, they do not, however, move outside the boundaries of the individual model of disability. Specifically, they fail to acknowledge that the social model of disability does not neglect the personal but rather seeks to transform the personal into a political tool for social change (Morris, 1991).

Feminist critiques of the social model find their origin in the work of writers such as Morris (1991), Thomas (1999), French (1993) and Corker (1999), who introduced into the social model of disability, the experience of feminism, especially in opposition to dominant views of male disabled scholars. Morris' critique takes as its starting point the feminist premise and assertion that we must incorporate the 'personal' as a political tool of analysis, claiming that the 'personal is political'

(1991). The feminist writer insists on the need to bring 'the private' into our under-standings, and to include such issues on the political agenda along with male 'public domain' issues. Morris (1991) and Thomas (1999) introduce the issue of gender into their discussions, arguing that the social model of disability is mainly concerned with barriers experienced by disabled men and that it usually underplays the needs of disabled women. They distinguish between the more materialist and economic needs usually prioritised by male commentators, such as employment, housing and other issues, such as home help and child care, that are more likely to be experienced by women. Morris (1993), in particular, acknowledges that although there is a rich literature relating to gender and disability regarding women, there are few publications about men and disability. This is evidence enough that men's histories of disability have long been considered as the 'general' approach to disability, valid for all disabled people, regardless of their gender. This position contrasts with Morris's view that, in reality, men and women have to face different challenges. Morris's argument leads her to suggest that masculinity serves as the dominant social construct in relation to men, and dependency as a social construct for disabled women (Morris, 1993). To put this another way, arguments such as this have given voice to female disabled activists' views, revealing indications and echoes of the same kinds of oppression experienced by non disabled women in a non disabled man's world. Female disabled theorists such as Jenny Morris have, in this way, contributed to the understanding of the complex phenomenon of disability in including experiential and emotional aspects, usually left out of discussion by male disabled activists in their attempts to theorise disability.

Thomas's critique (2002) of the social model entails the inclusion of impairment effects in the social model of disability. At the same time, she acknowledges that the limitations of the social model, such as being 'over-socialised', leaves room for attacks and critiques that merge into the creation of the classification schemas. Drawing on scholars' misinterpretation of the meaning of 'restrictions of activities' and 'disability', Thomas is concerned with the conflation between what she defines as the 'social relational approach', developed by the UPIAS and the social model theorists, and the 'property approach' which insists on the role played by impairment on the restriction of activities. The 'social relational model', she explains, considers the restrictions caused exclusively by social factors, from which it follows that disability is a form of oppression. On the other hand, the 'property approach' refers to the definitional schemas developed by the WHO and considers restrictions caused, in part, by impairment as well – from which it follows that disability is also related to bodily experience. Thomas (1999) confronts the two models with a third one, named the 'impairment effects'. In this final theorisation of disability, she affirms that although we cannot deny the consequences of impairment in our life, the latter are the 'effects' rather than the 'disabilities' per se. It is not 'disabilities' that are our difficulties, but a society which fails to provide us with alternative tools to fully participate in daily activities. Disability, she argues:

> …is about restrictions of activity which are socially caused. That is, disability is entirely socially caused. But some restrictions of activity are caused by illness and impairment. Thus some aspects of illness and impairment are

disabling. But disability has nothing to do with impairment. (Thomas, 1999:39)

As other scholars have indicated (Barnes, Oliver and Barton, 2002), the above critiques have come mostly from disabled people and their uneasiness when confronted with the difficulties deriving exclusively from their impairment and their lack of opportunity to discuss their conditions and feelings [such as those expressed in the conference organised by the Great London Action on Disability in London (GLAD, 2000)]. At the same time, it is crucial to remember that the initial critiques were manly elaborated by women, such as Liz Crow (1996), Jenny Morris (1991; 1993), Carol Thomas (1999; 2001; 2002), Sally French (1993), Nasa Begum (1992) and Mairian Corker (Corker and French, 1999). Conversely, male social modellists (for example Shakespeare and Watson, 2002) have engaged with such issues only subsequently, in what might be called a second phase of the debate. While common sense suggests that disabled women might gain considerable benefit from the arguments of the feminist movement described above, French (1993) has pointed out that women experience particular comfort when they confide in each other regarding their distress and problems. This inclination to talk without necessarily finding a solution may have contributed to critiques of the social model but also to new forms of conducting research based on biographical narration.

In the light of the above, it is not surprising, that Barnes, Oliver and Barton (2002) have noted that the "challenge to orthodox views came not from within the academy but from disabled people themselves" (2002:4) and it has drawn implicitly, if not explicitly, on both personal experience and sociological insights. They argue that the social model approach:

...does not deny the significance of impairment in disabled people's lives, but concentrates instead on the various barriers, economic, political and social, constructed on top of impairment. Thus disability is not a product of individual failings, but is socially created; explanations of its changing character are found in the organisation and structures of society. Rather than identifying disability as an individual limitation, the social model identifies society as the problem, and looks to fundamental and cultural changes to generate solutions. (Barnes, Oliver and Barton, 2002:5)

Arguments such as this one suggest a need to revive the personal and experiential dimensions in social theorisation. Such dimensions were never, of course, denied. On the contrary, they resulted from a pragmatic initiative taken to comply with political strategies (Barnes, Mercer and Shakespeare, 1999). The difference between Barnes, Oliver and Barton's argument (2002) and the one, for example, supported by Crow (1996), is that the latter gives priority to the individual 'experiential dimension' rather than to the communal social dimension. Instead, leaving out the personal and experiential domains in the conceptualisation of disability would strengthen the political interventions of disabled people based on common grounds for collective actions (Barnes, Mercer and Shakespeare, 1999). Personal experiences, although very meaningful, may risk becoming 'diversionary forces' which leave room for medical interventions (Thomas, 2001:49) and thus, reducing the focus on disability to a direct consequence of impairment only.

A third important critique of the social model of disability derives from the capability approach (Terzi, 2005b; 2005a; 2008) which can be described as another way of approaching the dilemma of difference in education. It is concerned not only with access to education, but to the type of education actually provided to all students – and, most importantly, to students identified as having 'special educational needs' as well as disabled students. These students, because of their particular individual conditions, are perceived as requiring additional resources. Given these considerations, this approach views disability as an element of human diversity, which may require a just distribution of resources based on the actual capabilities of each person. Although such an approach acknowledges the political role played by the social model of disability in detecting a series of social and economic barriers, it suggests that the social model of disability fails to remove the very barriers it has detected. This position is based not only, as other critiques of the social model of disability have shown, on its being 'over-socialised', but by denying the existence of normality – a standardised and normal functioning of human beings widely shared and recognised. Possibly, one way of understanding the critique developed by the capability approach is that it may act as a moderator of those positions of the social model that are perceived as being too extreme. In particular, I refer to the critiques which identify the social model as an overly materialistic and political approach (Tremain, 2005). Tremain (2005) argues that the social model should also address the issues around the paradox of benefits and requirements provided for disabled people on the basis of their impairments, and how, by benefiting from these provisions, disabled people may inevitably become part of that system that they are seeking to overthrow.

At the same time, the critiques of the social model of disability as being over-socialised (such as focusing on social dimensions) and over-politicised (such as using disability as a political banner) can be better understood if we consider that these critiques are part of a well-designed project. Put simply, there is a joint effort to focus on the commonalities and the political claims of disabled people as a group in order to contribute to the creation of the disability movement as a new social movement (Oliver, 1990). Oliver (Barton and Oliver, 1997) draws on the work of Gramsci (1971) and the concept of 'civil society' – private and corporate pressure groups alternative to the State - to explain the potentialities for change represented by a social movement. A social movement is capable of overturning dominant ideologies based on principles of assistance, dependence and cure. Consequently, the disability movement can be seen as a counter-hegemonic force capable of influencing society by suggesting alternative and radical changes that may benefit both disabled people and other historically marginalised social groups (Barton and Oliver, 1997). A disabled people's movement capable of transforming disability into a tool for social and political activism, whose impact for example can be found in the creation of the motto 'nothing about us without us' (Charlton, 1998) and in the promulgation of the Convention of the Rights of People with Disabilities (UN, 2006). In this way, the social model becomes a sort of political manifesto of the disability movement: an example of self determination that can pave the way for a shift from the deficit model of education that locates the problem within the disabled child, to a process of restructuring education in order to respond to all students based on the experience of disabled people.

Internal Critique of the Social Model of Disability

The internal critique concerning the social model of disability comes from a number of Disability Studies theorists (Reiser and Mason, 1990; Shakespeare and Watson, 2002; Matshedisho, 2005). Some of these scholars have argued, for example, that the social model of disability is only a model providing a specific understanding about a phenomenon:

> A model is a framework by which we make sense of information...the same event can appear very different to people who have been brought up with different models of understanding. (Reiser, 1990:14)

What is most interesting about this critique of the social model is the acknowledgment that the social model of disability is not a theory but an attempt to explain phenomena by reference to a particular system of ideas (Llewellyn and Hogan, 2000). However, although a model may not provide solutions or explanations in itself, it nevertheless may 'help to generate an explanation in some way' (Llewellyn and Hogan, 2000:157) which may contribute to the understanding of a phenomenon and, subsequently, the promotion of solutions. In line with these views, Oliver (1996b) argues that the social model of disability is not:

> ...a social theory of disability and it cannot do the work of social theory. Secondly because it cannot explain everything, we should neither seek to expose inadequacies, which are more a product of the way we use it, nor abandon it before its usefulness had been fully exploited. (Oliver, 1996b:41)

From this perspective, the social model of disability is neither right nor wrong 'per se' but rather, it is the way in which it is used and interpreted, that may or may not contribute to the progress of the people using it for the development of an inclusive society. Despite the social model having limits in the explanation of a phenomenon such as disability, its influence to change 'consciousness' can be paramount. This result can be achieved, for example, in suggesting alternative frameworks of analysis to those provided by the medical model of disability that has played such a dominant role in all Western and industrialised countries.

Shakespeare and Watson (2002) argue that it is necessary to find a more adequate and sophisticated 'social' theory of disability that moves from what has been achieved with the social model of disability, to a new model that takes into account the diversity of disabled people's individual experiences. They argue that the flaws of the social model of disability are what once were considered its strengths, such as the benchmark idea of the social model that disabled people represent a diverse minority. The conceptualisation of disabled people as a social minority, as argued by Shakespeare and Watson (2002), fails to take into account the fact that the experiences of disabled people are significantly different from those of other minorities. Although it is possible to learn from the struggles fought by black people, feminists, gay and lesbian people to obtain their rights of full citizenship, disabled people also experience an oppression which comes from their impairment, and their own health conditions. In line with this consideration, they advocate the creation of a new model that takes into consideration the individual experience of disability, the effects of impairment and the identity building process (Shakespeare and Watson, 2002), yet always within sociological rather than individualistic boundaries. In this regard, they take into full account the position of those disabled people who do not perceive their condition as a form of social oppression and whose purpose is to belong to the supposed condition of 'normality'. To put it simply, as Liggett (1988) also argues, some people may choose to reject transforming their 'label' into a political badge.

In conclusion, Oliver suggests that 'our child - the social model - is not yet grown up and that if we turn her out into the world too soon, we do so at both our and her peril' (Oliver, 1996b:32). Thus, the social model of disability should not be considered as the 'only valuable' approach to the study of disability, rather as another possible approach to understand and investigate such a phenomenon. Although different theoretical frameworks (such as medical/individual model versus social model) may, arguably, be equally valid, they nevertheless focus on different aspects, providing different explanations and related solutions for similar phenomena (for example 'disability' and 'school failure'). For this book, the social model of disability has played a crucial epistemological role in the study of inclusive education. For example, it allowed me to identify different origins of the same problems – such as micro-exclusions in the mainstream - and looked for different types of solutions and interventions – such as beyond the redistribution of resources. As a result of this new theoretical perspective a series of revelation took place which were fundamental to my undertaking, such as a new theorisation of the concept of disability, a new understanding of the policy making process and of the principles of inclusion. Consequently, this perspective was particularly relevant when applied to the investigation of the policy of *integrazione scolastica* and the extent to which it can be defined an inclusive policy.

THE ITALIAN MODEL OF DISABILITY: THE INTERNATIONAL CLASSIFICATION OF FUNCTIONING, DISABILITY AND HEALTH (ICF)

As emerging from the Policy Guidelines for the Integration of Pupils with Disabilities (Ministero dell'Istruzione dell'Università e della Ricerca, 2009), the International Classification of Functioning, Disability and Health (ICF henceforward) is the model used to identify and conceptualise disability in Italy. Evidence of this position can be found in the recent ministerial policy guidelines for the development of the integration of 'pupils with disabilities' (MIUR, 2009) that promoted the use of the ICF for the assessment of disabled pupils. The ICF model is perceived as the new theorisation of the social model of disability and in line with the principles highlighted in the UN Convention (2006). Disability is therefore described as resulting from the 'interaction between the functional deficit and the social environment' (Ministero dell'Istruzione, dell'Università e della Ricerca, 2009:3).

At the time in which the research was conducted (2004–2008) the schools investigated seemed to be only marginally aware of the existence of this new classificatory tool. However, discussions about the ICF and the possibility to apply it in schools were already held. Debates also included the discussions about the International Classification of Diseases Revision 10 (1990) manual (ICD henceforward) and the previous ICIDH (1980) manual, both used as a tool to identify, assess and conceptualise disability in schools. Evidence of the use of the ICD could be found in the Individual Education Plans collected for the research which reported the same diagnostic definitions and classifications as used within the ICD. Similarly, evidence of the use of the ICIDH model could be found in the way in which disabled pupils were called, namely students in a situation of handicap, hence emphasising the difference between the biological condition (impairment and disability) on the one hand, and the social condition of disadvantage (handicap) lived by disabled people on the other hand.

In the schools investigated for my research, however, there was very little awareness of the existence and use of the social model of disability. There did not seem to be any publication or ongoing discussion concerning the existence of the social model as theorised by the UPIAS movement, neither in the school settings nor in conferences/seminars held in the area in which the research was conducted. Debates were mainly concerned with the application of the international classification tools, such as the ICD (1990) and the ICIDH (1980). These tools were and are currently used as eligibility criteria according to which local health units decide to issue a 'certification of handicap' (or statement of special educational needs) to redistribute resources to mainstream schools where disabled pupils are integrated.

In 2002, in the attempt to break with the medical/individual model of disability strongly embedded both in the ICD and the ICIDH, and the subsequent *Atto d'Indirizzo* Decree 1994, many educators (Canevaro and Malaguti, 2002; de Anna, 2002; Hanau, 2002; Ianes and Banal, 2002; Pavone, 2002; Ricci, 2002) including myself (D'Alessio, 2002), encouraged the adoption of ICF as the new classification tool to identify and classify 'disability' and in general to improve the life conditions of disabled people in society. At that time, the ICF seemed to represent the lesser evil to shift the pathologising gaze from students' deficiencies to health conditions (for example what disabled people could do, rather than what they could not do) and to screen environmental limitations and societal barriers that could act as hindrances or facilitators of individual performances. Nevertheless, very much akin to the false promise of the school effectiveness project in England during 1990s (Slee, 1998), the ICF model seems to remain embedded primarily within a functionalist approach to disability which does not challenge discourses about normality as inclusion should do. As already argued elsewhere (D'Alessio, 2006), although the ICF model of disability can be conceived as an attempt to introduce a new model of disability which could compensate for societal failings, it nevertheless still presents a series of contradictions and problems that need to be carefully addressed.

The ICF model of disability is broadly considered (Bickenback et al., 1999) as representing a fundamental shift forward from the limitations embedded in the medical model of disability – such as focus on impairment only - as well as being a move forward from the 'flaws' encapsulated within the social model of disability – such as losing sight of individual impairments. Unlike the previous classification tools (see the ICIDH, 1980 and the ICD-10, 1990) the ICF seems to be capable of identifying circumstantial and environmental factors rather than focussing only on individuals and their functional characteristics. Whilst the ICIDH identified disability with impairment and constructed disability as a disease, the new model is concerned with health-related conditions and constructs disability as an inter-relational pheno-menon caused by the interaction between the individual and the environment (Barnes, 2003:1). The ICF model rejects the use of the word 'handicap' and substitutes it with the definition of 'participation restrictions and activities limitations' in every-day life (WHO, 2001:10). To put it simply, ICF supporters and experts (Bickenback et al., 1999) also in Italy (Ianes, 2004), argue that the ICF model of disability overcomes the limited scope of individual aetiology as a starting point to identify barriers to participation and incorporates societal barriers and how they could be effectively removed.

As Bickenback et al. (1999) illustrate, the ICF widens the scope of normality by universalising – hence normalising - disability purely as a variation of human functioning. It also provides experts and professionals with a standardised language to address disability and related issues at an international level. It is therefore not entirely surprising that the ICF model can be used as an international tool to assist with the development of 'universal' disability policies. However, although ICF supporters (Bickenback et al., 1999; Ianes, 2004; Canevaro, 2008) believe that the ICF is a tool that could identify aspects of social environments responsible for disadvantage and disability, they fail to understand that the final version of the ICF still categorises 'disability' – in terms of individual impairments - rather than 'disablement' – environmental barriers limiting normal forms of participation. More-over, although it should address all people and their health conditions, in the end it is only used by those individuals who are the objects of the health and welfare systems (Rossignol, 2002). Despite the fact that the word 'disablement' was inserted in the penultimate version of the ICF – known as ICIDH- beta 2 version (1997) – the final version has instead maintained the word 'disability' with its inevitable conse-quences. Without this change of terminology, and its legacy, it is hard to believe that a paradigmatic shift from normal individual functioning to normal forms of human participation will actually occur, or that there will be a clear distinction between impairment (biological) and disability (social). The ICF at least claims to be moving in this direction. This problematic is also visible in the fact that the ICF model is also named the 'bio-psycho-social' model, with the terms 'bio' and 'psycho' listed before the term 'social'. The emphasis seems to be on the individual biological conditions rather than on the societal and environmental factors.

At the same time, despite the contrasting positions concerning the adoption of the ICF model within the Disability Studies, Italian scholars (Canevaro and Mandato, 2004; Ianes, 2004), have chosen to adopt the ICF model within the educational domain, particularly as a new way of assessing students - with or without a statement - who encounter difficulties in accessing the curriculum (Ianes, 2004; 2005). The ICF will promote the development of a new assessment tool which, for the first time, will envisage the participation of a committee of experts, rather than one expert only, for the issuing of a disabled student's 'functional diagnosis', and which will include contextual factors which are not envisaged in the diagnostic model currently in use (see the Presidential Decree 1994). It will also facilitate the provision of support to those students identified as having 'special educational needs' who still face difficulties at schools but who are not eligible, according to the current legislation (such as Law n. 104/1992 and the Presidential Decree 1994), for a statementing procedure (for example pupils identified as having dyslexia, behavioural and emotional disorders, mild learning difficulties). Furthermore, the ICF will provide teachers and educationalists with an assessment tool capable of identifying, describing and increasing students' competences, especially those required for disabled pupils and their transition from school to employment (Ianes and Biasoli, 2005). In this way, Ianes and Biasoli (2005) claim that, not only social cohesion will be promoted as a result of the integration of disabled people in the work-place, but it will also improve country competitiveness by focusing on the development of human capital (Lisbon European Council 2000).

Recently with the publication of the International Classification of Functioning – Children and Youth – ICF-CY henceforth - (OMS, 2007), some scholars (Ianes, 2008; Nocera, 2008) have underlined the importance of adopting the ICF as the new classification tool to promote the development of *integrazione scolastica* at the school level as it focuses on issues concerning individuals at a developmental stage. The need to review the diagnostic procedure drawing on the ICF-CY seems to suggest that pupils will gain from a new process of assessment which is based on the participation of different stakeholders (family, school practitioners and support services) including pupils. The process should trigger the issuing of a holistic 'functioning profile' (Ianes, 2008), rather than a labelling medical diagnosis. It should support the disabled pupil throughout his or her life career (Canevaro, 2008) as it takes into account environmental, social and personal barriers and fosters formative, re-habilitative and school interventions.

The ICF approach to disability in Italy is conceived as the fundamental effort to renew a system of classification and categorisation of disability which is still strongly based on the severity of the impairment (see the Framework Law n. 104/1992) and does not adequately address issues concerning the interaction between the impairment and the context, and hence how the impairment could become a disability within a context which had not yet removed societal barriers. The ICF attempts to take into account pupils' participation (Iosa, 2008) and the need to break with a history of corruption (such as issuing of 'fake' clinical diagnosis in order to obtain state resources and assistance). Nevertheless, drawing on the sociological approach used to conduct this research, I argue that the ICF still stems from the same medical/individual model from which it seeks to disentangle itself as it does not problematize the need to categorise and classify people on the basis of impairment in order to obtain additional resources. There is no sense of the fact that categorising and classifying procedures are actions of power (those who categorise and those who are categorised) which do not challenge the existing ways in which society is structured and schools are organised, but work in ways which focus on *compensation* through *adaptations* and *adjustments* rather than in ways which support the development of strategies for fundamental change. It is against this background that a new reading of the policy of *integrazione scolastica* and of the theoretical premises in which it is embedded become to emerge.

FOUCAULT AND GRAMSCI

In order to overcome the limitations of the social model of disability, such as its being a model rather than a theory, the conceptual framework of this research required a critical involvement with the works of Gramsci (1971) and Foucault (1972; 1977) and how they could inform an analysis of the policy of *integrazione scolastica* from a sociological perspective. Their works enabled the study to make sense of the dominant ideologies and discourses impacting upon the policy of *integrazione scolastica* in schools. Essentially, both authors were central for their radical contributions to educational research and critical pedagogy. For example, their input to educational studies was particularly visible in the analysis of the social and political purposes of education beyond schooling, and in the interrogation of educational sites as political places where power is exercised (Mouffe, 1979). To investigate educational sites as political sites, is to 'affirm the ubiquity of relations of force' (Foucault, 1980:189) and to become aware that all relations are basically relations of power, not only conceived within the framework of eco-nomic production. Interestingly, both theorists suggest alternative ways of theorising education systems beyond the enlightened pedagogical discourse of teaching and learning, and they question the origin of self-evident and taken-for-granted phenomena, such as compulsory mass education and apparently neutral state institutions. It was with this in mind, that I have started to problematise a policy such as *integrazione scolastica* and to go beyond a traditional interpretation of this policy as a humanitarian policy that allowed a previously excluded minority to access regular schooling.

Drawing on a recent work of Olssen (2006), one must acknowledge that Gramsci and Foucault are formally associated with two different theoretical frameworks, respectively, Marxism and Post-structuralism (although Foucault always rejected any label). Hence, this 'combination may appear incongruous' (Kenway, 1990:172) and, I would add, ambitious. My effort to combine different foci to carry out my investigation of the policy of *integrazione scolastica* was intended to increase the possibility of looking at things through different lenses and to avoid the pitfall of blindly embracing one way of thinking to the detriment of another. Although these theorists offered different conceptualisations of the same notions (e.g. power), such divergence could be used as a way of complementing the two scholars, as 'each moderates the weaknesses of the other' (Olssen, 2006:96). Thus, despite the differences, I am much in agreement with Olssen (2006) when he states that the two authors are reciprocally illuminating, rather than in opposition.

The works of Foucault and Gramsci were revealing as both scholars have engaged with concepts of power, resistance, change and language, that were all significant themes to analyse the policy of *integrazione scolastica* and the extent to which it may lead to inclusive education. So for example, in relation to power, both theorists describe its productive, rather than repressive impact upon societies and historical processes, thus suggesting to look at the process of decision making, policy discourses and the issue of self-advocacy when investigating the policy of *integrazione scolastica*. Whilst Gramsci focuses primarily on structural sources of power and on macro-mechanisms of social control (for example political parties, the state and the Church), Foucault writes about the micro-technologies of power in everyday life (for example disciplinary forces and individual agents in different domains). Similarly, whereas Foucault underlines the role of individuals, Gramsci links individuals together within a collective conscience necessary to interrogate and change existing discriminatory social conditions. These insights become crucial for understanding how the school subjects and their identities are constructed through pedagogical and discursive practices, and to investigate practices as the effects of power relations:

> Between every point of a social body, between a man and a woman, between the members of a family, between a master and a pupil, between who knows and every one who does not, there exist relations of power which are not purely and simply a projection of the sovereign's great power over the individual; they are rather the concrete changing soil in which the sovereign's power is grounded, the conditions which make it possible for it to function. (Foucault, 1980:187)

As emerging from this extract, unravelling relations of power become a disclosure through which one may start looking at things critically, and to understand where the boundary between 'caring for' particular children and 'controlling' them is located (Barton and Tomlinson, 1981). Similarly, Gramsci's insights concerning relations of force (social, political and military) and the division of powers between the ruling and the ruled groups are relevant. Gramsci's conceptualisation of social relations into a hegemonic bloc discussed beyond the issue of economic confrontation between opposing social classes was crucial when investigating school practice beyond the confrontation between segregation and integration.

In relation to resistance and change, although Foucault underlines individual agency as a way of opposing subjectification and societal constraints, he does not seem to provide a clear explanation of how agency could bring about change (see Giddens, 1987 in Olssen, Codd and O'Neill, 2004). Yet, as Olssen (2006) also indicates, Foucault chose not to get involved with ready-made solutions, and preferred supporting localised interventions and individual freedom in order not to contribute to the reproduction of power mechanisms. Gramsci, on the other hand, suggested social and intellectual forms, through which social agency was possible, such as the organisation of political movements and the role of organic intellectuals (Gramsci, 1971). Here Gramsci becomes crucial since he envisages a space for solutions that are able to trigger change that Foucault fails to suggest so concretely. An example of this are the actions promoted by disabled people movements and their allies. This position is also evident considering that in contemporary society, disabled people cannot be identified any longer with the docile subjects of the nineteenth century, since they have campaigned and have organised themselves into social movements (Hughes, 2005). Thus, if Foucault can help us to understand past conditions and how disabled people were made into passive subjects, current analyses of disabled people requires an understanding of changed historical, social and political conditions which must recommend possible actions for change, as anticipated by Gramsci. Nonetheless, I am in agreement with Allan (1996) who argues that Foucault offered a space of hope for social change located within the individual sphere of self-reflection and critique of one's own thinking, as inclusion, she remarks, 'starts with oneself' (Allan, 2005). Finally, in relation to language, the works of Foucault and Gramsci are crucial as they underline the importance of discursive formations in the construction of reality. Such an approach has been relevant when addressing the consequences of using the 'language of special' (Corbett, 1996) in the educational field and investigating discourses that may foster or alternatively hinder, the development of inclusive features.

For the purposes of this book, I have drawn on Foucault's notions of discourse, power and normalisation. Foucault identifies 'discursive formations' (1972:46) as statements constituting the same objects they describe:

> 'Words and things' is the entirely serious title of a problem; it is the ironic title of a work that modifies its own form, displaces its own data, and reveals, at the end of the day, a quite different task. A task that consists of not – of no longer – treating discourses as groups of signs (signifying elements referring to contents or representations) but as practices that systematically form the objects of which they speak. Of course, discourses are composed of signs; but what they do is more than use these signs to designate things. It is this 'more' that renders them irreducible to the language (langue) and to speech. It is this 'more' that we must reveal and describe. (Foucault, 1972:49)

Discursive formations should not be considered simply as linguistic enunciations but as epistemological facts that construct the same reality which people speak of (Taylor, 2001). Discourses are both constraining and enabling of a particular form of knowledge and they play a crucial role in the process of managing, producing – and reproducing - a social system. Thus, discourses are not merely interpreted as statements, but rather as practices enshrined within historical contexts and social rules. Clearly, discourses constitute what counts as a 'regime of truth' (Foucault, 1980:131), the articulation of what can be and cannot be said at a particular time (Kenway, 1990); they sanction what mechanisms and practices are available and valued. Consequently, it is through discourses that 'the social production of meaning takes place and through which subjectivity is produced and power relations are maintained' (Kenway, 1990:173).

Additionally, discourses elucidate how power is exercised, as 'relations of power cannot themselves be established, consolidated, nor implemented without the production, accumulation, circulation and functioning of a discourse' (Foucault, 1980:93).

61

Although, Foucault does not provide a clear definition of what power is (Foucault, 1978; 1980; 1988) he seems to conceptualise it as a productive and a circular force:

> Power is not about repression. It is not negative, it is not about who exercises power but how does it work...Power uses techniques that make it possible to locate people, to fix them in precise places, to constrict them to a certain number of gestures and habits, in short it is a form of 'dressage'. (Foucault, 1988:105)

As suggested in this excerpt, the book investigates power relations occurring in the case study sites as a force of relations, a discipline/knowledge (or a form of dressage), with a relational nature and how it contributes to the production and reproduction of specific discourses about disability. Perhaps, by becoming aware of the modes in which this relational force permeates all domains, including the education settings, it will be possible to understand the interplay of unequal relations of power, and their consequences. Power becomes fundamental, as it requires an analysis of the ways in which it works, independently of the political association of a given historical period:

> Where Soviet socialist power was in question, its opponents called it total-itarianism; power in Western capitalism was denounced by the Marxists as class domination; but the mechanics of power in themselves were never analysed. (Foucault, 1980:116)

In this statement, Foucault argues for the need to investigate the mechanisms of power and how they are reproduced in different systems and institutional bodies. In so doing he underlines the importance of unmasking those mechanisms whose influence increases according to their level of invisibility and in relation to the capacity of individuals – the subjects - to internalise those mechanisms:

> Take for example an educational institution: the disposal of its space, the meticulous regulations which govern its internal life, the different activities which are organised there, the diverse persons who live there or meet one another, each with his own function, his well-defined character – all these things constitute a block of capacity-communication-power. The activity which ensures apprenticeship and the acquisition of aptitudes or types of behaviour is developed there by means of a whole ensemble of regulated communications (lessons, questions and answers, orders, exhortations, coded signs of obedience, differentiation marks of the 'value' of each person and of the levels of know-ledge) and by the means of a whole series of power processes (enclosure, surveillance, reward and punishment, the pyramidal hierarchy). (Foucault, 1982:218–219)

From this excerpt, schools become loci of investigation, as they are places where power is exercised. It is the social researcher's interest to bring to the fore those disciplinary mechanisms which contribute to the creation of docile bodies and subjects through 'perpetual assessment' (Foucault, 1977) such as surveillance modalities, hierarchical observation and examination procedures. A critical analysis of how such procedures can be found within the policy of *integrazione scolastica* will be provided in the following chapters.

One of the mechanisms of power, which is central to Foucault's work is that of normalisation. This mechanism draws on Foucault's 'principle of coercion' (Foucault, 1977:184), a normative framework of reference, to which individuals are required to adapt by means of disciplinary forces – subtle forms of control and power. This is particularly evident in the Western world which Foucault defines as the 'society of normalisation' (Foucault, 1980:107). He explains that procedures of normalisation follow a type of logic associated with medical treatment and to a particular scientific knowledge by which difference from an established norm can be measured and compensated. In alignment with this observation, the normalising society becomes a 'structure of domination' with the medical sector playing the impartial arbiter of redistribution and compensation (Stone, 1984; Liggett, 1988).

Finally, as Allan (1996) pertinently writes, Foucault's contribution to the study of education and, specifically of special needs education, can be found in the strategy of 'reversal' (1996:226):

> This entails examining official discourses which point to a particular conclusion, usually positive, and considering the implications of an opposite outcome. (Shunmay 1989 in Allan, 1996:226)

In alignment with the above consideration, therefore, this study of the policy of *integrazione scolastica* entails an analysis of the implications of a policy at school level. In order to understand these implications, it is necessary to disentangle the study from the old debate that simplistically positioned integration versus segregation. The question to ask is not 'why we have become integrationists, rather how did integration and not something else come to be the dominant discourse within special education' (Allan, 1996:225).

On the other hand, Gramsci's writings played a significant role in understanding the conditions that led to the passing of the policy of *integrazione scolastica* and its leading role as a major policy initiative in the Italian context. It was Gramsci's interests in ideological hegemony, the merging of different corporate interests, the focus on culture in the struggle for social, economic and political domination, which suggest alternative ways of looking at an educational policy beyond its explicitly stated humanitarian principles. Furthermore, Gramsci's insights concerning the conceptualisation of schools as political sites, the spur towards a more comprehensive school – the 'common school' (1971:29) – the role of intellectuals as mass educators, the collaborative work, the development of critical thinkers and of creative schools, are all significant in understanding potential factors involved in the development of inclusive education. With this in mind, if inclusive education is about restructuring and modifying the educational system in order to allow the participation of all students, then Gramsci's original thoughts seem to contain some of the seeds of such new thinking:

> If our aim is to produce new stratum of intellectuals, including those capable of the highest degree of specialisation, from a social group which has not

traditionally developed the appropriate attitudes, then we have unprecedented difficulties to overcome. (Gramsci, 1971:43)

Here, arguably, Gramsci envisages a process of radical educational change despite the many difficulties it may encompass. The link with inclusive education, which should also support change of current education systems, then, becomes evident.

Of equal interest within Gramsci's political theory is his conceptualisation of notions of hegemony, consent, and struggle. Like Foucault's interpretation of power, Gramsci only (1971) defined hegemony in a scattered way throughout his work. It is therefore difficult to provide a definitive use of the concept by Gramsci. Drawing on his political writings, he often seems to emphasise the concept of 'collective will' by which different, also contrasting, positions are stitched together to achieve the interests of a ruling class. Hegemony, however, should not be interpreted as only representing the dominant ideology of a ruling group, but rather:

> ...the spontaneous consent given by the great masses of the population to the direction imprinted on social life by the fundamental ruling class, a consent which comes into existence 'historically' from the 'prestige' (and hence from the trust) accruing to the ruling class from its position and its function in the world of production. (Gramsci, 1970:124)

An important issue that this insightful citation raises is the relational and fusion-like quality of hegemonic domination (Mouffe, 1979). What emerges is the dismissal of totalitarian and coercive means, substituted by popular consent, and based on common sense thinking. Hegemony, although identifiable with a ruling class, does not constitute one group's interests, but rather the 'ability of one class to articulate the interest of other social groups' (Mouffe, 1979:183). Similarly, Boggs (1976) argues that hegemony can be defined as 'the "organising principle" or world-view (or combination of such world-views), that is diffused by agencies of ideological control and socialisation into every area of life' (1976:39); a cultural ideology which permeates our life and our consciousness, and structures our system of values and beliefs. This principle, Boggs (1976) comments, is internalised by the population until it is transformed into popular 'common sense' (1976:39), allowing the perpetuation of a ruling class ideology, which comes to be perceived as the natural order of things (Burke, 1999). Consent, therefore, is the social mode through which hegemony is achieved, supported and maintained and an instrumental factor for the creation of a political unity. Thus, hegemony is a pervasive force which is maintained and reproduced through all social, intellectual, political, moral and economic functions, such as state apparatuses (such as schools or universities) and civil society (such as means of communication and of production). This perspective became crucial to understand the role played by the philosophy of *integrazione scolastica* thirty years on after its first enactment in Italy.

At the same time, however, the notion of hegemony (as power in Foucault) is not to be conceived only as a repressive force. On the contrary, hegemony is also a potentially subversive force (Burgio, 2007) as it encompasses two apparently incompatible approaches. On the one hand it is a reactionary force that reproduces existing relations of power, whilst on the other hand, it is a progressive force that may open up spaces for a counter-hegemonic action. Hence, it becomes a transformative tool that overthrows existing relations of power 'through means of self-consciousness and reflexivity necessary to modify ways of thinking' (Burgio, 2007:135).

With the above considerations in mind, the notion of struggle becomes central. Gramsci envisages the possibility of how to bring about radical changes in society by creating a new hegemony - a counter-hegemony - which counter acts with the pre-existing hegemonic ideology. He does write about terrains on 'which men move, acquire consciousness of their position, struggle etc...' (Gramsci, 1971:377). However, a radical change does not result from coercive imposition, neither does it result from a modification of the economic conditions only. On the contrary, Gramsci moves the battlefield of class struggle from the economic to the cultural and intellectual domain to promote an 'ideological transformation' (Mouffe, 1979:191). The intellectuals then, become fundamental in the struggle for change as they play a crucial role in the contestation of old collective will and in the elaboration of new theories (Gramsci, 1952; 1970; 1971). It is here that the work of Gramsci can be linked to the quest for the development of inclusive education as a paradigmatic shift from the tradition of special needs education. In particular, the role of educators (Apple, 2008) and of disabled people's movements (Oliver, 1990; Barton, 2001; Barnes, Oliver and Barton, 2002) and their alliances, as potential organic intellectuals for change, become evident:

> It will be said that what each individual is able to change is very little indeed. But considering that each individual is able to associate himself with others who desire the same changes as himself, and provided the change is a rational one, the single individual is able to multiply himself by an impressive number and can thus obtain a far more radical change than would first appear (Gramsci, 1970:78)

What this citation elucidates is the potentiality to bring about change, whenever it is sustained, negotiated and acted upon by means of alliance. By drawing on the work of Mouffe (1979), the process of hegemonic replacement is doubled and it entails the fostering of self-awareness as a class and the search to enlarge the basis for consensus (for example allies of disabled people). For the scope of this study, the concept of hegemony was employed to investigate the policy of *integrazione scolastica* and the possibility of deconstructing the latter in order to construct inclusive education.

Bearing in mind the effort to apply the social model of disability and to address the limitations of such a model, the work of Gramsci were exemplary of how the social model of disability could be put into practice, whilst Foucault's insights became central in order to address the critiques that this model is over-socialised and materialist (Tremain, 2005). On the one hand, Gramsci indicated how a collective subjectivity, as the one theorised by Disabilities Studies in the common cause of oppression of disabled people, could lead to a collective action that aimed at radical change (such as disability politics). On the other hand, Foucault's reappraisal of individuality – and not of individualistic aspects – paved the way for the recognition of the politics of identity (Fraser, 1996) and the work of those potential agents of change who reject to use their condition as a political badge (Liggett, 1988). Moreover, while Gramsci managed to identify where the struggle for change should be located – such as structural barriers – Foucault emphasised that educational systems are historically and geographically situated contexts in a state of continuous flux.

CONCLUSION

In this chapter I have set out and discussed the epistemological standpoints within which the book is located. Combining the different foci, such as the social model of disability and the works of Foucault and Gramsci, has been an attempt to apply the social model of disability to an educational enquiry. By mixing the ideas from different thinkers and the social model of disability, the research could benefit from a new understanding of previously taken-for-granted phenomena and from identifying domains of oppression and openings for subversion.

In conclusion, the reason why Gramscian and Foucauldian concepts were relevant for a critical analysis of the policy of *integrazione scolastica* was that both scholars stressed the material status of ideas and discourses embodied in social practices and institutions. A sociological analysis of the policy of *integrazione scolastica* could identify on the one hand the material consequences of the implementation of this policy in schools, and on the other hand, the processes through which this policy began to play a hegemonic role, that of a unifying principle maintained and perpetuated by a hegemonic group of special pedagogues. The following chapters will show how the scholars' insights provided a fertile terrain to critically investigate the policy of *integrazione scolastica* and its leading role more than thirty years since the policy was first enacted, the proliferation of discourses that followed its enactment and the consequences of them for the people the policy purports to safeguard.

POLICY ANALYSIS

Mistaking the Means for the End

Social policy analysis has been slow to recognise the role of ideology in the development of social policies…. (Oliver, 1990:79)

By investigating the different legislative measures that led to the policy enactment and its further development, this book shows how the policy of *integrazione scolastica* has been transformed into a shared philosophy which made education for all disabled pupils in regular settings a reality. However, when exploring the policy in greater depth, it emerges that *integrazione scolastica* still encompasses a series of limitations embedded in the way it is formulated, the language it utilises, the ideological framework to which it refers and the social context in which it is rooted. For example, the policy is characterised by the use of a disabling language that contributes to the reproduction of biases and assumptions concerning disabled people. Moreover, it seems to be embedded in a deficit-oriented rationale, which identifies disability as an individual pathology, and it does not seem to acknowledge the differences between impairment (individual) and disability (social).

As already discussed in Chapter One, the historical turn in favour of the education of disabled children in regular settings occurred in the 1970s. At a European level, while international bodies were still investigating *whether* it was possible to integrate disabled students in ordinary classrooms (Helios, 1980; the Eurydice network, 1980) Italy was already exploring ways of *how* to improve the quality of education for disabled pupils in mainstream settings (Law n. 517/1977). For this reason, the Italian policy of *integrazione scolastica* has been internationally characterised within the field of education as being very progressive (Booth, 1982; Hegarty, 1987; Buzzi, 1993; Meijer and Abbring, 1994; OECD, 1994; O'Hanlon, 1995; de Anna, 1997; Mittler, 2000; Thomas and Loxley, 2001; Segal, Maigne and Gautier, 2003; OECD, 2005; Ferri, 2008). As acknowledged by national and international literature in the field (Buzzi, 1993; Meijer, Soriano and Watkins, 2003) disabled children have been integrated in regular schools, as a matter of national policy, for more than thirty years (Onger, 2008) and any other alternative educational provision for disabled students is considered as a 'denial of basic human rights' (Adams, 1990:151).

This chapter is concerned with policy analysis at a micro (e.g. school and teachers) and macro (e.g. statistics) level. In the first section, I will address the process of policy making and I will challenge the dominant view that the problem with *integrazione* lies in its lack of implementation at school level. Secondly I will provide an overview of the different interpretations of *integrazione scolastica* and how these may coexist and overlap according to historical imperatives, financial crises and political contexts. I will therefore provide a brief outline of the many different inter-pretations concerning *integrazione* provided by the teachers interviewed in the schools. In the remaining sections I will provide an analysis of the main legislative measures that paved the way to the current policy of *integrazione scolastica*, suggesting reasons for their re-formulation. This is particularly crucial as policies and statistical data concerning *integrazione scolastica* keep focusing on pupils who experience difficulties at school, rather than on the inadequacies of an education system.

INCLUSIVE EDUCATION AS A POLICY MAKING PROCESS

Most Italian literature (Canevaro and Ianes, 2001; Nocera, 2001; Canevaro and Ianes, 2008) concerning the policy of *integrazione scolastica* indicates that the problem lies in the lack of the implementation of this policy at a school level. In contrast, this book suggests a different reading of the problem. As a starting point, the investigation of this policy disentangled itself from a traditional interpretation, which still differ-entiates between policy and practice. Practice is interpreted as another form of policy which is made at different levels (Fulcher, 1989) and via the struggles occurring in teacher councils, governing bodies, staff rooms, classrooms and in meetings with parents and practitioners. The analysis of the process of policy making in the school context is strongly linked to how people and contexts respond to policies:

> ...responses indeed must be creative...Given constraints, circumstances and practicalities the translation of the crude, abstract simplicities of policy texts into interactive and sustainable practices of some sort involve productive thought, invention and adaptation. Policies do not normally tell you what to do; they create circumstances in which a range of options available in deciding what to do are narrowed and changed. (Ball, 1993:12)

The varied actors operating in the different school contexts commit themselves to the enactment of policy according to their own expectations and understanding. There-fore, for example teachers' attitudes towards inclusion are crucial factors that need to be carefully considered. It is noteworthy to remind however, that changing attitudes is a very difficult task as it concerns itself with the changing of strongly rooted habits (Wiliam, 2007) that reflect the ways in which teachers themselves were taught when they were students. Yet, schools and teachers cannot be considered the ultimate responsible individuals for implementing inclusive practice, since they are subject to pressures from external forces, requirements and ideologies that may hinder their attempts to be inclusive. Furthermore, much of the response to a policy depends on who exerts the dominant role in the struggles occurring in the process of policy making – although these struggles are responsible for outcomes in practice, in much of the policy analysis literature there is 'no sense of the political struggles involved in developing and implementing policy' (Fulcher, 1989:3). In the process of this tug of war among different policy makers, only the dominant discourses are likely to be articulated into the policy (Ball, 1993). It is, consequently, of critical importance to understand which voices are heard and which voices are disempowered (for example students).

In terms of inclusive education, advocacy for those populations at risk of exclusion must occupy a relevant position in the formulation of new policies if we want to secure specific desired outcomes at the level of practice. The issue of *advocacy* is as relevant as the process of legally enforcing anti-discrimination laws via sanctioning. Essentially, in relation to sanctioning, Vlachou (2004) indicates that for policies to be effective and promote effective practices they must be 'enforceable and under-written by appropriate sanctions if they are breached' (2004:6). For example the UN Convention on the Rights of Persons with Disabilities (United Nations, 2006) required its signatory countries not only to sign the Convention but also to ratify its Optional Protocol in order to transform the Convention from a mere 'declaration' of rights, into an enforceable treaty to protect the human rights of disabled people from violation. Prior to the sanctioning, however, advocacy, by the people for whose 'benefit' the policy is intended, must be guaranteed. Thus, the issue of representation becomes fundamental. Very often, the advocacy of disabled people, as many disability scholars (Barton and Tomlinson, 1981; Aspis, 1997; Barton, 2005; Arnot and Reay, 2007) also argue, is limited and this limited representation provides room for those supporting discourses against the interests of the very people the policy should 'safeguard'.

Within the educational field, policy-making should entail an analysis of how policies are made and interpreted in different arenas and by whom. Drawing on this interpretation of policy-making, schools, and in particular classrooms, can be considered as the ultimate arenas in which policy is made. Not surprisingly, one of the most debated dilemmas concerning policy making is how to transform inclusive values into practice (Lindsay, 2003; Meijer, 2003; Wedell, 2005; Ainscow, Booth and Dyson, 2006). Teachers and practitioners themselves often report how difficult it is to translate policy directives into everyday practices, particularly within a context of challenges and constraints (Armstrong and Moore, 2004). Corbett (2001) argues that although problems may exist in addressing how inclusive theory can be applied in practice, it is necessary to explore how different schools seek to implement inclusion to obtain a sense of possibilities. In order to pre-empt and challenge the critique of inclusive education as idealistic, Corbett suggests that 'the time has come' to focus on *pedagogy* as the central strategic route to implementing inclusive education and the radical changes it requires (Corbett, 2001:XIII). This said, it is equally true that awareness (of the problem, as well as of its possible solutions) is a fundamental pre-requisite for implementing change and in giving power to key actors. To become aware implies that practitioners choose to contribute to change rather than to per-petuate existing forms of 'folk pedagogy' (Bruner, 1996). That is to say to reproduce common-sense ideas about teaching and learning that serve a conservative function of maintaining and supporting existing understanding and practice (Apple, 1990; hooks, 1994; Moore, 2004). At the level of schooling, it would be advisable to investi-gate alternative forms and processes of teaching and learning in contrast with the traditional rigidity of schooling procedures (Ainscow and Booth, 1998; Corbett, 2001). Inclusive education scholars (Slee, 1993b; Ainscow, 1997; Clough, 1998; Ainscow, 1999; Ainscow, 2000; Corbett, 2001; Slee, 2001; Ainscow, 2005; Slee, 2007) underline how the work on pedagogy, classroom practice and the re-organisation of mainstream schools in general are crucial factors to suggest ways forward in relation to inclusive policy-making in schools and classrooms as something feasible and not only advisable. There is the need to be able to answer the question of *how* you are going to implement this inclusive policy, rather than *if*. In this respect, the Index for Inclusion: Developing Learning and Participation in Schools (Booth and Ainscow, 2000; 2002) and the work of Education Queensland (in Slee, 2001) could be considered important exemplars in terms of translating inclusive education into practice.

Given the reflections highlighted above, the study of the extent to which a policy such as *integrazione scolastica*, can be considered an inclusive policy must address issues which do not concern only the application (or otherwise the lack of application) of regulations at a school/classroom level, rather they should entail an investigation of the discourses embedded within this policy and that may reproduce exclusionary practice. As the following sections will show, evidence of exclusionary practice in the Italian policy of *integrazione scolastica* can be found in the perpetuation of dominant discourses about disability (such as medical model of disability) and schooling (such as the principle of homologation), the role played by different actors participating in the process of policy-making (for example disabled people and students being often excluded in the process of decision-making) and the investigation of the theoretical premises supporting the policy (such as special need education), which may determine the implementation of a specific form of practice notwithstanding the official objectives articulated within the policy.

INVESTIGATING MEANINGS: ONE *INTEGRAZIONE* OR MANY *INTEGRAZIONI*?

There is a general understanding that while 'integration' aims to find a way of supporting students perceived as having 'special educational needs' in 'unchanged' ordinary schools, inclusion instead aims at a radical restructuring of the school system (Armstrong, Armstrong and Barton, 2000; Dyson and Millward, 2000). Consequently, whereas integration concerns mainly disabling conditions at an individual level, inclusion encompasses social and systemic disabling conditions that may oppress the individual and may have a decisive impact on his/her difficulties. In international contexts the meaning of integration has usually been associated with a process of normalisation (OECD, 1994) and as Derrick Armstrong (2003) claims, with assimilation. A similar position to that of Derrick Armstrong emerges from the work of Slee and Corbett who argue that:

> Integration is inherently assimilationist. It holds firm, to a traditional notion of ideal types, both of people and institutions. According to this model the emphasis is upon deficit, diagnosis, categorisation and individual treatment. (Corbett and Slee, 2000:134)

In this statement, Corbett and Slee articulate the underlying fear that inclusion could be transformed into a new label for integration, with the risk of perpetuating assimilationist and normalising discourses embedded in the concept of integration. Although, in principle, I am in agreement with such a position, it is important to mention that integration is not a static condition. Just as inclusion has to be understood in relation to specific contexts and people, so does integration whose meaning may also change, depending on the conditions and the historical period in which it is considered. Therefore, although reductionist notions of integration may prevail today, it is necessary to acknowledge that there might have been alternative interpretations of the notion of integration that have not been necessarily assimilationist.

Most Italian scholars in fact strongly argue (de Anna, 1998; Canevaro, 2001; Malaguti Rossi, 2004) against an assimilationist interpretation of *integrazione* and urge educationalists to distinguish between 'integration' – assimilation of a minority group into society - and *integrazione scolastica* – a process of reciprocal adaptation undergone both by society and the individual with impairments contemporaneously (Larocca, 2007). In line with the above considerations, Booth (2000) observes that both concepts (such as integration and inclusion) need to be seen as 'unending processes of transformation' (Booth, 2000:88). Moreover, by investigating the Italian context it is necessary to underline that unlike the English definition of integration, which generally refers to placement, *integrazione scolastica* carries the sense of *putting things together*, for both learners and systems. The latter idea, one may argue, is a more powerful suggestion of change than is often seen to be implied by inclusion (Booth, 2000). Clearly *integrazione* has a strong social and community based dimension (Gaspari, 1999) which the English word 'integration' does not possess. However, the main limitation of the notion of *integrazione* in Italy is that, although disabled people's organisations campaigned for the passing of the national policy, academics, educators and policy makers who have debated issues concerning its implementation, have done so, I argue, in a way which was often 'divorced from the views of disabled people themselves' (Oliver, 1996:83).

Currently, in Italy, there have emerged two main interpretations of the concept of *integrazione scolastica*: a theoretical one and a pragmatic one (Canevaro, 1997), elsewhere defined as institutional-legislative and educational-didactic conceptualisations (Sbarbati, 1998). Whereas the theoretical vision seemed to identify *integrazione scolastica* as a structural aspect of Italian schooling aimed at improving the quality of schooling in general, the pragmatic vision insisted on the importance of providing additional resources to schools in order to promote the integration of students who did not fit in with the established norm. We might say that the theoretical conceptualisation of *integrazione scolastica* is concerned with a continuous change in the education system developing out of successful experiences of mainstreaming disabled people in ordinary schools (de Anna, 1997; Malaguti Rossi, 2004). It is also, however, concerned with the removal of cultural, economic and social barriers that prevent disabled students from actively participating in the process of learning. Drawing on Malaguti Rossi (2004) the theoretical concept of *integrazione* could not be interpreted only in terms of additional provisions to compensate individual deficiencies. She argued instead that schools implementing *integrazione scolastica* were starting to understand 'diversity not in terms of inferiority, but as something that belongs to all human beings' (Malaguti Rossi, 2004:38). The pragmatic conceptualisation of *integrazione scolastica,* on the other hand, refers to the process of placing disabled students in ordinary schools, in ordinary classrooms, and providing them with extra resources necessary to access the curriculum.

Other interpretations of *integrazione scolastica* identify three main concept-ualisations of this policy: strong, moderate and weak *integrazione* (Ricci, 1999). The first definition is very similar to the radical inclusion position as described by Cigman (2007). Such a position argues for the policy of *integrazione* to be imple-mented in all schools notwithstanding the difficulties and the limitations that the schools may have to face. Strong *integrazione* rejects any other alternative solution to regular schools for all students and supports the dismantling of all special schools. The second definition of *integrazione*, the moderate one, argues that integration should only occur in specialised and 'prepared' contexts and classrooms, which must be adequately equipped with all resources necessary to welcome the diversity of the student population. Finally, weak *integrazione* focuses only on the outcomes of this policy rather than on the pre-conditions of learning. This interpretation supports the maintenance of forms of 'special schooling' (Ricci, 1999:207), if the latter is perceived as the only way for learning to occur.

Recently, however, other interpretations of the notion of *integrazione scolastica* have appeared in the Italian literature (Medeghini, 2008). These critical analyses have attempted to indicate that what was once conceived as the theoretical meaning of the process of *integrazione* has slowly slipped away into more reductionist inter-pretations. The latter identify *integrazione* with the process of allocating additional resources and differentiated educational provisions to disabled pupils and they put aside the urge towards school change. In this concern, Medeghini (2008) identifies four types of *integrazione*: participatory, conditional, differentiated and progressive. The *participatory* type of *integrazione* can be identified with the original notion of the process of *integrazione scolastica*. It envisaged a process of transformation of the mainstream school as a result of the 'reciprocal' change that both educational settings and pupils with impairments should undergo in regular classrooms. The *conditional* type of *integrazione* refers specifically to the process of allocating resources to schools in order to promote the adaptation of disabled pupils into mainstream settings (i.e. subjected to the allocation of resources). Thirdly, the *differentiated* type of *integrazione* is based on the severity of pupils' impairments and it envisages the possibilities of alternative learning pathways for disabled students within or outside the mainstream system (for example special units and *scuole potenziate*). Finally, the *progressive* type of *integrazione* envisages a compensatory approach to disability as it supports a linear conceptualisation of learning and claims that disabled students need to develop specific abilities necessary to be progressively 'integrated' within the able-bodied society. These interpretations of *integrazione* have clearly prevailed, as the following chapters will also indicate, over an original conceptualisation of *integrazione* intended as a process of change.

Despite the differences among the many definitions used within the literature, all the different interpretations of *integrazione* seem to remain imbricated in the old debate between segregation and integration as they suggest 'responsible' ways of going from special to ordinary schooling. Moreover, these different notions of *integrazione* seem to distance themselves from the notion of inclusive education, as theorised in Chapter Two. Whilst *integrazione* is constructed in terms of participation of disabled children in mainstream schools, inclusion should be about the well being of all students and the consequent *transformation* of educational sites. Furthermore, these interpretations of *integrazione* embrace an orthodox vision of policy which claims that 'achieving integration is only a matter of policy' (Oliver, 1996:86). As a consequence of such an understanding, debates primarily address issues of allocation of resources, support and training of personnel, while there is no sense of the power relations, inequality and conflicts that represent the nature of social reality today as the works of Foucault and Gramsci have also indicated. In the end, the policy of *integrazione scolastica* seems to be concerned with issues about the delivery of provisions rather than with the struggle for a change of education systems (Slee, 1993a).

Teachers' Interpretations of the Policy of Integrazione Scolastica

The differences in the interpretations of the notion of *integrazione scolastica* were particularly visible in the interviews with teachers who have attempted to provide a *working* definition of *integrazione*. Despite the differences, a common feature emerged from participants' responses concerning the meaning of *integrazione* and this was the awareness of the difficulties of putting this policy into practice in the classroom. At the same time, not only did some school actors suggested that *integrazione scolastica* failed disabled students in ordinary classrooms, but they also envisaged the possibility of re-opening special or differentiated classrooms for students with impairments:

> *Integrazione* is very difficult to explain. For example for those students who are not Italian they are placed in ordinary classrooms, they cannot speak a word of Italian, they are sitting the whole morning in the classroom, without understanding what is going on. While some schools have managed to get funded, and have good teachers, other schools haven't. ...I should say that *integrazione* is something that in some schools is easier whereas in other schools it is not easy at all and depends on good luck ...If it weren't for the teachers who take the issues of these children at heart, their integration would not be successful. But what happens if you have more rigid teachers?.... In the city of Bologna where I used to work, there are special schools for blind and deaf people. Pupils are all employed after they finish schools.... A colleague of mine, a blind Italian literature teacher, he had attended a special school. I am not arguing that our disabled students attending mainstream schools remain outside the labour market, but sometimes I do find that special schools might be more successful for children with sensory disabilities. (Interview 04, Art teacher, *Don Milani* School)

Similarly, another participant remarked upon the difficulties in implementing *integrazione scolastica* in practice by making reference to special settings as a potential way forward to promote the learning of disabled people:

> You need to have the necessary tools to implement *integrazione* at school, otherwise you are socialising students and not integrating them. *Integrazione*, I believe is when the others understand that your diversity is not a hindrance.

For example in our classroom we share this principle and we are trying to achieve this, but on a practical level we did not succeed. I do not know what happens in other countries, I know that they have special schools and that maybe this is not good as they have ghettos....but if you look at Emanuele, the student with a certification of handicap, he attends the ordinary classroom with his peers. Of course this is very good, he manages to participate in most lessons. But still his integration is 50%. Because of his intellectual deficit, he often beats other students, he is often very aggressive and he breaks the usual unfolding of a lesson. Especially with the girls, he would like to approach them, to talk to them but he does not know how to do it and they reject him as he may become rather annoying. If Emanuele were attending a special school, like the centre for vocational training we have here in *Adriazzurra,* he would not perceive the difference with his peers, as he does when he is at school. That vocational centre is a ghetto-non-ghetto since you learn but you do not feel that you are different. You can still perceive that your mate is different from you but he is not 'Mount Everest', he is not that different! (Interview 03, English teacher, *Fellini* School)

In these extended extracts, the teachers were sincerely uttering their opinions concerning the limitations of implementing *integrazione scolastica* in mainstream classrooms, in particular in relation to the opportunity for disabled people to affirm their identity in regular schools. Although they both seemed to approve of the policy of *integrazione scolastica* as a principle, they explained that this policy lacked a series of resources and material tools that could support the work of strongly motivated teachers. Without this support, they argued, the process of *integrazione* was destined to fail, along with the disabled pupils who attended ordinary schools.

Other participants chose to align themselves with official discourses, and reported about the policy of *integrazione* as a process of reciprocal adaptation between the child with impairment and the context around him/her:

Integrazione is a path in which each individual develops his/her potentialities and grows. *Integrazione* is not only about the handicapped student who is integrated inside the class, but it is also about the class, which must change to welcome the handicapped child. (Interview 17, head teacher, *Fellini* School)

This definition constructs *integrazione* as something that is not made, but continuously negotiated, until the very moment in which it enters the classroom. Although the head teacher puts the emphasis on the disabled student and his/her attempts to fit with the school environment, she introduces the topic of change - a mutual adaptation between disabled and non-disabled pupils – thus, suggesting that school transformations are under way.

In line with the concept of *integrazione,* which was not made until the very moment in which it entered the classroom, one support teacher discusses *integrazione* in terms of local struggles between support teachers and mainstream teachers:

T: It would be good if *integrazione* were real. I have to admit that my support colleagues, they are much better than myself; they make a lot of efforts. In my opinion they are doing their best to change the attitudes towards 'their' pupils so that these pupils can be accepted and seen in a different way, I have to say that they are struggling for it.

R: Struggling with what or whom?

T: They are struggling against the mainstream teachers who keep delegating, and send these students outside their classrooms whenever they can. (Interview 12, support teacher, *Fellini* School)

This extract is reminiscent of the work of Ball (1994) on micro-politics, and how policy results from struggles fought in different arenas by different contenders (Fulcher, 1989) such as those fought between mainstream and support teachers. Furthermore, participants report about their fears concerning the process of *integrazione scolastica* and that what should be considered as a legacy of the Italian education system is only an illusion:

I believe that *integrazione scolastica* does not exist; at least not here. We still tend to withdraw the 'problem' outside the classroom and possibly without making too much noise. *Integrazione* is to make people understand that we are all different, even those who believe that they are normal. We all have our differences. Some people have more difficulties than others. There is the student with handicap, the student who comes from a different country, the student who is often distracted in the classroom. *Integrazione* concerns every subject, all of us, and not only the pupil with handicap or the foreign one or the one who comes from another region...in this school if you come from Sicily they consider you as someone to be integrated! (Interview 13, teaching assistant, *Fellini* School)

The teaching assistant provides a theoretical interpretation of *integrazione scolastica* which seems to be very inclusive, as she reports that *integrazione scolastica* is concerned with 'all of us'. However, she also states that this type of interpretation is an illusion, as prejudices and cultural biases about diversity and otherness have not been adequately addressed. She also suggests that the school under investigation marks each type of 'difference' – 'if you come from Sicily they consider you as someone to be integrated' and by doing so she identifies one possible barrier to inclusive education not only in the rigidity of the school system, but also in teachers' prejudices and difficulties in questioning old assumptions.

At the same time, some potentially inclusive features of the notion of *integrazione scolastica* can be found in the following extract:

Integration is an encounter; or better, a confrontation. I mean, not necessarily a confrontation, but certainly, a confrontation is a process of *integrazione* ... sometimes it may lead to an encounter but it should never be considered as a visit to pay to somebody. Let's make an example: you and I are two friends who live in different cities, I live in Rome and you live in Milan and we are planning to meet somewhere... If you are in Milan and I stay in Rome I will not say 'come and see me in Rome', but I'd rather say 'Let's meet in Florence'. Thus, I leave from Rome for Florence and you will do the same from Milan.

This movement to reach the other is crucial. But it is very difficult to move from one's own positions, because, you see, if you want to meet somebody you need to move from your convictions in order to meet someone else's, that is what you have to do, there is no choice. You must leave the house of your convictions and this requires a big effort! We try to do it but it is so difficult to achieve it! (Interview 12, support teacher, *Fellini* School)

The support teacher seems to suggest that despite the passing of legislative measures, policy requires a process of 'internal' change of those actors involved in the process of policy making (Allan, 2005). Therefore, unless teachers became aware of assumptions, no matter what the national policy would say, the outcomes of this policy would still be discriminatory. The space for counter-hegemonic actions, therefore, could be found in the personal journey that educationalists and practitioners have to undertake in order to question not only the external and systemic barriers to inclusive education, but also their own positions.

In conclusion, teachers' interpretations of the meaning of *integrazione scolastica* and how it could be implemented and improved in practice indicate that this policy is fundamentally perceived as an educational measure which concerns the process of mainstreaming disabled students in ordinary settings. Although some statements suggest that classrooms as well as pupils with impairments are supposed to undergo a process of transformation, participants never concretely address what these changes are and how they can impact upon the usual unfolding of traditional lessons. It emerges that integrazione is primarily about disabled pupils' rights to obtain support and resources within the mainstream settings, without any sense of the changes that traditional pedagogy, curriculum and assessment should undergo as a result of integrating a heterogeneous student population. The policy of *integrazione* seems to have lost its original target, which was concerned with the reformulation and the development of mainstream settings. As I will attempt to show in the following chapters, practitioners, as well as policy makers, seem to have mistaken the *means* of this policy, which are and were related with the process of mainstreaming disabled students into regular classrooms, for the *end* or *purpose* of it - that of improving the quality of mainstream settings and of contributing to the construction of a more just and equal society.

NATIONAL STATISTICAL DATA: CHALLENGES AND DEVELOPMENTS.

Evidence of misunderstanding the means of this policy for its purpose can also be found in policy documents concerned with the presentation of statistical data on the integration of disabled students in regular classrooms. In most national policy documents concerning *integrazione scolastica* there is still a predominance of official governmental statistics displaying figures showing an increase in the number of disabled students enrolled in ordinary classrooms (see Table 1).

The apparent increase in the number of disabled pupils enrolled in ordinary schools is officially considered to be a 'significant' indicator of improvement in the quality of *integrazione scolastica* and of the education system in general (Ministero dell'Istruzione Università e Ricerca, 2003; 2005; Ministero Pubblica Istruzione, 2006).

Table 1. From 'La scuola in cifre 2006', Ministero Pubblica Istruzione, Italia 2006

Number of disabled pupils expressed as a total and as a percentage of total pupils enrolled in ordinary schools (*)		
Italy 2000–2006		
* special schools not included		
Disabled pupils	Disabled pupils (%)	
2000–2001	132.646	1,5
2001–2002	142.774	1,6
2002–2003	156.009	1,8
2003–2004	161.159	1,8
2004–2005	167.804	1,9
2005–2006	178.220	2

Many official policy documents have chosen to adopt particular 'discursive tactics' (Fulcher, 1989) to convince the audience of the reliability of a quantitative approach as an indicator of the high quality of *integrazione scolastica*:

> After twenty-five years since the promulgation of Law n. 577 in 1977, which triggered the process of *integrazione* of disabled students into regular state schools, we can show figures that indicate that the number of disabled students placed in ordinary schools has increased. This data refers to the past ten years and shows that there has been an increase in the number of disabled students, with an average growth of 2% in primary and lower secondary education, and slightly less of 1% in upper secondary education. (Ministero dell'Istruzione Università e Ricerca, 2003:2)

> Today, the *integrazione* of the 'handicap' in schools seems to be a largely shared concept, which cannot be questioned anymore. There are more than 140.000 handicapped students attending all grades of schools, with an increasing rate of 34,4% in the last ten years (Aprea, 2002:4–5)

> [by referring to statistical data] ...there is a consolidated will to continue the process of *integrazione scolastica* and to improve its efficacy by analysing the results achieved till now and by confirming that if *integrazione scolastica* is good for the students with disabilities, it is also good for all those who share this communal experience. (Tinagli, 2003:1)

Clearly these extracts, and the table I from the Ministery of Public Instruction are attempts to put forward the political agenda of the Italian government to show that there 'has been an increase' in terms of quantity (such as the number of disabled students enrolled in regular classrooms), and consequently, of the quality of the education system. The problem arises, however, when there is no information concerning what is meant by 'quality' and how this should be measured. There is, for example, no reference to the experience of teaching and learning or to the ways in which students' diversity is addressed and valued in ordinary classrooms. What seems to emerge from policy texts, is instead the use of reification (Nicholl and Edwards, 2004) – to repeat things in order to *naturalise* them and turn them into 'real facts'.

By referring to *integrazione scolastica* as something which has been in place for more than 'twenty five years', 'a shared concept' and a 'consolidated will' that belongs to the Italian culture, policy makers add to the construction of the policy of *integrazione scolastica* as a powerful governmental discourse used to administer and manage disability, starting with the identification of disabled students 'placed' within the regular system. Nonetheless, having reified something does not necessarily imply that a policy is being adequately supported and implemented. In contrast, some discourses related to *integrazione scolastica* could have been used as 'conduits for marshalling consent' (Armstrong, 2002:52) and maintain practices unchanged, and consequently to keep barriers in place. Although policy documents provide some indications concerning how the government wishes to improve the policy implementation (for example by increasing funding and personnel), they do not address the requirements of all students, what actions should be taken to promote school changes (Ainscow, Booth and Dyson, 2006) as inclusion should do.

Given the above considerations, statistical data seem to be presented only 'to excel in comparison with other countries' (D'Alessio, 2007:53) as they do not provide relevant information concerning the quality of *integrazione scolastica* in schools. The increasing number of disabled students, and of 'statements of special needs education' (*certificazione di handicap*) could instead be a symptom that schools are struggling even more to comply with their educational tasks. As previously stated, statistical descriptions not only do not provide information about the quality of the education system for disabled students, but are also redundant when we consider that special schools in Italy have almost completely disappeared, and that those which are still operating are not counted in the data collection (see Table I). Whereas in some countries, where segregating institutions are the rule, the numerical description of the number of students integrated into regular settings could be an indicator of an apparent rising trend towards inclusive education, yet in Italy, where placement into ordinary education systems is the norm, the number of integrated students should be considered as a pre-requisite of an effective process of *integrazione* rather than as an indicator of any 'qualitative' improvement. Possibly, there are two underpinning assumptions in relation to the gathering of statistical data as an indicator of 'quality' for *integrazione*. Firstly, the notion that exclusion equals segregated education; thus suggesting that there is no sense of the micro-exclusions that can be reproduced within the mainstream settings. Secondly, there seems to be the belief that *integrazione* starts with placing disabled people within the ordinary settings, rather than with a re-conceptualisation and transformation of ordinary settings and education systems for all pupils, as inclusion implies. Although, placement was a relevant factor when *integrazione* was first enacted in the 1970s, today it does not seem to add any valuable information concerning the current state of the policy and/or of its level of application or implementation in schools in Italy.

Another common aspect of national policies is that statistical descriptions seem to reinforce the claim that policy makers prefer hard data (Ritchie and Spencer, 2002) – figures about the number of disabled students placed in ordinary classes – and fail to interrogate the reasons why a policy has to categorise students into two separate groups: disabled and not disabled pupils – in order to educate them. By choosing to classify particular students rather than others, these texts indicate that, although many anti-discrimination laws have been passed and have contributed to the dismantling of separate institutions, there still exists a dichotomous vision of reality that pathologizes disability.

Quantitative studies that rely on statistical data, should sometimes be considered as a topic of investigation themselves rather than only as a resource for research (Prior, 1997). For example, from a sociological perspective, the focus on statistical descriptions of the increasing number of disabled students currently attending mainstream schools, should be questioned as a way of organising and assembling reality by experts, rather than interpreted solely as research evidence for the effective implementation of a policy.

Additionally, by assuming that the increasing number of disabled students in regular schools is the most relevant indicator of an effective process of *integrazione scolastica*, national documents marshalling *integrazione scolastica* constructs the disabled person as being the sole and final 'consumer' of this policy (Ministero Pubblica Istruzione, 2006):

> Since 1977, with the enactment of the policy measure that ensured disabled students the right to education and instruction by placing them into regular schools, the presence of disabled students has increased conspicuously in regular schools, and we believe that this is enough evidence of the growth of the process of *integrazione scolastica*. (Ministero Pubblica Istruzione, 2006:64)

Although this extract suggests that there is a shared agreement that disabled students are entitled to education in ordinary schools, yet it fails to explore how the policy of *integrazione scolastica* could contribute to the development of the entire school system. This approach inevitably exacerbates the special status of *integrazione scolastica*, as it constructs it as something additional to normal schooling. It also fails to question other reasons that could possibly determine the increase in the number of disabled students with a statement in regular settings. From an inclusive perspective, the increasing number of *certificazioni di handicap* might instead exemplify the rising number of failing schools, rather than the growth of 'problematic' pupils. This latter assumption distracts attention from the limitations and the barriers that may be inscribed within the school organisation and/or pedagogical practices that may determine the onset of 'special educational needs'. Similarly, in the data provided by the Ministry, there is little sense of the several constraints and administrative pressures impacting upon school practitioners and local bodies. As the following statement also indicates, governmental concerns mostly refer to how many disabled people are being certified and catered for in terms of allocation of resources and provisions of special aids, thus transforming the policy of *integrazione scolastica* into a redistribution policy:

> The data from the Ministry – which shows that there has been an increase of the number of statements, from 1,5% to 1,8%, in the last six years – along with other sources, indicate that the concept of handicapped person drifted away from a notion of someone who has got psycho-physical and sensorial impairments, to a notion of 'social disadvantage', or rather socio-educational

disadvantage. However, disadvantage is not covered within the sections of Law n. 104/1992 (sections 12, 13, 14) and this should, therefore, be a problem dealt with by the school itself, within its autonomy of organisation and teaching methods rather than the final object of specialised intervention. Disadvantage requires different methodologies, resources and personnel from those mastered by support teachers. (Aprea, 2002:6–7)

This statement suggests that the education system manages to blame disabled pupils, and their deficiencies, rather than questioning its structure. It also reinforces the special status of *integrazione scolastica* as something to be dealt with by experts, such as 'support teachers', whilst regular staff should take charge of students with social and economic 'disadvantages', a 'problem' to be dealt with by the school without any additional resource by the government.

The Italian model of gathering statistical data is based on a medical approach that identifies failing students without any attempt to problematise the process of classification and categorisation. In contrast, Felicity Armstrong (1999) indicates that there exist differences in the way in which groups are categorised. Categorisation procedures, she argues (ibid.) are linked to the historical development of a country and are not related to an individual pathology, but rather to dominant social norms and practices that define disability in particular ways in a given cultural context. Much in agreement with Armstrong, Daniels (2006) observes that categorisation procedures in special education are not necessarily linked to students' health conditions. Very often categorisation procedures, and the issuing of statements, result from the vested interests of professionals and their need to address difficult problems or alternatively, they may represent a school strategy to obtain additional resources. At the same time, it is not surprising that parents may also require the issuing of a statement for their children, either as a way of obtaining extra funding and support or as a form of psychological respite from perceived parental inadequacy to deal with complex situations (Daniels, 2006). Put simply, 'categories of impairment or difference are socially constructed' (Armstrong, F., 1999:91) and categorisation can be defined as a 'socio-cultural process' (Daniels, 2006:5), which reflects political, administrative, social, economic and systemic priorities rather than mirroring pupils' requirements. This is also visible in the lack of any pedagogical advice that should accompany the issuing of a statement of impairment from the local health unit specialists.

Similarly, international organisations such as the OECD (2005) and the European Agency for Development in Special Needs Education (D'Alessio and Watkins, 2009) put the emphasis on the different classificatory systems in use in each member country and how these differences impacted upon the process of comparing statistical data across different national education systems. The discrepancies in the incidence of a particular type of impairment or of a disease cannot be dependant on individual medical conditions, especially in Western countries where there are similar levels of hygiene, medical assistance and health policies. What the organisations reported was that discrepancies in the number of disabled students and related statements of 'special educational needs', often resulted from different interpretations of the definition of 'special educational needs' and most importantly, from different administrative, bureaucratic and political measures which influenced assessment procedures and did not reflect variations in the number of disabled pupils across countries. With this in mind, in the collection of official national statistics in Italy there does not seem to be any sense of the complexities that lie behind the procedures of classification and categorisation of disabled students and no attempt to question why statistical data are collected, how, by whom, for what purposes and with what consequences.

CONCLUSION

This chapter suggests that the policy of *integrazione scolastica* is both a cultural and structural component of the Italian education system. However, policy analysis conducted so far, has mostly focused on issues about placement such as the percentage of pupils integrated in regular settings, the implementation of this policy into practice, and the redistribution of resources, without addressing issues of what this policy actually means in terms of curriculum, pedagogy and assessment for the mainstream settings. Although policy documents seem to acknowledge that *integrazione scolastica* is a fundamental aspect of the Italian education system, it emerges that *integrazione scolastica* means different things to different people and that most scholars and practitioners alike have mistaken the means of this policy (placing disabled pupils into regular classrooms) with its purpose (change schooling).

As will become evident in the next chapters, policy makers and school practitioners mostly focussed on the issues around the debate of segregation versus integration, rather than changing the teaching and learning routines starting from the experience of integrating disabled pupils into regular schools. With this in mind, the policy of *integrazione scolastica* has been transformed into a rhetorical and official discourse of educating disabled pupils in ordinary classrooms without any sense of its implications for the amelioration of current education systems.

INVESTIGATING INCLUSIVE PRACTICE IN THE SCHOOLS OF *ADRIAZZURRA*

This chapter presents the research context in which the study was conducted, the methods used to collect data, and a discussion of the findings emerging from the analysis of empirical data. The approach used for this book is very distant from the traditional positivist idea where the researcher is the one with power, orchestrating the exchange with informants. Rather it focuses on an equal relationship between the researcher and her/his participants, with intentionally loose and unstructured methods designed to leave participants space to manoeuvre. To investigate inclusive practice, this chapter interrogates the everyday practice of *integrazione scolastica* implemented in the two schools selected as a case study, bringing to the fore the tensions and limitations raised by participants. Finally, the chapter makes a case that micro-exclusions may happen in mainstream settings, although very often disguised as forms of inclusion.

RESEARCH PROCESS AND METHODS

When reflecting on the research process and methodology used to generate the findings presented in this book, I had to develop an awareness and understanding that the process of research is not a linear one. It does not follow an evolutionary trail, which merely encompasses asking the right questions, collecting the data and answering those initial questions. On the contrary, I have experienced continuous pitfalls and have learnt to live with uncertainty. As a social researcher interested in reflexivity I have experienced the collapse of my alleged 'reality', to discover other possible accounts of reality. This has been both fatiguing and exciting.

In the light of these reflections, I have to acknowledge the slight change of trajectory that my study followed as a result of engaging reflexively with my own preconceptions. At the beginning, I wanted to investigate the policy of *integrazione scolastica* to identify which features could be considered inclusive. This view was based on the assumptions that the policy of *integrazione scolastica* was potentially an inclusive policy as it provided an alternative and valid option to segregation. During my field-work, however, I realized that my expectations concerning the 'inclusiveness' of the policy of *integrazione scolastica* did not correspond to my preliminary findings. What my data brought to the fore was instead, features of a policy that may produce marginalisation and exclusion, despite its 'genuine' stated purpose of doing otherwise. During the research process I had to face two minor route deviations. Firstly, when I was collecting my data in *Adriazzurra*, and secondly, when I was analysing the data. With hindsight, these changes impacted upon the research questions. At the beginning of the field-work phase, I collected examples of innovative examples of teaching and learning procedures that I perceived as facilitators of the process of inclusion.

However, I soon realised that although teaching methods were critical factors, their effects were impacting upon school change only at a superficial level. With this in mind, I shifted my focus from the 'technicalities' of teaching and learning to the pre-conditions that would make innovative procedures possible. It was schools, and education systems in general, that needed to be changed so that teachers could be relieved from pressures and constraints. Having understood this, I sharpened the focus of my research questions to examine those institutionalised impediments that could hinder teachers' innovations and, consequently, students' participation in learning.

My decision to draw from ethnographic methods and case study approaches to generate my data was not made at the very beginning of my fieldwork, when, due to time constraints, I had primarily chosen to conduct two case studies of two lower secondary schools. During my fieldwork, however, the case study approach slowly began to extend into the ethnographic terrain. What became evident was that although the case study approach could address the complexity of the contexts along with the singularity of the cases investigated, it could not adequately capture the extent of involvement of myself as a researcher.

The issue of time was a relevant factor of the research in the schools. Traditional ethnographers spend prolonged time in a place, even before they actually 'go native' (Colic-Peisker, 2004) and it may prepare them to understand the context more fully. Without being acquainted with this tradition, and before visiting the schools, I actually spent more than a month in the research context and I tried to get accustomed to the place and its local culture. Although I am Italian, it is important to bear in mind that there is a significant difference between northern (where the schools were located) and southern regions of Italy (where I come from). Consequently, you might often feel a foreigner in your own country simply by crossing regional borders. With this in mind, I spent days going around the town centre, reading local newspapers, cycling and trying to do the things 'natives' were also doing. I went to all local initiatives and I attended local university conferences and seminars concerning *integrazione scolastica*.

Drawing on Val Colic-Peisker (2004), while I was conducting the research I could identify myself as being a 'halfie' – part of the researched group and simultaneously distanced from it (2004:93). Over the six-month period of intense observation and visits to schools, I frequently experienced a continuous shifting of identity, between that of a researcher and that of a teacher, and also between my background as an Italian and the new formation of identity as an 'English' social scientist. My identity as an insider and a teacher was strengthened by the fact that my Italian background allowed me to contact gatekeepers through pre-existing networks and acquaintances, and inevitably, this made the initial phase of my research more fluid. At the same time, my other identity as a social researcher from England made many participants feel very reluctant to engage with the research in a more informal way.

Throughout my visits the level of my engagement with participants was particularly high. One of my participants burst into tears while I was interviewing her and on that occasion I felt that:

> ...what I invested in that 'session' were true emotions, not just researcher's curiosity: she struck a chord in me, and we together experienced a sort of

catharsis. This human attachment, rather than just engagement in 'role playing' made the inevitable retreat from the research field akin to betrayal, and the research itself akin to manipulation. (Colic-Peisker, 2004:89)

As Coffey (1999) indicates in her study of the self and the researcher's identity, emotions and feelings do not only address the target of completing the fieldwork. By acknowledging the emergence of emotional tensions one contributes to the construction of the self as a researcher. Moreover, such tensions may also influence further decisions and research questions. For example, these incidences piqued my curiosity and led me to interrogate teachers' biographical accounts and how these might ultimately influence their pedagogical choices.

Establishing meaningful relations with participants was very productive from a research point of view. As Coffey (1999) also argues the quality of the data collected is very often 'dependent upon the formation of relationships' (1999:57). It soon becomes clear that the relations are reciprocal and that as much as the fieldworker is influenced by the social world in which he or she is engaged so are the participants. In my experience, this reciprocity emerged from conversations with many participants who revealed that my presence helped them to reflect upon their work. Moreover, some of the participants explained that they had gained benefits from my 'inquiring' presence, as they had become more aware of their role as educators and as individuals in a particular social context.

Choosing the Research Context

In order to gain access to the schools, I relied on one Italian academic who gave me advice on how to best identify suitable sites for my research project. His name became my 'credentials' for the rest of my research in the field, whenever I had to negotiate permission and access for interviews, observation and other research related activities. He put me in contact with the head teacher of a local primary school in *Adriazzurra*, better known for being the headquarters of a network of state schools whose mission was (and is) to improve the quality of *integrazione scolastica*. This school soon became the gatekeeper to the secondary schools in which my study was actually conducted. Like the experience led by A.S. Neill and the Summerhill school in Britain, the primary school I was put into contact with, the school *Arcobaleno* – pseudonym - was renowned for being a very forward looking educational site. Inspired by the pedagogy of Freinet, Cousinet, Frobel, Laporta and Borghi, education in the school *Arcobaleno* has always been based on the principles of 'active learning' - such as children learn through practical experience and by making mistakes. What made this primary school particularly interesting for my research was that it carried out a networking project that drew together many local state schools. This net-working project aimed to equip local schools with additional support (for example continuous professional development, special aids and materials) required for a successful application of the policy of *integrazione scolastica*.

I am very grateful to the staff of the school *Arcobaleno*, whose mediation was fundamental for getting in touch with the lower secondary schools I had chosen to conduct my two case studies.

My actual school visits started in February 2005. The two schools selected for my case study were the school *Fellini* and the school *Don Milani* (pseudonyms). By having joined the networking system of the *Arcobaleno* School, these schools represented exemplars of educational sites that clearly stood out for their policies and practices of *integrazione scolastica*. Although the two schools shared much in common in terms of humanitarian ethos and staff commitment to the policy of *integrazione scolastica*, there were also some differences that needed to be addressed. These differences became evident from the first appointment with the head teachers. The head teacher of the *Fellini* School was very welcoming and talked to me for almost an hour. In contrast, the head teacher of the *Don Milani* School was much more formal. The meeting did not last longer than twenty minutes and he asked me many questions concerning the modalities in which I intended to interview teachers, students and for what purposes.

The *Don Milani* School, a state comprehensive school, consisted of five different buildings situated in different parts of the town and welcoming students from the age of three to fourteen. The lower secondary school building was situated in a quiet suburb that used to be the agricultural province of *Adriazzurra*. This school building happened to be temporarily located in a religious seminary situated on a hill. At the time in which my research was conducted the suburb was undergoing a general transformation, which intended to turn the original agricultural village into a trading and service centre. During the school year 2004–2005, 346 students attended this school. Ten students were classified as having a statement of special educational needs (or *certificazione di handicap*). There were sixteen classrooms for a total of 36 teachers. The curriculum (the same in both schools) envisaged the teaching of the following disciplines with a priority in terms of teaching hours given to Italian, Mathematics and Science, followed by a Foreign language (usually English), Geography and History, Music, Arts, Technology and Design, Physical Education, and Religion (optional). The school week consisted of thirty hours of lessons (twenty seven compulsory plus three optional) or thirty three hours (thirty compulsory plus three optional) depending on the curriculum chosen by the family (among the optional hours: Latin, Environmental Education, Second Foreign Language and Citizenship). The school plan reported on two main educational projects carried out by the *Don Milani* school: 1) Music, arts and theatre education and 2) Transition to upper secondary education and academic success. Despite the commitment to *integrazione scolastica*, personalisation of learning and celebration of diversity, as indicated in the school development plan (the *POF*), the *Don Milani* School seemed to pursue conflicting agendas. This was evident because a great deal of attention was given to school projects aimed at improving students' academic performance in subjects such as Italian, Mathematics and English, exemplified by several remedial work courses held in the afternoon hours. On the other hand, initiatives supporting music, arts, creative writing (with the publication of a school magazine) and sports education were also addressed and promoted, but mostly as an additional way of fostering students' cognitive development and personality, rather than in terms of improving academic standards. The latter initiatives, therefore, were usually promoted within the space of extracurricular activities, and appeared to be considered as marginal ones, especially when compared to core subjects. From an architectural perspective, all buildings of the *Don Milani* School were accessible for wheel chair users, at least on the first floor. Thanks to the small dimensions of the school building, the way in which classrooms were positioned and the availability of ancillary personnel, all students (with the teacher's permission) could move freely within the school site. For example, they could go from one floor to the other, access the school library and other classrooms, and they were often allowed to do physical education classes in the park surrounding the school.

In the *Don Milani* School development plan *integrazione scolastica* was discussed in terms of special resources required to support 'differently able children with diverse pathologies' (cf. POF). Drawing on the POF, a team of support teachers were 'in charge of' these pupils. Support teachers were required to help class teachers to plan activities through the compiling of an individualised education plan (IEP henceforth) containing all the information about the 'differently able' student. Facilities to promote the policy of *integrazione scolastica* included:

1. A small special unit with two computers and special needs education software
2. A kitchen laboratory
3. An arts laboratory
4. Horse-riding courses
5. Special needs education books

What distinguished the POF of the *Don Milani* School was its committed ethos to the policy of *integrazione*, yet this was articulated within a separate section of the school plan. Possibly, this separation reinforced a binary division between ordinary teaching practice for those students without impairment, the 'real end-users' of the school plan, and *integrazione scolastica* practice for those students with impairments, a separate category of students. This dichotomy between disabled and non-disabled students was also underlined by the use of the term 'differently able' that, as I have argued elsewhere (D'Alessio, 2007), ended up reproducing old prejudices under a new label rather than challenging the concept of normality.

The *Fellini* School was composed of two main buildings located in two different districts of *Adriazzurra* (one not far from the city centre and one in the suburbs) both welcoming a lower secondary school grade with students between the age of eleven and fourteen. The broader catchment area of the *Fellini* school contributed to welcoming a great variety of students with different social, economic and cultural backgrounds. In 2004–2005 about 879 students were enrolled in the school with a total of 103 teachers. Drawing on the POF, the school registered and classified students according to specific characteristics. Thus, 4,4% of students had impairments (thirty nine in total, ten of whom had severe impairments) and 11% of students were without Italian citizenship (ninety five in total), most of whom belonged to the Roma community. Among the students at risk of being excluded, the school development plan also included students from the Southern regions of Italy (in particular Sicily and Calabria) who had faced initial problems of integration in the new setting. The main building of the school was situated near to the sea and welcomed students from the maritime area of *Adriazzurra*. The POF reported on the strengths of the school by listing a series of structures, facilities, and the availability of human and material resources provided by the school. Amongst others, school priorities included:

1. Setting up of a formative contract between the school and the parents to ensure the academic success of the pupils.
2. Promoting initiatives to prevent school disruption
3. Improving the integration of those students who are disadvantaged, particularly those who are not Italian or who belong to the Roma community.

The school provided the students with the same curriculum of thirty, or thirty-three hours, as the *Don Milani* School. The only difference being that there was also an option to choose a curriculum of 36 hours depending on the amount of optional courses selected by the family. As with the *Don Milani* School, Mathematics, Italian and Science were prioritised, followed by the other subjects. Unlike the *Don Milani* School plan, however, the *Fellini* School had a main, although still a separate, section of the POF in which the historical and traditional commitment of the school to *integrazione scolastica* was reported. This section, entitled 'School of All and for All' addressed issues concerning disability and intercultural studies – identified under the main umbrella term of diversity. The emphasis was on a policy of 'full integration', which consisted of mainstreaming all students including those with severe impairments. As the following sections will indicate, this policy of 'full integration' was carried out by a team of effective and willing teachers, and its main purpose was that each disabled or migrant student had to belong to the local community. Although in the POF, the *Fellini* School claimed to support change in order to welcome all students, as we shall see in the following sections, the school had to resort to create 'alternative' spaces and 'special' practices for those children who could not gain from ordinary teaching. Possibly, the school was struggling under the pressures of an educational system that on the one hand promoted autonomy and diversity, but on the other hand identified effective and successful schools with standardised attainments and traditional knowledge.

Regarding the differences between the two schools, whilst the *Fellini* School was a community-like institution, with several links with the provincial education authorities and support services, the *Don Milani* School instead seemed to be more like an appendage of central government. It seemed that despite their shared commitment to *integrazione*, the two schools had a different agenda of how *integrazione scolastica* was to be implemented in practice. For example, the *Fellini* School had set up an internal policy, which made explicit its full commitment to *integrazione*. This was particularly visible in the efforts made for the creation of a fully equipped special unit, which was often the object of frequent visits by foreign and national observers researching the policy of *integrazione scolastica* in Italy. On the other hand, the *Don Milani* School had chosen instead to operate inside the national boundaries of the national policy, without putting any particular emphasis on the implementation of this policy in its venues. Put simply, whilst the *Fellini* School stood as the 'flagship' school of *integrazione scolastica* in the area, and exemplified the policy through creating additional spaces, recruiting external specialist and human resources, the *Don Milani* School instead was not dissimilar from the average Italian state school.

CONTRADICTIONS AND TENSIONS ARISING FROM THE IMPLEMENTATION OF *INTEGRAZIONE* SCOLASTICA AT A SCHOOL LEVEL

When investigating the implementation of the policy of *integrazione scolastica* in the two lower secondary schools chosen as my case studies, some contradictions could be found in the way in which this policy was carried out in the classrooms and what national policies supported. So, for example, whilst governmental policies were committed to *integrazione* through the means of increasing the allocation of funding, school actors reported a lack of specialist support (especially in terms of financial resources) and the absence of clear regulations from central bodies. More-over, despite policy statements claiming that disabled children had the same rights to education in the mainstream classroom as any other 'normal' student, data from my interviews and from my observations, shows that disabled children were often considered candidates to be catered for by support teachers and specialised personnel only.

The Issue of Resources

The interview with the local policy makers (Municipality and Province) indicated that *integrazione scolastica* policy is funded by the State through regional education boards – the *Ufficio Scolastico Regionale* (also known as USR). Funding is allocated according to the number of disabled students with a *certificazione di handicap* (corresponding to the English statement of special educational needs) located in a particular school. After the passing of the legislative measure n. 440/1997 and with the enactment of the Autonomy Law n. 275/1999, schools could be allocated extra funding:

1) On the basis of the number of projects aimed at fostering the *integrazione scolastica* of disabled students and other 'disadvantaged' groups (for example migrants)
2) Through local agreements and school networks (for example the *accordo di programma*) with other institutional bodies – local health units, municipality boards, voluntary organisations and other schools.

Similarly, local policy makers reported that two main regulations, the Regional Act n. 26/2001 and the local Action Plan measure n. 328/2000, were two crucial policy documents which sought to maintain the level of resources available for the *integrazione scolastica* of 'vulnerable' groups into regular schools at relatively stable levels.

Head teachers and teachers of both schools, however, argued that the resources allocated for the integration of disabled students were not sufficient to address all the problems that the schools had to face. For example the head teacher of the *Don Milani* School explained that:

There are no conflicts concerning the sharing of the principles underlying *integrazione scolastica*. There are different local bodies in charge of the imple-mentation of this policy (municipality boards, local health units and schools).

> This is visible from the signing of protocols and local agreements such as the *accordi di programma*. We are all committed, but the problem is another one, and it is that *resources are limited*! For example the Deputy Secretary of the Ministry of Instruction said that we should certify only those students who have a physical handicap and not those with a learning difficulty or handicap! This means that we have to cut down the number of support teachers! The Deputy Secretary does not understand that there are disorders, like the hyper attention deficit disorder, which are more problematic for the school than a physical handicap. (Interview 08, head teacher, *Don Milani* School - emphasis added)

As shown in this statement, the quantity of resources allocated to schools in order to implement the policy of *integrazione scolastica*, seem to have been reduced. Cutting resources to schools on the basis of the severity and/or of the type of impairment, not only underlined that the funding of *integrazione scolastica* remained linked to the process of statementing, weighted toward the medical legacy which allocates more money and more teachers whenever there is a more severe physical pathology. It also indicated that there was very limited understanding of the challenges that teachers have to face when they integrate pupils in mainstream settings, as severe physical impairments do not necessarily imply the presence of particular educational requirements. At the same time, although the head teacher suggested that schools, and not governmental bodies, should play a leading role in the process of decision making concerning the allocation of resources he, nonetheless, still acknowledges the need to tie these resources to individual needs. This approach was also reinforced when he identified 'hyper attention deficit disorders' as another category to label problematic students and thus, obtain more resources. In line with the debate over the reduction of resources, the head teacher of the *Fellini* School remarked:

> I am satisfied with the legislation we have in Italy but I am not satisfied with the resources, *which are limited and ridiculous*. At least, we have many teaching assistants but this is not enough! I understand that students with disabilities should attend the nearest school and should be distributed everywhere in the local area. But on the other hand if the resources are limited and the schools do not have infrastructures, students may have less significant experiences. I mean from a theoretical perspective it is better that students, even immigrant students, are located in all schools but from a practical perspective, if I have a greater number of students with disabilities and difficulties than another school, then I can ask for more resources and I obtain them! And I can build up infra-structures necessary to welcome them! I can look for partnership with external bodies. Instead, if I have a few students then I cannot do anything to face the problem of *limited resources*! (Interview 17, head teacher, *Fellini* School – emphasis added)

Here, the head teacher sought to clarify that the main problem did not lie in the reduction of resources, but in the fact that they had not been increased, whereas schools had to respond to more requirements when compared to previous years (such as more migrant students). Unlike the head teacher of the *Don Milani* School, however, the head teacher of the *Fellini* School suggested how the school could possibly tackle its problem of limited budget by grouping together larger numbers of disabled students in one venue. By acting as a flagship school for integration, the *Fellini* School, inevitably welcomed a larger number of disabled students and this situation would enable the leadership to establish 'partnerships' with local bodies that could provide the school with extra support and resources.

The head teacher was genuinely seeking to investigate alternative solutions to provide students, particularly those with severe impairments, with more resources and chances to learn, especially when compared to the learning experience of disabled people who are dumped into ordinary classrooms and deprived of the necessary resources to learn. These endeavours, arguably, aimed to impact upon the rigidity of the school system and to explore new ways of financing education. Furthermore, the head teacher's problem solving approach to public expenditure cuts could indicate that schools have got many alternative solutions within their own reach, before looking for outsourcing. However, although with the best intentions of helping disabled students, the head teacher of the *Fellini* School suggested solutions that were much more aligned with a special needs education approach to *integrazione scolastica* rather than to an inclusive one. Evidence of this can be found in the fact that a concentration of disabled pupils in one venue could possibly lead to the re-opening of special schools (such as *poli specialistici* or specialist schools). If equipment and personnel are located only in a few well equipped schools, this decision could inevitably run counter to the right of all children, including disabled children, to attend their local school, as they will be required to register in those schools – such as specialist ones – that can adequately meet their 'needs'.

Another tension, emerging from the issue of resources was related to the micro-policies of resource allocation. For example, a support teacher of the *Don Milani* School once reported the difficulties of using funding to meet the requirements of a disabled pupil:

> Once I asked for a laptop for a pupil with muscular dystrophy. I thought that this laptop could help us to work wherever we were. You see the laptop was allocated to this school when the student had already left the school! And the laptop is now here in this school while the student is in the upper secondary school! Or take the Braille keyboard. We asked for it last year and it arrived almost a year late. You see the problem in my opinion is not the lack of resources, but the difficulties in using them according to current rules. There are, for example, three thousand euros to be spent but you must spend this money in a particular way, you cannot do as you like, you must write projects, you must spend it according to a given calendar and the deadlines are either too tight or too loose. Maybe you have some money left from a project but you cannot spend it for another project, which requires more money than that allocated in order to be done! Honestly, I would do with less money, but I would like to choose when and how to spend it; when there is a need to be met, and not when I am required to do so by the local board. (Interview 10, specialist teacher, *Don Milani* School)

In this extract, it seems that the problem was not concerned with the reduction of resources, but with the systemic constraints that locked resources and did not take into account the views of teachers or the requirements of schools. Conversely, the allocation of resources was influenced by budgetary restrictions and limitations of local bodies. Another example was the delivery of human resources that, as school-teachers reported, were often delayed and/or inefficient. This was because different bodies were in charge of the allocation of different resources, such support teachers by the regions and special aids and teaching assistants by the local municipality. Most importantly teachers were not consulted, or that if they were, they struggled to make their voices heard. Resources were allocated following a process of decision making which left power relations in place, with the medical and the municipal personnel occupying a leading role while teachers had a very marginal one.

Arguably, the issue is whether decision-making is to be driven primarily by educational or by economic priorities. If collaboration with local bodies such as municipalities and regions is another form of state control and if such control brings into educational sites budgetary and economic priorities which are different from those traditionally associated with learning, this leaves open to question the issue of whose interests schools actually serve. In the interviews with local policy makers there was no mention of the role that teachers, parents and, most importantly, students should play in the process of decision-making, in particular in relation to the setting up of priorities in the allocation of resources.

Another local body, which identified budgetary priorities for the allocation of resources (financial, personnel and material) to schools, was the psychiatrist from the local health unit:

> Resources are being reduced dramatically; when I have to make decisions concerning the statementing process of a child, my priorities are the amount of work and commitment that that particular student requires to the school. You see, you have some 'behavioural' students who can stop the school routine for one day, if you are not able to manage them. And this is one of the biggest problems of our system of provision and of our legislation, which is based on the old systems of classification that still classifies physical deficiencies as the most problematic ones and does not encompass other deficiencies. In this old system there are three main categories: physical, sensory deficits, and cerebral palsy. However, these categories have registered a dramatic decrease in the last few years. There has been instead an increase of mental retardation and behavioural disorders. You see a boy with behavioural disorders is more difficult to manage at school than a tetraplegic child. (Interview 23, local health unit, Psychiatrist, *Adriazzurra*)

As we can see from this statement, although the doctor seemed, genuinely, to consider disability from a school perspective – 'a boy with behavioural disorders is more difficult to manage at school than a tetraplegic child' – he nonetheless contributed to the creation of two mystifying notions of disability. When reading this statement from a social model perspective, three reflections seem to emerge. Firstly, the psychiatrist produces another socially constructed category of impairment, when he labels students 'with behavioural disorders'. Secondly, he locates the problem within the pupil, rather than in the school or the teaching and learning routines that may have produced those 'behavioural' disorders. Thirdly, when addressing the problem of the lack of resources, this statement indicates that there is a system of classification, and a record of distribution of resources linked to it, which constructs the notion of disability as an administrative category attached to the medical sector. This situation suggests that re-distribution policies were not only obsolete - 'old systems of classification' - but that they were mobilised by interest groups according to who 'shouts the loudest' (Thomas and Loxley, 2001:90) in the ears of medical practitioners and policy makers. Arguably, the psychiatrist brought to the fore a submerged conflict between different lobbies which represented different types of impairment, some of which were entitled to receive funding (such as physical and sensory impairments), and other types which instead were not entitled to it (such as 'behavioural disorders'). On the one hand, the psychiatrist acknowledged that the categorisation system should be changed in order to serve the needs of the school. On the other hand, he did not question the procedure of statementing children as the only available administrative device to allocate provision. Conversely, what the participant observed was the need for a new consultation between old and new lobbying bodies such as associations for disabled people, new specialised personnel.

What seems to have increased, I would argue, is not, for example, the number of children with 'behavioural disorders', but, possibly, the power that their representative bodies currently play in the struggle for the re-distribution of resources. Here, however, when addressing the issue of the lack of resources, all local policy makers and practitioners fail to question the reasons why a policy like *integrazione scolastica* must resort to classification systems rather than interrogating the modalities of classification themselves which do not encompass, for example, listening to the voice of teachers, parents and students alike. Also they did not question the policy, or its rationale 'I am satisfied with the legislation we have in Italy' (Interview, 17) or the ideology which constructed disability and put disabled people at the margin, whereas they sought to develop tactics and procedures to tackle what seemed to be a contingent problem since 'resources are limited' (Interview, 08).

The tensions at the level of implementation indicated that the policy of *integrazione scolastica* was often transformed into a struggle for more resources:

> The implementation of policy frequently is reduced to disputation over resources, which it is argued, will facilitate integration... such debates sustain the flawed notion that integration is simply a technical issue to be achieved through deployment of special equipment and personnel to regular schools, recommending a further consideration of the contribution of pedagogy, curriculum and school organisation to disabling and enabling educational programmes. (Slee, 1993b:351)

Funding was perceived as being the most important strategy to implement *integrazione* and it was still geared to the number of students who were identified as disabled. Nonetheless, what the interviews seemed to show is that this complaint about the lack of resources was transformed into a discursive formation that deflected attention from other alternative debates that could influence the policy making of *integrazione scolastica* in the long term. For example, discursive formations distracted attention from exploring alternative mechanisms of allocating resources, which are not necessarily tied to students' medical needs. Inevitably, the debate concerning the lack of resources was very common and it wandered off the point of how, for instance, to improve and change schools, to promote curricular teacher training, to experiment with integrated pedagogy and to revise classroom practices (Slee, 1993a; 1993b; 1998; Ainscow, 1999). In this way, policy makers and school practitioners failed to take into account that the problems may arise not in the lack or reduction of resources, but in the way they are spent. I am not suggesting here that funding should not be increased or that it is not fundamental for the development of inclusive schools. Education is clearly expensive, and money, which is not spent for education today, might be spent later on in the shape of incapacity benefits, redundancy funds, care institutions or even prisons. However, in the struggle to obtain more resources, school practitioners often failed to address ways of how to improve and change schools that might have been already available within the school (Ainscow, 1999). Put simply, if resources were spent in different ways and followed different procedures, they might not always appear to be insufficient (Ianes, 2005). For example, it would be interesting to consider how to avoid those 'perverse incentives' that strangle provision by tying them to statement procedures. In contrast, by focussing on the lack of resources, the risk is to remain entangled in a debate of how to increase funding rather than engaging with a debate over the nature of the mechanisms of funding themselves.

Drawing on the social model perspective and the works of Gramsci and Foucault, my argument is that local bodies and schools should challenge those routines that are considered self-evident and should further explore the nature of the struggle for 'special' resources for example by including all teachers, parents and possibly children, when they have to establish priorities and procedures. In conclusion, when looking at these tensions and struggles over the allocation of resources for *integrazione* and the way in which they are spent, disability is constructed as a medical and an administrative category which is tied to the processes of redistribution of accumulated capital (Stone, 1984; Oliver, 1990; Stiker, 1999) following eligibility criteria established by the medical profession. This is not surprising or new, as following Oliver (1990), the alliance between the medical sector and that for the allocation of provisions (for example administrative, welfare, care and third sector) represented a 'historic bloc' that still exercises control over disability and society. One of the major distortions imposed by this construction of disability is that the role of medicine and of welfare systems are taken for granted and they go unchallenged (Oliver, 1990). From an inclusive perspective it would be advisable to engage with these ideologically constructed meanings of disability and system roles that reproduce old prejudices in new administrative mechanisms.

Tensions among Different Collaborating Bodies and Actors

Italian policies (for example Law n. 328/2000, *accordi di programma* and *piani di zona*) have put great emphasis on *integrazione scolastica* as a systemic policy

(Iosa, 2000) that should encourage collaboration, rather than competition, among schools and local bodies. In this concern, *integrazione scolastica* does not arise from a single intervention of one stakeholder, such as the school, but on the statutory collaboration among many different stakeholders of a local community. This legislative framework is an important factor for the development of *integrazione scolastica*, since it indicates that there is awareness that schools alone cannot tackle the increasing number of challenges that they have to face under the pressure of national guidelines. Specifically, in the Province of *Adriazzurra,* a series of local initiatives, supported by the Autonomy Law, clearly delineated the enactment of this systemic principle, which included collaboration among different schools (for example the networking project of the primary school *Arcobaleno*) and the enactment of agreements with local bodies (for example voluntary organisations for disabled people, municipal bodies).

Given the above considerations, the schools could be identified as community-active institutions that relied on a series of collaborations as a means to implement the policy of *integrazione scolastica*. However, it is important to distinguish between external collaboration, among local bodies working in partnership with schools (local education bodies, local health units and municipalities) and internal collaboration within the schools among different school actors, in particular between class teachers and support teachers.

The following extract from an interview with a representative of the provincial education authority, is relevant in terms of understanding how collaboration was interpreted:

> The Law n. 328/2000 was a Copernican revolution for those who wanted to carry out projects in the local area. According to this law all local bodies must take charge of the implementation of the policy of *integrazione* and they must collaborate. Thus, for example, if you need more support teachers, then the regional board must provide them, if you need more teaching assistants, there is the municipality board, if you need specialised aids and materials there is the local health unit in charge of it and of course a wide number of voluntary organisations. We diagnose the situation taking into consideration the environmental conditions, and then we identify the needs. Afterwards we try to respond to these needs all together. (Interview 19, Provincial Education Authority, *Adriazzurra*)

What this statement illustrates is that educational policies have undergone an important change – 'a Copernican revolution' – as far as the collaboration among different local bodies was concerned with a shift of responsibilities from centralised, ministerial bodies to local bodies. The enactment of a statutory regulation such as the Law n. 328/2000 along with the passing of reforms (such as the Autonomy Law 1999), signalled what Benadusi and Consoli (2004) drawing on Giddens (1997) and Putnam (1993), identify as being the new model of the Italian education system which must rely on a complex system of social networks to support innovation and educational development. Conversely, head teachers remarked the lack of external support in the implementation of the policy. Thus, for example, the allocation of personnel to schools via provincial and municipal bodies was given on the basis of pupil 'needs' that had to be compensated. In this way, the different stakeholders of the process of *integrazione scolastica* struggled against one another in relation to 'who should give what, when and how' and they failed to address issues concerning where these needs come from and how they could be pre-emptively addressed (for example short-sighted municipal housing policies which concentrate Roma population in some districts of the town and consequently in one school). If students with impairments should, as a right, be able to attend local schools, then their participation should not be considered a contingency that requires 'extra funding'.

Thus, the policy maker from the municipality reported that:

> The regional education authority is the ministerial body at the local level and the one that is in charge of the allocation of human resources, I mean the support teachers. The municipality instead provides the teaching assistants [i.e. *educatori*]. So, there are three professionals rotating around the child with a handicap: the support teacher, the teaching assistant, and the ancillary who may be used in particular situations and for particular purposes. The main expert, however, is the support teacher. In fact the school hours that the teaching assistant spends with the child with a handicap must be less in terms of quantity than those spent with the same child by the support teacher. Therefore we provide our resources (the teaching assistants) only after the regional education authorities have taken their decisions about how many support teachers they will allocate to each school. What happens instead is that the regional education authority wants to know in advance how many teaching assistants will be allocated for the pupils with handicap in a particular school. Then if you are asking me this question, I say, 'none'! First you must tell us how many support teachers are provided for that school on the basis of the number of the children with a handicap and then, afterwards, we will set up our meetings with the schools and the local health units to decide whether that child also needs a teaching assistant or not. We need to know if there is a support teacher. We cannot pay for the teaching assistants when there should be a support teacher working with that child! (Interview 20, municipal policy maker, *Adriazzurra*)

The municipal representative was articulating the conflicts that existed within local bodies in their management and delivery of resources allocated to teach disabled students (in particular personnel). The problem, however, did not reside in the conflict per se, but in the consequences that these conflicts may have in the schools where resources could be delayed and decisions could be made on the basis of dominant discourses and pre-determined procedures. The procedures for recruitment and the annual allocation of specialised staff to schools showed that teaching personnel were appointed as a result of struggles between different stakeholders (including teachers' trade unions) whose 'needs' may not necessarily correspond to those of the students. It also emerged that three different professionals, such as the support teacher, the teaching assistant and the ancillary employee, catered for the child with impairments but the municipal policy maker does not mention the class or curricular teacher. This is evidence enough that there was still a pre-conception, despite legislation, that the disabled child was a matter to be dealt with by specialised personnel only. This view clearly did not take into account possible structural and organisational barriers that concerned teaching routines and that could have been at the origins of pupils' problems at school.

Another important factor emerging from the analysis of different forms of collaboration was the tension expressed by many support teachers when asked to describe their work and their professional partnership with curricular teachers. Officially, the support teacher is also a class teacher who should participate actively in teaching routines. Support teachers' work consists in supporting the class teacher in the process of individualising teaching and adapting the curriculum for those students with a *certificazione di handicap*. The relationship between the class teacher and the support teacher should be one of partnership in which two equal professionals organise their teaching in order to promote all students' learning. My observations in the classrooms, however, showed that some support teachers were often struggling to find their own identity in the educational establishment irrespective of what written policies might say. Thus, support teachers, teaching assistants and policy makers talked about the reproduction of the practice of delegation according to which the statemented pupil– or *alunno certificato* - was literally shifted into the hands of the support teacher:

> There is still a tendency to delegate the tasks concerning the individual with handicap to the support teacher, and this is evident also because the hours of special teaching provided to schools and families are considered as insufficient. On the contrary, I do not believe that *integrazione* means to give more hours of special teaching to a statemented pupil. If this were the case, then the support teacher would be transformed into a guardian angel of the pupil with handicap, rather than a specialist for the whole classroom. I do agree that we need resources, including more personnel and hours of special teaching, but the effort is to make the whole school context responsible for the individual with deficit, and this includes the class teacher, the ancillary and the teaching assistant, not only the support teacher. (Interview 19, provincial education authority, policy maker *Adriazzurra*)

This extract illustrates the rhetoric used by policy makers who argue for effective partnerships and who oppose the transformation of the support teacher into a 'guardian angel'. At the same time, this statement indicates that the practice of delegation was known and was widespread in the province under investigation. Yet there was little suggestion concerning how such a phenomenon could be tackled, beyond denouncing it. This was also evident from my interviews with support teachers who reported feelings of isolation and of a lack of support experienced in their every day job.

During my observations in the schools, I could witness abdication of responsibility on the part of the class teacher, whenever the task concerned disabled students. Evidence of this could be found in the feedback provided by the students during the focus group interview:

> R: Can you tell me about your teachers? Who are they?

S: We have the teacher of Italian, Miss …, Mathematics & Science, Miss .., History & Geography, Miss…., History of Art, Miss…, Technology and Design, Mister…., Physical Education, Mister…, Music Education, Miss… and Religion, Father….and that's all!,

R: What about Mister… (and I mention the name of the specialist teacher).

S: Him?? But he is not our teacher; he is the support teacher for Emanuele only! (Focus group interview with students 04, *Fellini* School)

The same question was presented during all focus group interviews (6 in total) and all students provided a similar response. Only one group of students spontaneously reported the name of the support teacher in the list of the class teachers but then a student immediately added, 'but she is here only for Sandro, - a boy with Down syndrome - not for us' (Focus group interview 06, *Don Milani* School). The marginalisation experienced by support teachers always rebounded on students. Another support teacher also reported about the practice of delegation:

I have experienced delegation many times. In the past, it took place much more often than today, although I must say that it still happens sometimes. Today, class teachers have changed a bit, they are more positive. In the past you were considered as an intruder inside the classroom. I was often told to leave the classroom with 'my' student since I was making too much noise! Or I was told to withdraw the student from the class since 'she does not have a clue!' and with the student next to me who used to ask me 'why the teacher does not want me?' (Interview 10, specialist teacher, *Don Milani* School).

In this statement, the word 'intruder' explains the lived experience of the support teacher and the tensions between two, supposedly, equal school actors. Although, as the support teacher suggested, there had been an improvement in the class teacher's attitudes towards support teachers, this change had not been systematic. On the contrary, it seemed to be left to the personal initiative of teachers, thus suggesting an unequal power relation between a class teacher who could ask a colleague to 'leave the classroom' and the specialist teacher who was struggling to help the pupil with a *certificazione of handicap* belong to the class group. Similarly, the practice of delegation was also an example of the way that formal procedures concerning disabled students were usually carried out and of the perpetuation of a special education mind-set. This situation was clearly described by a teaching assistant:

Yes, it [delegation problem] exists. And the evidence can be found in the fact that the support teacher always writes the individualised education plan, while it should be a joint plan produced by all teachers. (Interview 13, teaching assistant, *Fellini* School)

Here, the support teachers carry out the compiling of the Individualised Education Plan alone. In line with this statement most participants confirmed that they were writing the individualised education plan for the disabled student on their own, although, some of them acknowledged that they often integrated the plan with comments and recommendations from Italian or Mathematics teachers.

In the following extract, a support teacher looked for explanations about the practice of delegation:

> The problem is that class teachers do not consider the disabled pupil as one of their students! And this is a cultural bias, which is difficult to change. You must make them understand that 'that' student is one of their students. They do not have 24 students plus 1. They have 25 students. I am sure that we are improving, and that class teachers' sensibility will slowly change, but it will take a long time before it happens. (Interview 07, support teacher, *Fellini* School)

What is interesting in this statement is that the support teacher provides a clear description of classroom routines and how they produce support teachers' frustrations. Nevertheless, he seemed to identify the main problem with the attitudes of class teachers who were not willing to take charge of the disabled student, but there was no mentioning of the role that support teacher could play in the process of changing those attitudes. Conversely, the support teachers of the *Don Milani* School seemed to suggest the counter-hegemonic role that specialist teachers could play in the process of modifying how class teachers perceive their colleagues, and also as support teachers perceived themselves and their work:

> I heard about the practice of delegation and of the frustration of most of my colleagues, but I, personally, have not experienced it. I consider myself a teacher, 100%, especially because I take the same salary as curricular teachers do. Some colleagues like to complain about everything. I think that it depends on you, and how you situate yourself in relation to your colleagues. The collaboration among teachers is a delicate issue and you need to understand your class colleagues. It is not a problem of the support teacher, but a problem of the mainstream teacher. They have someone; an adult in their classroom and it is not easy. I think that I am actually more specialised than my class colleagues, I do not want to say that I think that I am superior to them, but I certainly know things that they do not know because they have not had extra training like I have. (Interview 11, support teacher, *Don Milani* School)

This statement shows how collaboration is still conceived in terms of a contra-position between colleagues rather than partnership in which each individual should be equally valued and respected for the accomplishment of common goals. Although the support teacher claimed that he was not facing any problem, he nevertheless reinforced the idea that there was a division between 'them'- class teachers - and 'us'- support teachers and the difference in teacher training pathways inevitably maintained such a division.

Support teachers were not partners but were more often playing alternative and/or subordinate roles to those of the mainstream teachers.

Pursuing this interpretation further, it is possible to identify three main roles played by the specialist teachers that are respectively that of warders, assistants, and guardians of disabled children or, alternatively of those children deemed as being difficult to teach. The evidence of being treated as warders arose from an examination of my observation notes in which I took notice of the frequency with which support teachers were required to control the classroom and to keep the students seated and silent while the class teacher was away. Another example of being qualified as warders was due to the fact that they were often required to substitute for their colleagues, to fill in the 'gaps' as supply teachers for mainstream teachers, even when they had their own teaching schedules and timetables. In contrast, class teachers never substituted for support teachers. As far as the role of assistants is concerned, I was struck by how frequently the support teacher was required to leave the classroom to make photocopies for the class teacher. Support teachers very often left the classroom for an average of five minutes almost every lesson either to make additional copies or to adapt the teaching materials for 'their' pupils. The role of guardians – as already anticipated by the policy maker - was evident when support teachers were associated with everything that concerned the disabled pupil, with the consequences that this association inevitably brings:

> When the class teachers give tasks to do or when they collect homework done at home they come to you and say aloud 'does your student have to do it? Then, I myself wonder if you have collected 24 papers why don't you also collect the 25th? By asking if 'your student has done it or not' they frustrate your efforts to make that student feel part of that class! The kid feels he does not belong and this behaviour tells me that these teachers don't think about him (the student with statement of needs) at all! What happens is that the support teacher should help the student to belong to the class, whilst he inevitably emphasises the pupil diversity and makes him/her feel different from the rest of the classmates. (support teacher, Interview 07, *Fellini* School)

The issue of belonging is central here as it is for the process of learning to occur and for inclusion to be promoted. At the same time, belonging is a fragile condition which can be broken by behaviours, words, the presence of individuals or alternatively by the absence of them. It is worth commenting, however, that belonging cannot be made, but only felt and lived by students and that pupils often 'receive subtle messages from their teachers that suggest that they are not valued as learners' (Ainscow, 2003:19). These teachers' attitudes were a barrier to belonging and participation and needed to be carefully avoided.

Interestingly enough, the hierarchical relationship between the support teacher and the curricular teacher was mirrored in the relationship between the teaching assistant and the support teacher:

> I have been working many years as a teaching assistant, but it took me many years before the teachers learnt to value my job. (Interview 22, teaching assistant, *Don Milani* School)

> I am learning a lot from to the support teacher. She is leading me in my everyday work, she gives me the tasks to do and I follow her instructions step by step. I know that if I have a problem I can always rely on her. (Observation notes, teaching assistant, *Don Milani* School)

> R: How is the teaching assistant perceived in this school?

TA: We are considered like support teachers, we are 'equal'. We work in parallel with them. They work on adapted didactics and we work on the autonomy of the pupils. It is inevitable that they (the support teachers) treat us as equal. We work so many hours together and without us they could not do their job.

R: Do you take part in the writing of the individualised education plan?

TA: No, I don't

R: Do you take part in the staff meetings concerning the class?

TA: No we are not allowed to. We are not 'allowed' to participate in the class council meeting unless it is explicitly required by the support teacher. We are not allowed to read the child's documentation and we cannot write the individualised education plan. However, we asked for permission to do it, but we could not obtain it and honestly I think that they do not want us to be in the meetings, I mean the class teachers. They keep thinking that the disabled kid is the 'problem' of the support teacher only. (Interview 13, teaching assistant, *Fellini* School)

These extracts indicate that teaching assistants were excluded from the process of decision-making in relation to the disabled pupil and that although they felt that they were 'equal', the very need to mention it implied that equality was still an issue. It also showed that although teaching assistants were possibly situated as hierarchically 'inferior' when compared to support teachers they, nevertheless, represented a unified front with the latter in relation to class teachers.

Unfortunately, the reproduction and maintenance of power relations do not foster inclusive systems, but rather oppose them. Inclusive systems require an inclusive ethos that should not only concern children, but all personnel. If support teachers and teaching assistants do not feel included in the establishment, how can they help the children to feel part of the school? At the same time, educational establishments are hierarchical institutions that are built for purposes other than learning (Foucault, 1977). Both schools seemed to be working as 'integrated systems' (Foucault, 1977) in which each member, such as the teaching assistant and the support teacher, was an agent in charge of maintaining order and reproducing power relations already in place:

It [disciplinary power] was also organized as a multiple, automatic and anonymous power; for although surveillance rests on individuals, its functioning is that of a network of relations from top to bottom, but also to a certain extent from bottom to top and laterally. (Foucault, 1977:176)

The emphasis upon observation and management reflected mechanisms of power which held people in a network of reciprocal hierarchized observation and which were often reproduced and embedded in the pedagogical activity of teaching and learning. For example, even non-disabled pupils were often part of this hierarchical organisation, as they were 'used' by class teachers as learning assistants for disabled peers, when the teaching assistants were not available. On the one hand peers' roles can be central in contributing to the shaping of their disabled peer as one of them rather than as 'other' (Allan, 1999), and, I would argue to the improvement of learning as a social experience (Vygotskij, 1987). On the other hand, they may also become collusive agents in constructing difference as something hierarchically inferior as they may reproduce teachers' discourses and prejudiced views.

MICRO-EXCLUSIONS IN THE MAINSTREAM SETTINGS

As stated in Chapter Two, exclusion is not a straightforward notion and it may take different shapes. Although the most striking factors of exclusion have almost been completely dismantled (such as segregated institutions) exclusion is very resilient. With this in mind, in the schools chosen as case studies, I was often faced with micro-policies, teachers' behaviours, practices and language that could provide evidence of forms of micro-exclusions, often camouflaged as inclusive features.

The practice of 'withdrawal' – disabled students withdrawn by their support teachers and taught separately in special units - has been almost completely eradicated in the schools investigated, as support teachers rejected teaching disabled students outside of the classroom and re-affirmed the student's right to be taught along with their non-disabled peers. Although this intervention concerned mainly 'where' education took place, rather than the quality of education, it nevertheless indicated how support teachers' initiatives could impact upon schooling. At the same time, however, this modification was time-consuming, especially as it depended on teachers' personal choices, leaving enough room for other forms of exclusion to take place, even within the classroom itself. Conversely, structural changes such as clearer definitions of the class teachers' tasks and responsibilities, could accelerate the change of curricular teachers' attitudes and of schools in general, thus limiting the perpetuation of disguised forms of exclusion:

> The problem is that the child is not withdrawn from the classroom anymore, but this does not mean that the student is really integrated. We keep him inside the classroom but this may result in something worse. There is no *integrazione* if you have to leave the room, but equally there is no *integrazione* if you remain inside the classroom, but in a corner and doing something on your own with your support teacher, while your peers are doing something else! This is far worse than leaving the classroom I believe! I mean I am inside the classroom but I am doing something else, maybe it would be better if I had left the room and done it somewhere else. Do you think that *integrazione* is about staying in the same classroom with your peers? I am not with my class-mates because I am sitting next to them but because I am doing something together with them. (Interview 12, support teacher, *Fellini* School)

This support teacher brought to the fore the complexity of the process of *integrazione scolastica* and how it has often been misinterpreted in terms of placement, rather than of modifying teaching and learning procedures. By explaining that withdrawal was not taking place in the *Fellini* school and in the school he had taught for some years, he seemed to corroborate the idea that there has been an improvement in the way *integrazione scolastica* was implemented in schools. Nevertheless, he argued that forms of micro-exclusion were still taking place, although in a disguised form. They were the latter that my research sought to investigate and reveal.

As a flagship school for the implementation of the policy of integrazione scolastica, the Fellini School was particularly known for the creation of a special unit or a workshop room, called the Sunflower room – a pseudonym - situated on the ground floor of the school building:

R: When was the Sunflower room created?

T: It was set up in the year 2000. I started it, although I have to say that the climate was ready for it. I mean that the school was ready for it. Before I arrived here there was a very good art teacher who had organised a great deal of art exhibitions. What was missing was the carrying out of structural projects and the creation of labs. Someone who could be in charge of these activities. Now I am the one in charge of the laboratory activities. When I first arrived here, in this school, there were many students with severe impairments who spent the whole morning in an empty room on the ground floor. It was 1997. Since the year 2000 instead these children have to attend at least the first two hours of the day in the classroom with their classmates and then they can go downstairs to the Sunflower room, if they need to or want to do so. Honestly with you though, the biggest change, has occurred with the class teachers. First they did not even know about the existence of this workshop room with its activities and now they come downstairs and look for you because they want to work with us jointly and do projects with our pupils.

R: can you tell me more about the activities?

T: On Mondays we do activities with clay, on Wednesdays we do mosaics, the students come down from their classrooms and on Fridays. But if you want the schedule, this is available in print if you would like to have a copy of it.

R: Do you think that the *Sunflower* room and the activities carried out in there have favoured the process of *integrazione*?

T: Yes I do think that they have! The *Sunflower* room has shaken things and people; different students come down and work with us, Roma students and migrants as well. I remember that once there was a Roma girl who was very good at doing mosaics. She had a lot of problems with Italian and other subject matters, but she was extremely good with her hands and the *Sunflower* room gave her the possibility to show this to the rest of her classmates and teachers alike. It was then that the process of 'acceptance' began. (Interview 07, support teacher, *Fellini* School)

Significantly, the special unit actually seemed to have favoured spaces and time to promote alternative forms of teaching and learning, to those associated with traditional core knowledge, but which were equally important for learning to develop – such as arts education and social skills. The experiences of alternative forms of teaching and learning within the special unit were actually improving the learning opportunities of the pupils educated within the unit. When discussing with support teachers I often wondered why these new types of teaching and learning were not transferred into ordinary teaching as in the long term, they would have proved to be conducive to inclusive education. For example, teachers could have investigated what was successful about the *Sunflower* room that made even the most 'vulnerable' students capable of learning and then, for comparison, examined what was absent within the ordinary classroom. The special unit seemed to have modified the attitude of some class teachers who were now looking forward to working jointly with support teachers. Yet this possibility appeared only illusionary as the experiences of the special unit remained confined within the boundaries of the *Sunflower* room, and the opportunities for changing teaching and learning were carefully held back. The 'shaking' suggested by the support teacher, did not seem to have occurred as the work done in the special unit did not impact the pedagogical repertoire of the mainstream classroom:

> R: how are these activities assessed? I mean, are they assessed in the same way as the activities the students do in the classrooms?
>
> T: no, the assessment procedures are different. There is still a long way to go before we can actually assess these activities, as they deserve. It is true, these activities are not assessed in the same way (basically there are no marks), but they have the same value! Maybe we should work in the direction of valuing these activities also through assessment procedures for the main-stream. In my opinion it should be the work that the students do 'there' (in the workshop room) that should be assessed, the class teachers should see what their students, the same students who are not very good in the classrooms, what beautiful things they do 'there'! (Interview 07, support teacher, *Fellini* School)

Again the special unit fails to be transformed into a space and a tool for counter-hegemonic action. Assessment is an important aspect of teaching as it is the basis for taking decisions regarding students' careers; it devolves authority to support teachers' initiatives and is a relevant device to promote learning. The learning occurring within the *Sunflower* room instead was not accounted for and was considered as occupying a second place when compared to the learning that took place in the ordinary classroom. Consequently, the potentially innovative influence of the activities not only remained situated within the four walls of the special unit, but it ended up producing opposing outcomes to the ones it purported to achieve. What emerged was that there was still a spatial separation between what happened in the classroom and what happened in the special unit, as if they were two separate education systems within the mainstream school, one for those pupils perceived as being 'normal' and one for those who instead differed from the norm. Consequently, this polarisation of student population and spaces impacted upon students lives and the way they were perceived inside the school:

> R: When you say 'our students' what do you mean?
>
> E: Those ones [students] who do activities in the special unit. It is an institution now! We even gave it a name: the *Sunflower* room. At the beginning it was

only 'the special unit'. At least now they [disabled students] know they go to a room where they do workshop activities. At the same time we gave a name to a special class inside the school and we missed our target. We made a choice. From the outside you may think 'oh! Good you have additional space for 'these' students!' but in reality we have re-created a *differentiated class*. (Interview 13, teaching assistant, *Fellini* School – my emphasis)

Although the workshop room was initially perceived as a successful initiative, the very existence of a 'dedicated' place reinforced, rather than counteracting, the problem of delegation. To put it another way it justified statements like 'I am not good enough for 'these' students' (Interview 15, Mathematics teacher, *Don Milani* school) but 'there are people [and places] that have the right expertise for this' (Interview 01, Mathematics teacher, *Fellini* School). Two different interviewees when asked to provide an account of their experiences with disabled students articulated similar statements. As the teaching assistant also suggested, a separate room where alternative activities are carried out inevitably transforms what was once intended as a resource for learning for all students into a differentiated class:

The more the *Sunflower* room grew, the more I could see the practice of delegation. Whenever a class teacher has got a problem, they call you. The *Sunflower* room is not a support for the class, as originally designed, where disabled students could have an additional space to work with their peers, where the whole class used to work together. It is a way of handing the 'hot potato' from one floor to the other until it reaches the ground floor where the special unit is located! (ibid.)

Here, the teaching assistant indicates that the very presence of 'specialised' places and people not only reinforces the existence of traditional teaching and learning by means of opposition to those activities held in the special unit, but also justifies the reproduction of forms of micro-exclusions.

Similarly, the *Don Milani* School had a small, special unit where disabled children were often withdrawn. However, the special unit in the *Don Milani* School occupied a very marginal role within the building and it was often used in alternation with other spaces such as the library room and the gym where disabled children were often doing activities along with a group of non-disabled peers. Nevertheless, although with different emphasis, both schools identified 'spaces for *integrazione scolastica*' to be carried out, clearly a contradiction in terms. *Integrazione scolastica* continued to have a special status rather than being considered as something structured within the education system. When looking at the management of 'space' (for example special units) in these schools, the Foucault's concept of 'enclosures' (1977) becomes relevant. As Foucault puts it, the organisation of space is a mechanism of power and control which society uses to contain and order diversity, a place in which those who cannot be controlled are deemed to be contained. As Armstrong (2002) puts it, this could be reminiscent of a:

'[…] discourse of power which has its roots deeply entrenched within the complex apparatuses of the state education, health and welfare system, and it is used as a mechanism for spatializing procedures which sort and place people in different sites' (2002a:450).

CONCLUSION

In this chapter I have shown the methodology chosen to conduct the research and how the process of analysing empirical data took place. By seeking to provide vivid accounts of schools and participants, I have brought to the fore some of the contradictions and tensions arising from the implementation of this policy at a school level. In this respect, this chapter indicates how crucial it is to develop the debate over the nature of inclusion and the processes of exclusion, by investigating power relations and assumptions concerning education, particularly in relation to the education of disabled pupils. Although partly anticipated within this chapter, the next chapter is an attempt to identify the discourses articulated within the two schools chosen as case studies and their consequences for the participation of students in the process of learning.

DECONSTRUCTING INTEGRAZIONE SCOLASTICA

In this chapter I articulate my endeavor to deconstruct the policy of *integrazione scolastica* by identifying cultural and systemic barriers that emerge from the analysis of empirical data and policy documents. In the first section, I investigate how discourses can be used as data to investigate current principles and practice of *integrazione scolastica*. In particular, I suggest how discourses that ostensibly support the development of inclusion are instead reproducing earlier, restrictive ways of thinking. Secondly, I engage with a series of institutional barriers that have been in place for many years and are perceived as natural and unchangeable mechanisms and devices of the Italian school implementing *integrazione scolastica*. Finally, I articulate the possibility that the policy of *integrazione scolastica* has been transformed into a powerful discourse that constructs, manages and controls disability in education.

DISCOURSES AS DATA

Discourses can be analysed as evidence of truth, claims of truth or 'structures of thoughts' (Olssen, Codd and O'Neill, 2004:46) capable of explaining a phenomenon under study in its present state. By extension, language is connected to social practices, as exemplars of the exercise of power, and it becomes a relevant indicator for social researchers. As my research interests were represented by social practices, language was understood as a means through which social processes and power relations occurring in the school contexts could be identified, captured and analysed as data. In addition, the analysis of discourses must encompass the interrogation of material forms and structures of language through which power is exercised. Therefore, the data I gathered were mainly represented by language and how that language was used to construct the reality in which the enquiry was conducted. Along with discursive formations, the study included the examination of material objects and devices, through which practices were performed (such as individualised education plans, educational tools and spaces).

Discourses may become a way of discovering what lies behind, or as Foucault (1972) argues, discourse becomes the 'allegorical' thought referring to something else which is fixed and symbolic and which cannot be understood differently in that particular context and time (ibidem:27). In line with this, Olssen, Codd and O'Neill (2004) argue that discourse analysis is particularly relevant in school contexts where specific discourses have been used as instruments of power to prioritize particular theories, structural organisations and pedagogical practices. A discourse analysis therefore should aim to bring those discourses to the surface and interrogate the forms of knowledge from which they stem and which they reproduce.

Carabine (2001) argues, following Foucault, that discourses are always ideologically and historically situated and that they set the boundaries of our reality.

As Carabine (2001) puts it, discourses always have a purpose, as they meet the needs of a community and are responsive to people's expectations. Consequently, discourses not only articulate people's ways of making sense of their own reality, but they are also indications of a particular structure – a powerful discourse – with which respondents choose to align themselves. They not only exemplify personal discourses, but they also reveal the wider structures within which people situate themselves and through which they are influenced.

Given the above considerations, I was interested in exploring policy discourses of *integrazione scolastica* that offered particular solutions to contingent problems of education. In particular, I was concerned with interrogating why certain school actors, such as teachers, chose to align themselves with particular discourses – for example medical discourses - both intentionally and unintentionally, and with what consequences, especially for the education of disabled students.

In the following sections I identify some discourses, which have been articulated in relation to the policy of *integrazione scolastica* and I examine the impact of such discourses and their possible influence for the realisation of inclusive education. Understandably, some discourses are more problematic than others for the development of inclusive education. Depending on the type of discourses being used by different school actors and policy makers, *integrazione scolastica* can be identified as encapsulating more or less inclusive features and therefore, of being more or less conducive of inclusion. Similarly, just as discourse analysts search for regularities in language, so too I explore why certain statements are chosen among the plethora of possible linguistic enunciations provided, for example, in the texts of government policies. Furthermore, I establish whether the choices made have produced a specific pattern and have sought to ascertain what this pattern might represent in terms of practice (Taylor, 2001).

The Discourse of Celebrating Diversity

The policy of *integrazione scolastica* has always been recognised as a policy that, based on the experience of 'mainstreaming' disabled students into regular schools, aims at valuing diversity as a resource for learning rather than as an obstacle. Consequently, the policy of *integrazione scolastica* has usually been associated with the practice of celebrating diversity in education (Canevaro, 1999a; Canevaro and Ianes, 2003; Canevaro, 2006). In the schools I visited, teachers and head teachers alike often reported that they were valuing diversity, as indicated in their school development plan, and that students were 'assessed according to their potentialities rather than their limitations' (Interview 01, Mathematics teachers, *Fellini* School). However, whenever I entered the classrooms to conduct my observations, I could rarely find examples of how difference was being valued in terms of pedagogy, curriculum and assessment. As Slee (2003) also observed in relation to the findings of the Queensland School Reform Longitudinal Study (2001):

The researchers also concluded that although teachers were generally able to enter into informed and engaging discussions about student diversity, there was little evidence of teaching for diversity in the classrooms they observed (Slee, 2003:216)

Although teachers conveyed in principle, the need to celebrate students' different abilities and cognitive skills, I rarely found evidence of such an approach in their everyday routines. Very often, the discourse of celebrating diversity was only deployed in relation to a specific 'category' of students, such as those with a statementing procedure and/or the immigrant students, and articulated in order to make decisions concerning the allocation of teaching hours and additional resources. Here, diversity was not celebrated but, rather constructed as a marker of difference (Allan, 1999).

An interesting example of the difficulties encountered by schools to really celebrate diversity by marking *all* students' potentials could be found in the distribution of teaching hours. My classroom observations showed that support teachers were only assigned to disabled pupils, rather than to the school, and depending on the severity of the impairment and this was according to the classification manual ICD-10th Revision (1990). This procedure, not only indicated the limitation of a system of provision tied to statement scales, but it failed to impact upon the teaching routines. What was being marked was the weakness of the child rather than his/her strength. Moreover, what was also alarming was that for some children with severe impairments, the process of celebrating diversity, and the support linked to it, clearly appeared to be limited to an administrative action of physical containment:

R: What about Asia?

T: She has been given a support teacher for 18 hours; she is catered for throughout her school time. Last year she was *contained* by the teaching assistant and the support teacher. Most of the time she was in the special unit. This year I have two hours with her and then my colleague Giorgio has got two hours with her as well. The rest of the time the teaching assistant caters for her. We try to work together with her, because we want her to walk and we need to be two in order to move her and help her to stand. But to be honest with you, we do not have the right competences to work with Asia. That is why, at the end of the day, she is there in the special unit *like a plant*! She smells so bad. You cannot work with her unless you wash her first. They do not do it at home and we must do it here. If you work with her, her smell stays with you for the rest of the day. Nobody wants to work with her. (Interview 06, support teacher, *Fellini* School – emphasis added)

Usually the distribution of hours to disabled children provided by support teachers ranges between a minimum of 2 hours to a maximum of 18 hours per week for each disabled pupil. For Asia, a girl with severe impairments, diagnosed as partially deaf and blind, and using a wheelchair since she was born (although she could walk if adequately stimulated by correct physiotherapeutic exercises), the discourse of celebrating diversity was unmasked and dissolved into mere rhetoric. This situation was exacerbated, and at the same time made visible, because Asia generated physical repulsion ('nobody wants to work with her') and because her means of communication were entirely different from those used by the teachers who described her as a 'plant'.

Asia was not Italian but Albanian, and this 'supplementary label' added to the difficulties in communicating with her. When sitting in the special unit with Asia, I could observe how teachers failed to consider the fact that the difficulties in communicating with her were not only related to Asia being severely impaired, but to the fact that she might have developed alternative forms of communication (for example tactile) and that she did not speak Italian. No attempt was made to investigate any of these possibilities. By arguing that 'they do not possess the right competences', the support teacher brought to the fore the underlying assumption that severely impaired children should be better 'catered for' by specialists. Although such a comment was understandable considering the feeling of impotence for the injustice that was being perpetuated towards Asia, such reaction ended up adding to the marginalisation of the student even within the special unit. Finally, although some support teachers showed a serious commitment towards Asia, they became bogged down in a vicious loop of how to obtain more external resources and teaching assistants rather than administering already existing resources within the school.

A further problem relating to the discourse of celebrating diversity emerged from the allocation of hours of teaching for support teachers in relation to different subject areas. Drawing on my data, only some subjects such as Mathematics, Italian and English usually envisaged the presence of support teachers in the classroom, while other subjects like Physical Education and Art, were usually required to do without the attendance of support teachers. This was particularly evident in the following extract:

> Some subjects are considered more important than others because the disabled pupils are only allocated a support teacher for lessons when they are studying particular subjects, but not others. Strangely enough, those subjects where the disabled kid may have some potential, like art for instance, she or he is without the support teacher. Then I wonder, if we are supposed to work to develop the potentialities of these youngsters with disabilities why are we (support teachers) only allocated in those subjects where he or she is lacking something?' (Interview 09, support teacher, *Don Milani* School)

Here, the distribution of working hours (i.e. the *copertura*) of support teachers contradicts the concept of celebrating diversity. It also contributes to reinforce the assumption that some subject matters are more important than others and that there is a prioritised knowledge that need to be transmitted, notwithstanding students' diverse learning skills and potentials. What seems to be privileged is a compensatory type of support, which inevitably reinforces a deficit model of education. Moreover, this allocation of support teachers to disabled students is also part of the system of 'control' and maintenance of 'order' as discussed by Foucault's notions of disciplinary mechanisms (1977). The support teacher becomes the vehicle through which the disabled pupils is 'managed' in order to avoid any possible disruption of the smooth running of teaching in prioritised subject matters for the other students.

Both schools seemed to share a common sense notion of who was the 'ideal' student, and consequently both schools supported a unique version of 'school success' related to it. These understandings inevitably ran counter to any endeavour to value diversity:

> ...the ideal student is someone who is open, someone who has achieved a certain degree of maturity, someone who wants to study, someone who is yearning to know more, someone who asks questions, and you, as a teacher, you must answer him. I had many students like this, I do not mean only the student who has got good marks but also the student who is lively, well integrated in the classroom and who helps his classmates. (Interview 12, Mathematics teacher, *Don Milani* School)

> The concepts of the ideal student and the ideal classroom still exist. There are three aspects you must consider. First, the school must teach subject matters. Second, you must prepare students for life in this society, and then third, you must value the handicap. At the same time you must be aware that the disabled student cannot be a champion of competences, compared to what he can do, certainly he has also got competences, but if two students have to run a race, 100 metres, and one student has got the legs and the other student has not got the legs, it is obvious that the boy with legs is going to win the race. We all achieve our goals, but these goals must be different. (Interview 08, head teacher, *Don Milani* School)

From these quotations the interviewees indicated that the notion of the 'ideal' student still predominated and that he or she was usually associated with a particular type of success whose meaning was constructed according to older discourses of normality. As these participants argued, the student must be prepared for society 'out there' (Interview 12, Mathematics teacher, *Don Milani* School). Consequently, although the policy of *integrazione scolastica* is struggling to value different forms of school success based on formative assessment, which shows development and progression, schools still assess students on the basis of how much they respond to standardised forms of success which are socially privileged. Although disabled students can be considered as 'achievers', as the head teacher also remarked, they cannot 'win the race'. The use of a competitive language, such as 'champion' and 'win the race', indicates that the head teacher fails to understand that not only could goals be different but also that these same targets are dependent upon and could be influenced by, structural barriers. These barriers, in fact, are to be removed since they are the obstacles which deny some students the possibility of participating, and consequently, of winning, both in school and in life.

The discourse of celebrating diversity deflected attention from the consequences of different formal assessment procedures and examinations. Disabled students with intellectual impairments and who followed an individualised education plan were not provided with the same diploma as their 'normal' peers. They were instead provided with a certification of skills (i.e. *attestato*) that described the competences and the goals achieved during the school career. This certification was a legal credential to enter vocational training, but with basically no value in the job market. This type of school success seemed to be an illusionary one and it also became reminiscent of what Benjamin (2001) describes as being a 'consolatory type of success'.

Although disabled students participate in the process of assessment, their outcomes are still valued differently when compared to non-disabled children. For instance, disabled students' school success is defined in terms of *rendimento scolastico* (skills developed by the child at school) rather than in terms of *successo scolastico* (school success) according to standardised levels of performance. Unfortunately, diversity in this case is not celebrated, but it becomes a method of selection for gaining access to higher education and/or entering the job market. As Benjamin (2003) argues 'teachers are caught into the contradiction of having to value diversity but acknowledging that diversity never wins over dominant versions of success' (2003:44). Consequently, they may be faced with the challenge of having to choose between their need to comply with socially recognised norms and values and their will to respond to personal beliefs and educational priorities which might distance themselves from the former (Armstrong, F., 1998b).

In the following extract a Maths teacher reported about her experience with disabled students. Although this interviewee appeared to put forward a policy whose purpose was to celebrate diversity, and hence disability as an expression of such diversity, her statements, on the contrary, seemed to reinforce a construction of disability from an individual/medical point of view:

> Drawing on my experience as a teacher, I had many types of disabilities in my classrooms. The blind girl, the autistic child, the Down syndrome student, disabilities related to children with psychiatric disorders, I must say that I have a very wide sampling. Well, what we did was that, depending on the type of disability, the class council, with the great contribution of the support teacher, who I like to call the 'glue' teacher because I do not like the label of 'support' teacher. He is the glue because he keeps together the work of all teachers interacting with 'this' child. We have always tried to bring out the best from each disability, with the support of activities such as horse riding, the summer stay specifically designed for these students. We have always tried to offer the best to 'these students' as you have probably seen from their presence in the classroom and from their activities in the special unit. We managed to bring out what 'these' children had inside them. We have always tried to make school a pleasurable experience for 'these' children. With 'these' students you cannot appeal to their sense of duty, you must appeal to their sense of pleasure. I remember 'my' student with Down syndrome. When he sat the third year exam he came with a paper on volcanoes. Although he had language difficulties, he managed to explain what a volcano was. He had a *papier-maiché* volcano that he had prepared with the help of my colleague, the glue teacher. I still picture him; it was a very emotional time, and the way he passed the exam. We were almost crying when we saw him wearing his elegant jacket, his tie, all clean and tidy, with his copybooks as evidence of the things he had done throughout the school years. (Interview 01, Mathematics teacher, *Fellini* School)

By unpacking the teacher's long statement, it appears that this school has a successful tradition of teaching disabled students within the regular classroom by drawing together the support of different professionals, regardless of the type of 'disability' students might have. The pattern of speech and the use of 'we', however, seems to indicate that the Mathematics teacher is drawing on rhetorical speech in order to show what herself and the school have done with 'these kids'. Clearly, the teacher is highly motivated to provide all students with opportunities to learn. She also seems to be genuinely committed to the school success of the child with Down syndrome. Thus, the student with impairment is sitting the exam along with his peers and is awarded a school certificate of attendance – according to the Law n. 104/1992 - which indicates the type of skills possessed. I am not suggesting that the process of individualisation should not take place and that all students, including disabled pupils, have the right to be assessed according to individual progress. Nonetheless, the passing of this exam, when compared to the experience of non-disabled students, is clearly of a different type, such as 'especially designed for these children'. The problem is that the procedure of individualisation is only made in relation to disabled students whose 'exam certificates' have an 'inferior' value when it comes to the job market and the access to higher education. Moreover, students are referred to in terms of their pathology: 'autistic, blind, Down syndrome', contributing to an identification of the student with his/her impairment and without any distinction between disability (social) and impairment (individual). What seems alarming in this statement though, is that the teacher not only adopts a patronising language, but also a different way of speaking when referring to disabled pupils (such as 'with his elegant jacket') rather than to non-disabled pupils. This is particularly evident at the beginning of the statement where she shifts from a semi-professional register (such as 'drawing on my experience', 'sampling') to a non-professionalised lexical and grammatical framework, which is sanctioned by the adoption of the word 'glue'. The linguistic choice offers evidence for how separate she perceives this pupil to be from the rest of the class thus adding to the notion of diversity in terms of assistance and, even of inferiority.

Constructing a society that celebrates diversity, involves a real acceptance of the concept of diversity without any need for demarcation of different types of diversity, some of which are less disruptive – hence more 'acceptable'– than others. What is also contradictory about the schools I investigated, is that the discourse of celebrating diversity seems to extol some types of difference within the boundaries of 'normality' – such as migrant students - while others are 'tolerated' and contained – such as disabled students with severe impairments. Consequently, there is an invisible, but not necessarily less effective, line of division that indicates the limits of 'tolerance' between diversity and 'deviance' (Lemert, 1967 in Thomas and Loxley, 2001). Moreover, a discourse of celebrating diversity should disentangle from a description of the exotic character. Such a description is clearly an attempt to render 'the social agent politically innocuous' (McClaren, 1995 in Armstrong, D., 2003:33) and therefore, incapable of challenging forms of domination and oppression.

I argue that the limits of a discourse centred around 'celebrating diversity' is that it fails to challenge notions of normality and of normalisation of disability by means of categorisation, adaptation and compensation. Nevertheless, within the national literature (Ianes, 2001; Ianes, 2003; Canevaro and Mandato, 2004:23; Ianes, 2006) the discourse of *speciale normalità* - special normality - is an attempt to work in this direction. Central to this discourse there is the endeavour to blur the contours of and deconstruct the concept of normality. Canevaro (2004) pertinently writes that *integrazione* requires society to change in order to accept differences and that this change does not entail the effacing of diversity into normality, but on the contrary, the modification and extension of the concept of normality, by means of welcoming and celebrating diversity. This approach is arguably an attempt to incorporate philosophical (as well as religious) notions of frailty, mortality, vulnerability and impairment considered as essential elements of the human condition - hence their normality. Such a process, however, still identifies disability with a deficit within the individual. Consequently, the support provided to disabled students is very often inscribed within a dimension of extraordinariness and assistance. I argue that the very addition of the adjective 'special', to explain normality, inevitably abdicates inclusion in favour of ways of thinking associated with special needs education.

The Discourse of Need

School and national policies have identified among other priorities that of meeting students' needs in order to avoid school disruption and students' dropping out. However, as Thomas and Loxley argue, the notion of 'need' is seldom questioned' (Thomas and Loxley, 2001:48). 'Needs' are always attributed to the child, 'almost without thinking' (Thomas and Loxley, 2001:53) and no attempt is made to interrogate the way schooling is organised. Consequently, the discourse of need, not only transforms students with a 'statement of special educational needs' into a medical and an administrative category to be dealt with by extra services and personnel, but it also leaves systems and practices unchanged.

The notion of need is evident in the following extracts:

> We have 39 students with impairment out of 880 students in our school. This is a small percentage, but they are very *needy*. These students have some problems and the rest of their schoolmates must be informed about the type of pathology these students have. We must tell them that if a child, apparently normal, is not working as the others do, or leaves the room earlier than the others, this does not mean that he is being privileged but that he has got a problem and that he *needs* to be supported and catered for. (Interview 17, Head teacher, *Fellini* School – emphasis added)

In this statement there is the assumption that some students 'needs' are unproblematically different from the requirements of non-disabled students and that they are located within the child's deficiencies. Unquestionably, it is the school's duty to compensate those 'needs' by mobilising resources and procedures. The support provided, however, seems to be of an extraordinary type as it requires explanation that it is not a 'privilege' but a need. Evidently, the discourse of need, as indicated in this extract, is used to justify different types of teachers' behaviours in relation to disabled people, bringing to the fore the difficulty of impacting upon the rigidity of the education system and the need to resort to the notion of vulnerability to justify differentiation.

In Italy, the discourse of need has always been used, but it became very relevant with the introduction of a new terminology of *Bisogni Educativi Speciali* (*BES* henceforth) derived from the English definition of 'special educational needs'. Like the Warnock Report definition of 'SEN', the new Italian definition of '*BES*' (Ianes, 2005) seeks to create an umbrella term that encompasses all student 'needs' as they emerge in the school context and that may be soon detected by the ICF screening system. The new classification of '*BES*' does not concern disabled students with a medical diagnosis of impairment, but it includes all those students who may face problems at schools, although such problems are not the direct 'consequences' of a pathological condition:

> A special educational need is any type of developmental difficulty, either in the educational or the learning domain, which can be identified as a form of problematic individual functioning (following the different health domains identified by the ICF model developed by the World Health Organisation) and that may develop into a damage, obstacle or social stigma, independently from the aetiological condition of the individual. A problematic functioning, which requires individualised special education. (Ianes, 2005:29)

The clear implication here is that a child with '*BES*' is a child whose functioning, either in the sphere of learning and/or biological and cognitive development, does not work properly – according to the WHO standards - and that requires additional provisions. Although this *BES* assessment procedure seeks to expand the range of students who are entitled to receive additional resources without the need of a purely medical diagnosis, and beyond the limits of the eligibility criteria established within the Framework Law n. 104/92, it fails to grasp that the statement of *BES* is another form of labelling that can be transformed into an obstacle or a social stigma as much as the learning difficulties encountered by the very student:

> ...a discourse of having SEN fails to recognise that disability is not 'an individual pathology' but a form of oppression and exclusion produced by and within particular social and political conditions and relationships. (Armstrong and Barton, 2001:696)

Moreover, although Ianes (2005) attempts to provide suggestions concerning how existing resources could be best used before issuing a statement, he nevertheless does not seem to engage with issues of how education systems might themselves produce needs, and how those needs are linked to the vested interests of new professional practitioners (Armstrong, 2003). The discourse of *BES* fails to investigate the possibility that these 'special educational needs' could be social constructs which 'came into existence through the judgements and decisions of professional people' (Barton and Tomlinson, 1981:196).

At the same time, it is crucial to acknowledge that there are difficulties emerging when definitions – such as 'special educational need' – are exported in contexts other than the English one. Firstly, it is important to take into consideration that words may change meaning and have different outcomes depending on the context in which they are used. This would suggest that although the language of special education in England, is overburdened with biases and represents a hindrance for the development of inclusive education (Galloway, Armstrong and Tomlinson, 1994; Corbett, 1996), the same considerations may not be valid in another country. This view could be demonstrated in the case of Italy where the use of the language of *BES* could, arguably, be considered as a positive switch towards a more socially oriented model of disability. There is evidence that the *BES* language in Italy, despite its limitations – such as the problem is still located within the child – is an attempt to truly understand the difficulties that students face in learning and to improve school responses to them. Ultimately, although the language of *BES* may be deceiving and unsatisfactory, it seems to be an effort to struggle against the risk of re-opening special schools (Ianes, 2005; 2006). Indeed, the adoption of a '*BES*' definition is also an attempt to align Italy with international literature within this field of education as it emerges in the glossary section of the ISCED (International Standard Classification of Education) published by the UNESCO.

The underlining assumption is that the discourse of *BES* in Italy should overcome the traditional differentiation between students who receive extra support and those who do not receive it depending on their aetiological conditions. Although this new terminology seeks to reinforce the idea that disabled students do not necessarily have 'special educational needs', while other students, for example traveller children, may have 'special educational needs' and may need extra support, even though their functioning has not got any 'flaw', the focus is still located in the pupil 'mal-functioning'. This assumption, not only deflects the attention from structural barriers to learning, but also remains embedded in the old debate that links the allocation of resources following categorisation procedures. An inclusive way instead should question the need of categorisation and classification tools as a means to allocate resources. The language of *BES*, I argue, runs counter to such an attempt.

The Discourse of School Change

Drawing on the Italian literature (Canevaro, 1983; 1986; 1999b; 2001; Canevaro and Mandato, 2004) *integrazione scolastica* is based on the principle of reciprocal adaptation between the educational setting and the pupil with impairments. This principle is crucial in breaking with the idea that *integrazione scolastica* is something 'extra' and 'additional' to the education system. Rather, *integrazione* should trigger the process of change of the education system from within and by drawing on the experience of mainstreaming disabled students in regular classrooms.

The discourse of school change is one of the most employed discourses concerning the policy of *integrazione scolastica* thirty years on its implementation. As Malaguti Rossi (2004) reports in her research about educational changes, *integrazione scolastica* was intended to foster a pedagogical shift from teaching to learning and from a national prescriptive curriculum and a predominance of subject matter knowledge to a focus on processes of how students learn. According to official policy documents and legislative measures such as: Framework Law n. 104/1992, *Atto d'Indirizzo* in 1994, as well as the publications of research on 'good practices' of *integrazione* (Canevaro, 1999a; Nocera and Gherardini, 2000; Canevaro and Ianes, 2001; CDH Bologna and CDH Modena, 2003; Ianes, 2005), the policy of *integrazione scolastica* has at its core a concern to differentiate curricula and teaching so that all children can learn in the same settings and according to their ability (Ianes, 2007; Ianes and Cramerotti, 2007) although following different teaching modalities and assessment procedures.

After the passing of the policy, teaching and learning procedures in ordinary schools have sought to respond to different students' 'needs' by promoting the differentiation of the teaching procedures (Framework Law n. 104/1992, Circular n. 1996) and the individualisation of learning (Framework Law n. 104/1992; Decree n. 1994). In the former case, *integrazione scolastica* argued for the use of team teaching, full-time schooling (i.e. *tempo pieno*), active teaching and learning (i.e. *didattica laboratoriale*). In the latter case it supported the use of cooperative learning, peer tutoring and the teaching of meta-cognitive abilities.

In the schools investigated, many research participants employed the discourse of school change. For example, the head teachers of the schools argued that the policy of *integrazione scolastica* introduced new subjects and didactical methods that were not contemplated before. The following interview extracts encapsulate this observation:

> School innovation has also been promoted with the policy of *integrazione scolastica*. Let's consider for example the innovation brought about by support teachers who have introduced active learning emerging from the work in the laboratories or the workshop rooms. They work with the pupils in more concrete, rather than theoretical, ways and this is indispensable for pupils aged 11–14. In 1979, new curricula were introduced and new subject matters were taught: physical education, music education, art education, design and technology. It was then that the principle of learning by doing was introduced. (Interview 17, Head teacher, *Fellini* School)

> A lot of changes have occurred since I used to go to school. These are changes that mostly concern the interaction between students and teachers. These changes result from the enactment of the policy of *integrazione scolastica*. I remember my teachers were only transmitting knowledge, they were very authoritarian, beating us with a stick, and they were even smoking in the classroom! Today this is not the school of 'numeracy and literacy' anymore; it is an open workshop room. (Interview 08, Head teacher, *Don Milani* School)

In addition to the changes acknowledged by the participants, my observations in schools highlighted the experimentation of '*tempo prolungato*' (more school time allowed to learning) and the introduction of *compresenze* (co-teaching). Both these changes were introduced straddling two decades (the 70s and the 80s) and they aimed to break with the idea of dogmatism and didacticism developed during the Fascist period. These changes had been initially adopted to favour the *integrazione* of disabled children. Disabled students, in fact, were usually perceived as students requiring more time to learn and the adoption of differentiated teaching methodologies. Soon, these same changes were considered valid for all students and became school praxis (as the introduction of new subject matters previously mentioned in interview 17). For example, I could observe alternative forms of teaching from traditional teaching from the front, such as the use of cooperative learning, although only in a very few classrooms, which promoted the participation of disabled learners. The problem arises, however, when these alternative forms of teaching are used only as an exceptional means to allow the participation of disabled students, rather than as a normal school procedure to promote learning for all students, including disabled pupils.

Furthermore, I have to acknowledge that, every time I entered the classrooms for my observations, I could register very few examples of change concerning pedagogy, curriculum or assessment. Differentiation of teaching was difficult to achieve and the individualisation of learning was provided only for disabled students. Consequently, the process of individualisation constructed the experience of learning for disabled students as being essentially different - almost operating on a parallel but separate 'track' - when compared to that of non-disabled students. Moreover, no effort was made to formalise such changes in the attempt to break with the rigidity of the mainstream system, which may represent a barrier for learning not only for disabled students, but for many students who distance themselves from the established norm. There was no sense of how teachers could contribute to the construction of students' social identities and how some specific school outcomes were perceived as the only relevant factors with the potential to widen, or alternatively limit, students' life prospects.

Similarly, very few attempts were made to modify teaching and learning procedures in terms of education goals. The latter remained predominantly associated with the transmission of a prioritised kind of knowledge. To quote from my research diary:

> The teachers in the *Fellini* School show a high degree of professionalism and competences. They seem to know the best ways to teach to small heterogeneous groups of students. They use meta-cognitive didactic methods embedded in problem solving theories and constructivist pedagogies; all new teaching and learning techniques. But, I have a feeling that something is not working properly towards the development of inclusive features. Unless they do not modify educational objectives and if they are not aware of the discourses about what counts as knowledge and as learning, then these 'technicalities' will only reinforce existing assumptions. For example there is still a unique idea of school success in terms of achievements, there is still a mind-set that constructs a particular type of ideal student. There is an assessment system that rewards attainments rather than learning. Then how can we really value all students, diversity and diverse learning and promote a change of the education system? (Observation notes, April 20th, 2005)

Underpinning these observations are the statements of some class teachers who reported on their new teaching methods, but who, from my perspective, were transformed into agents of the reproduction of existing dominant forms of knowledge and power relations. Although some teachers stated that they did not feel the pressure of national guidelines on their daily teaching, my class observations suggested the issue of freedom was an apparent one since teachers were free to choose only 'how' to teach within the curricular boundaries set at a national level.

This was particularly evident in the debate concerning the delivery of the *programma* – the programme of study – representing the curriculum taught in classrooms. Although, officially, there was no statutory curriculum for lower secondary education schools, the following extracts indicate how the autonomy of teachers mostly concerns teaching methods rather than curricular choices:

'I must keep you going, we are almost at the end of the school year and I want to finish the programme of study. Quick, be quick' she says to the students. 'Let's finish this unit'. Then she looks at me and says: 'I know that some students would require more time and more attention, but I have to move forward'; 'Well done' she says again, 'We have almost finished the book! We have completed the programme of study for this year. I am very happy about it'. (Observation notes, English teacher, May 2005, *Fellini* School)

'You see, it is not that I do not know about these new didactical methods such as cooperative learning and peer tutoring, pair and group works, but the problem is that I have the programme of study to finish. And they need to go to the upper secondary school and I need to prepare them for it. There is no such thing as socialisation there, there is only content'. (Interview 15, Mathematics teacher, *Don Milani* School)

These statements suggest that the *programma* is transformed into a pedagogical discourse impinging upon daily routines. Thus, despite the passing of *integrazione scolastica* and the related introduction of new subject matters, support teachers and active pedagogy, the teachers interviewed choose to remain faithful to teaching traditional types of knowledge and pedagogy. The reasons for this decision, arguably, are explained in the second extract. Thus, the knowledge about how upper secondary schools may work, indirectly affects the possibilities for modifying the curriculum and changing teaching and learning routines in lower secondary schools. This runs the risk of transforming freedom into an illusion and converting the discourse of change into mere policy rhetoric.

Much in agreement with Canevaro (2004) I acknowledge that the process of transformation envisaged by the policy of *integrazione scolastica* was never fully accomplished as schools have continued to respond to disabled pupils as a contingency:

If the presence of a disabled person is still considered an exceptional event, the structure of schooling in general does not produce any fundamental change, which allows the school to welcome another disabled person not as a contingency but as a normality... Schooling has not yet entirely assimilated the new presence, which should trigger a change of the teaching methods for all students. Classroom organisation has still largely maintained its traditional front-of-class teaching. (Canevaro, 2004:59)

Paradoxically, the allocation of resources provided to schools via the policy of *integrazione scolastica* is not used as an opportunity to re-define schools and their pedagogical repertoire. What emerges is a systemic failure to translate resources into inputs for change and for improvements. This also reduces 'innovation to rationalised

forms of school management both at the levels of organisation and of teaching'
(Medeghini, 2008:81)

THE IDENTIFICATION OF SYSTEMIC BARRIERS

As the previous sections have shown, although some discourses were designed for
other purposes, such as those of fighting against marginalisation and improving
education, they seem to have served as reproductive agents of forms of knowledge
that hamper the realisation of inclusion. This possibility called for critical investigation
and analysis of the discourses that inform a specific form of knowledge relating
to disability and the education of disabled people in ordinary settings. Rather than
promoting inclusion, discursive formations investigated above seem to encapsulate,
construct and transform disability into something manageable and amenable for the
education sites, and by extension for society, in order to ensure the maintenance
and smooth running of the educational establishments and of the power relations
that constitute them. Through the deployment of discourses and discursive practices,
this section analyses the tools and the mechanisms that derive from such discourses.
These tools and mechanisms, such as the writing of individualised education plans,
could represent systemic barriers that perpetuate forms of micro-exclusion, as they
seem to be enshrined in a special needs education paradigm.

Reiterating Foucault's technique of 'management' (Foucault, 1988a:105),
Armstrong (1998a) writes that all institutions, including schools, are not neutral but
they are part of a wider system of social reproduction, control and management. It
is logical then to ask in what ways the implementation of the policy of *integrazione
scolastica* can be conducive to inclusive education, if regular schools per se are
already conceptualised as places for selection and surveillance (Foucault, 1977).

The Individualised Education Plan from an Inclusive Perspective

The policy of *integrazione scolastica*, enforced by the Framework Law n. 104/1992,
puts the emphasis on the writing of the Individualised Education Plan (IEP henceforward), as the main tool for the personalisation of learning. The IEP is an educational
tool that consists of an inter-institutional document – between school, local education
authority, local health unit and parents - containing the information for curricular
and organisational modifications necessary for the education of a disabled child in
ordinary settings. It can be defined as the organisational, didactical and pedagogical
plan – including rehabilitation, social and extracurricular activities – by which the
disabled pupil is 'integrated' into regular classrooms. Along with the clinical diagnosis
of impairment, it contains the functional diagnosis of what a student with impairment
can do (such as individual potentialities). The IEP is also the fundamental mechanism
for the allocation of resources to ordinary schools. This provision of resources,
however, has to go through the statement procedure (i.e. *certificazione di handicap*)
of the child with impairments from the local health unit, before it can reach the
school in which the disabled pupil is enrolled.

In the school investigated as my case studies however, the alleged beneficiaries
of the IEP, supposedly disabled students, were excluded from the participation at

the meetings concerning the writing of these plans. What was more alarming was that very often the individualised education plan sat on the shelf of the staff room and contained very few pedagogical recommendations for class teachers. Also, the IEP was mostly resulting from the work of support teachers and prepared only for disabled pupils. Consequently, it inevitably triggered a process of stigmatisation of some students because the main focus of analysis remained the person (Framework Law, section 12.3) and the way that he or she functioned. It failed to investigate school organisational and structural potentialities and/or limitations that may have affected students' performance.

As Galloway, Armstrong and Tomlinson (1994) also argued, the assessment procedure, upon which the IEP is written, accentuates child's limitations, whereas the 'reference to the school's resources, and to the ways they have helped either to meet or to create the child's problems, are usually conspicuous by their absence' (1994:37). Understandably, the IEP reproduces an individualistic approach to disability (Oliver, 1996), as the plan is only required for disabled children or children perceived as having 'special educational needs'. This has the effect of enlarging the discursive practices which differentiate between 'normal' and 'special' needs and consequently, between children with or without a statement. Moreover, there is enough evidence that the role played by the IEP is reminiscent of what Popkewitz and Brennan (1998) referred to as being a power technique (Foucault, 1977). Underpinning this position is the fact that the subject and, in this particular case, the disabled pupil, becomes known in details through 'forms of individualisation that segmented the person into discrete attributes and behaviours that could be supervised and observed to ensure progress' (Popkewitz, S., T., and Brennan, M., 1998:6).

Consequently, although the IEP is currently conceived by most Italian commentators (de Anna, 1997; Ianes, 2007) as an inclusive tool, I shall argue that it may risk reproducing the same discriminatory outcomes it aims to oppose. Unless individualised education plans are reconsidered as daily working tools to plan teaching and to facilitate learning for all students, not just those with a statement and unless they arise from the interaction between all school actors, including students, their presence and use will inevitably reproduce micro-exclusion within ordinary settings. As matters currently stand, they seem to be transformed into case histories of children with impairments, produced by the support teacher in the solitude of special units. The device of the IEP can therefore contribute to the reproduction of special education and all the structures that surround it within the mainstream system, sweeping away the inclusive potentialities of individualised teaching.

Unmasking Mechanisms of Power

The discourses analysed in this chapter indicate that although discursive formations might have been designed for other purposes, such as the promotion of inclusion, some of them ended up as legitimating 'strategies of power by which a decision is accepted and by which that decision could not be taken in the way it was' (Foucault, 1988a:104). Put simply, despite the benevolent humanitarianism, which supported the deployment of specific discourses in policy documents and literature, these

discourses are feeding and maintaining mechanisms and devices of control attached to a rational system – that of normalisation - which derives from the tradition of special needs education. What my data shows is the perpetuation of a series of mechanisms and related devices linked to the discursive formations previously analysed, which were mostly created to homogenise and normalise individuals. In summary, in the schools investigated, it was possible to identify three main mechanisms, and related devices of power of normalisation, that ran counter the development of inclusive education:
– Individualisation
– Categorisation
– Standardised assessment procedures

All three mechanisms, and their related corrective devices, come into effect as part of an apparatus of normative rationality, which individualises, categorises and assesses deviation from the norm. These organisational processes are reminiscent of what Ball (1990), drawing on Foucault, identifies with 'dividing practices' (Ball, 1990:4) which manipulate people and give them a social and personal identity (Kenway, 1990). Examples of such mechanisms were found in both schools investigated and they will be discussed below.

Individualisation could be interpreted as a benevolent mechanism celebrating the persons' uniqueness, and a possible way of re-distributing the resources equitably depending on students specific 'needs'. At the same time, as Foucault (1977) has repeatedly shown, individualisation can also be conceived as a powerful mechanism of social control. The individualisation procedures, as the ones identified by my study in the individualised education plans, increase surveillance through a system that investigates in depth the disabled pupil. Unless individualisation is transformed into a tool that takes into account the totality of the student population to promote the changes necessary to reform education it inevitably represents one of the first systemic barriers to be removed. One possible way forward could be the creation of educational plans which do not concern the individual pupil, or the writing of an individual plan for each pupil, but which foster the development of specific or group of competencies which concern all students such as educational plans for social skills, or for meta-cognitive abilities.

The issue of categorisation as a barrier to the development of inclusion and integration has been widely discussed both in the English literature (Galloway, Armstrong and Tomlinson, 1994; Armstrong, D., 1998; 2003; Ainscow, Booth and Dyson, 2006; Daniels, 2006), as well as in the Italian context (Canevaro, 1999b; Canevaro and Mandato, 2004; Medeghini and Valtellina, 2006). However, although in the English context the debate focussed primarily on the need to find alternative arrangements to allocate resources to schools, in Italy it mostly focussed on how to develop alternative forms of categorisation and classification to raise more funding to schools, as society 'cannot do without categories' (Canevaro and Mandato, 2004:170). This is particularly evident in the adoption of the ICF as the new form of identification and classification of disability.

The device par excellence of the mechanism of categorisation is the statementing procedure, following the Framework Law 1992. This is the administrative procedure that establishes the allocation of resources and personnel to a school where a disabled child is enrolled. I argue that we should start examining why we categorise, with what consequences for the people who are being categorised. Resources are a crucial factor for schooling. However, it is time to shift the debate over alternative ways of gathering and using resources, rather than increasing the number of categorised children.

Finally, assessment should be considered as a way of collecting information about student learning necessary to inform teaching and possibly bring about pedagogical changes and not solely as a means of selection based on pre-determined standards. Assessment systems such as principles, policies and practices, should always consider the totality of the student population and should aim to identify student progresses in learning in inclusive settings (Watkins, 2007). In contrast, assessment procedures in the two schools were very often used to measure and judge student attainments, to track and group students depending on their performances and to report about school accountability.

These assessment procedures become even more selective with disabled students as they are either excluded from assessment processes (see the *INValSi*) or are provided with alternative forms (Benjamin, 2003) of school success – for example certificates of attendance - rather than equally valid degrees. In the schools invest-igated, the class teachers provided students attending the last year of the lower secondary education with a formal appraisal. The teacher counselled them about what type of upper secondary education they could attend. Although these formal appraisals, or devices of power, as Polesel (2006) describes them, were not statutory documents, they influenced students' self-perceptions and self-esteem and their parents' choice regarding their child's school career. As will become evident in the following extract from my research diary, students seemed to be manipulated by teachers' assumptions about their own talents and skills:

> The room is formally organised with the teacher leading from the front. Here, however, it is not the answers to an orientation test for upper secondary school choice that is being validated and invalidated, but students' choices of school based on articulations of their own strengths, weaknesses and interests. Whereas students have presumably, until now, been encouraged to see and value the importance of doing well from a formative perspective in all subject matters, at the point of selection (to different types of high school) it suddenly becomes all right to be good at some things and bad at others, for us to be 'all different' (from one another) and to possess different skills. The teacher even references herself into the discourse, indicating that she was not very good at – or interested in – certain academic subjects as a school student. One thing that is achieved though, is the careful avoidance of any criticism of the system of selection and schooling for upper secondary education with an echo of Gramsci on education as a reproduction of class division. The teacher even talks about 'natural predisposition' – which is a naturalisation of socially constructed assumptions. (Observations notes, *Fellini* school, June 2005)

The appraisals, in particular for those students identified as having *BES* became a device that contributed to the reproduction of social inequalities. Here, lower secondary education was transformed into an agency of the State, which had to justify decisions and reinforce assumptions concerning higher education choices based upon natural skills and talents. There was no attempt to challenge such assumptions although, possibly this was with the best intentions to 'protect' students from school failure in upper secondary education. A formative type of assessment – or assessment for learning - should be promoted, not only as a way of adapting teaching and learning modalities depending on evidence of students learning (Wiliam, 2007) but also as a way of promoting procedures of self-assessment and self-advocacy for all pupils, including disabled children (Watkins, 2007).

THE HEGEMONIC DISCOURSE OF *INTEGRAZIONE SCOLASTICA*

As shown in Chapter One, the policy of *integrazione scolastica* arose from a series of post-war reconstruction initiatives designed to unify a poverty-stricken and culturally divided country. The merging of different political, social, and economic strands, might have transformed this policy into a hegemonic bloc – a common sense view (Gramsci, 1971) - that stitched together different social stakeholders with contradictory interests. This would need to include those social actors in search of democracy, justice and rights as well as those people supporting new forms of social control and power legitimated by different types of complex special needs discourses. Evidently, the crystallisation of *integrazione scolastica* as a common sense view prevented many educators from seeing the bigger pattern of which they were part and that they contributed to reproduce with their everyday actions. Primarily, the policy of *integrazione scolastica*, resulted from a political decision, which led some Italians to adopt an integrative frame of mind, under specific historical circumstances (Booth, 1982). However, this political decision was made without inquiring into the many different reasons which might have led to this integrative process beyond the humanitarian ethos of 'doing good' to 'unfortunate' minorities amongst the student population.

Most Italian commentators (Canevaro, 2001; de Anna, 2002; Onger, 2008) would agree that the policy of *integrazione scolastica* has slowly become a shared value and a widely accepted philosophy. Thanks to this policy, no child in Italy can ever be rejected from a local school, no parent can be required to justify the child's enrolment in the district school, no teacher can deny a pupil the right to full curriculum access, no head teacher can ever reject a child on the basis of impairment, ethnic origin or socio-economic disadvantage and no educational policy would be designed and put in place in order to exclude students from the mainstream, or disabled people from society. However, the realization that the policy of *integrazione scolastica* has been in place for more than thirty years, and has promoted the entitlement of civil rights to the benefit of previously marginalised sections of the population, halted the search and the interrogation of the values, assumptions and ideologies in which the policy was firstly enshrined. Indeed, what emerges is the lack of a critical engagement with the provisional nature of models, paradigms and realities resulting from the interplay of power and knowledge as was available at the time in which the policy was passed.

Similarly, there does not seem to be any acknowledgement that a reductionist notion of *integrazione scolastica,* stemming from a special needs education mind-set as indicated in the description of the history of special education in Italy, has prevailed over a systemic notion of *integrazione scolastica* which aimed to challenge the education system. As emerging from the discursive formations, practices and mechanisms of power examined within this chapter, it appears that what was once a liberating policy initiative has been transformed into an oppressive policy, or more specifically into a hegemonic discourse of normalisation which operates to construct, manage and control disability and diversity. For example, this issue becomes evident when investigating the notion of disability, which is uncritically constructed only in terms of individual deficiencies (Slee, 1996). Additionally, when exploring how the change of attitudes towards disability occurred, it emerges that an individualistic gaze was prioritized over a systemic one. The price of participation of disabled people in society was often sealed by a restriction of active participation, in particular in the process of decision-making, and by the introduction of compensatory measures rather than structural changes. A hegemonic discourse of normalisation also becomes apparent in the attempt of extending the notion of normalisation to include new standards of normality (see the discourse of special normality), rather than addressing common strands of oppression. Clearly, when the policy was first enacted, it envisaged liberating potentialities to fight against exclusion and the marginalisation of disabled people in society and to break with the rigidity of the Fascist school. However, unless a paradigmatic shift (Kuhn, 1970) from special education to inclusive education takes place, discursive formations will perpetuate existing power relations and will reproduce a mono-dimensional knowledge which has emanated from a historically situated frame of reference.

Given the above considerations, not only a hegemonic discourse such as that of *integrazione scolastica* maintains power relations in place, but it also functions as a barrier to innovative ideas and thinking such as those promoted by inclusive education. The insightful thinking of Gibson (2006) helps to understand the current Italian scenario:

> Inclusive thinking is steeped in philosophies of social justice and human rights discourse. The prevailing system is steeped in hegemony, where the culture of modernity and medical discourse still dominate. (Gibson, 2006:325)

This statement indicates the contradictory situation of Italy, the perpetuation of a mind-set that may limit the possibilities of critiquing the ideological foundations of mainstream education and of developing alternative theoretical conceptualisations leading to inclusive education. In the case studies investigated, despite the positive intentions of 'doing good' to 'fringe' groups of the population, the policy perpetuated micro-exclusions within mainstream settings.

At the same time, whilst acknowledging the exploitative and obscuring quality of hegemonic ways of thinking, I am not arguing against the deployment of a hegemonic discursive formation per se, as it may open up possibilities that have the potential to bring about radical changes. In this respect Gramsci, (1971) for example, identified the productiveness of a hegemonic culture for the unification of Italy.

In alignment with these considerations, the discourse of *integrazione scolastica* managed to outstrip the economic, social, political and geographical differences in a politically divided country after World War Two. This major Italian educational policy, allowed the modification of attitudes in relation to disabled people. Previously marginalised social groups were, for the first time, entitled to the same rights as any other Italian citizen and people's expectations were challenged by a modification of people's experiences of disability. There is hope that a new hegemonic discourse of inclusion might replace a reductionist notion of *integrazione* and lead to the development of inclusive education.

Consequently, to do so, it is crucial that spaces for counter-hegemonic actions are identified, in the light of new theoretical principles, such as the social model of disability, and then by listening to the voices of new intellectuals capable of breaking up the unity of traditional ways of thinking. For example, it would be crucial to promote the adoption of the concept of inclusion, as theorised within this study, not as a linguistic exercise, but as an attempt to confront the hegemonic discourse of *integrazione*. Possibly, by recovering the original purpose of this policy initiative, mainstream schools will be modified also by drawing on the experience of integrating disabled students in ordinary classrooms. By starting from the school setting, and the lessons learnt by non-disabled pupils sitting next to their disabled peers, society may undergo fundamental cultural changes [in this concern see also Armstrong's and Barton's argument supporting proximity and interaction between non-disabled and disabled students (Armstrong and Barton, 2001:706)]. However, unless, structural changes are made, old hegemonic forms of disablement are destined to be perpetuated. The identification of those everyday activities - small circumstances (Gramsci, 1971) - and of those rationalised relations of power (Foucault, 1988b) in the everyday life that must be challenged, is a fundamental step to start the process of change.

CONCLUSION

In this chapter I have shown how the policy of *integrazione scolastica* came to be deployed as the only valid 'regime of truth' which resulted from contingent, historical beliefs and values, and which produced a monolithic theory about how to run education and organise the participation of disabled people. I have engaged with the phenomenon of the proliferation of discourses and mechanisms of *integrazione scolastica* that have been hi-jacked by special needs education and which represent obstacles to the development of inclusive education. Consequently, although an anti-discriminatory policy is clearly a standpoint for the development of inclusive education, it does not guarantee its outcome at the local level. What was once intended as an ideological innovation to dismantle segregated education is now being deployed as a hegemonic and reactionary force restraining the development of inclusion.

Inclusive education is not an easy task (Barton, 2005; Barton, 2008) and cannot be guaranteed by the passing of legislative measures nor by the articulation of perceived pro-inclusive discourses and discursive practices. Inclusive education instead, results from struggles that are continuously fought in the process of policy making between different contenders and at different levels (Fulcher, 1989). The following chapter therefore, provides examples of the struggles that should be fought under the banner of inclusion and makes recommendations about how to overcome the present status quo and produce more inclusive settings.

CONSTRUCTING INCLUSIVE EDUCATION

Accepting that disability is a human rights issue requires us to broaden our horizons in fundamental ways. (Oliver, 1996:82)

Previous chapters have attempted to bring to the fore the cultural and structural impediments to the development of inclusive thinking within policies and the school context. In this chapter, though, I will provide reasons for an appreciation of the work done by the schools investigated. Taking into consideration the structural and cultural constraints in which the lower secondary schools operated, this chapter provides indications of how schools could promote inclusive education at a micro-level. Yet, inclusion is a contextually and politically situated process and it cannot be understood unless it is approached through the lenses of the people struggling for its realization.

With this in mind, in the first section I suggest ways in which the schools under investigation were coming to grips with the difficulties of implementing *integrazione scolastica* at a practical level and how some of these attempts could be interpreted as potentially inclusive features. Secondly, I recommend areas of investigation in order to move the debate over inclusive education outside the boundaries of the confrontation between integration and segregation (or special versus mainstream schools) at a macro-level. In this section, further insights to promote inclusive thinking are explored. Thirdly, I investigate the counter-hegemonic discourse of human rights as a possible way of constructing inclusive education.

SCHOOLS AT A CROSS-ROAD

What may distinguish the schools that I have investigated is that they were not familiar with the debates concerning inclusive education and the social model of disability, as conceptualised in this book. Nor were they familiar with the struggle for radical changes that derives from them. It was very difficult to engage with the investigation of inclusive features in a context dominated by the hegemonic discourse of *integrazione scolastica* in its reductionist interpretation. From my interviews, it was evident that most of the participants had never heard the words inclusion and inclusive education before. Similarly, school development plans did not report sections about inclusive education. Interviewees seemed to guess whenever asked to define inclusion:

I have never heard about inclusive education before. But, my opinion is that it (inclusion) reflects a desire to integrate, inclusion occurs before integrazione. Here in Italy we talk about *integrazione*, abroad they speak about inclusion, which means to put someone inside something, someone who is still excluded. Therefore it is a different discourse, something that must be conceived and designed from the very beginning. It is true that integrazione concerns mainly the handicap, while inclusion concerns a bit of all pupils; inclusion is a broader concept that takes into account society as a whole. (Interview 06, support teacher, Fellini School)

As this extract suggests, inclusion was understood as a different concept from *integrazione* and it was concerned with all students who were at risk of being excluded, not only disabled students. The teacher making this statement however, assumed that there existed one linear process of development that goes from segregation to integration, and inclusion was an intermediate step, as you cannot integrate unless you are included beforehand. Thus, inclusive education seemed to be interpreted as a former type of *integrazione*, although with a broader meaning as it addressed 'a bit of all' students. Conversely, a policy maker remarked that she did not regard inclusion as a previous type of *integrazione*, but rather as a new policy with a specific target: 'I think that *integrazione* is about disabled students, while inclusive education is about migrant students. It is time to use the legacy of *integrazione* in order to include migrant students' (Interview 19, policy maker, Provincial Education Authority). And it is here that the heritage of special education, perpetuated through the hegemonic discourse of *integrazione scolastica*, still looms over the attempts to change education and promote inclusive education. Without a re-consideration of the policy of *integrazione scolastica* and its limitations, any further application for other minority groups may risk reproducing discriminatory outcomes.

In alignment with the policy maker's observation, other participants in the school *Fellini* speculated that inclusion meant the integration of those students experiencing difficulties at schools such as those with other nationalities, students with learning difficulties or identified as having 'special educational needs', and Roma students altogether; 'I do not know what inclusive education means, but maybe it is about students who are socially and economically disadvantaged' (Interview 14, Italian teacher, *Don Milani* School). It seems that participants considered inclusive education as an extension of the *integrazione scolastica* policy. Arguably, the schools failed to engage in any critical questioning of the ideology in which the policy of *integrazione scolastica* was framed. Rather they conjectured about using the experiences of *integrazione* to promote the 'inclusion' – or better mainstreaming - of migrants and all students marked as 'other' in regular settings. These interpretations of inclusion seem to be enshrined in continuity with an ideology that still differentiates between those students who comply and those who do not comply with the established norm.

Given the above considerations, inclusive education was, 'still at a stage of discussion for a public which from the point of view of scientific ability is still in the first condition of youth and which therefore has a direct need for certainties' (Gramsci, 1970:98). It is necessary to acknowledge, however, that the schools genuinely showed a concern for all pupils and their process of learning, in particular for those deemed as being most 'vulnerable'. The problem raises considerations that these schools have been left with very few alternatives outside of the boundaries of *integrazione scolastica*. At the same time, inclusion is a school-based approach and concerns addressing barriers that hinder the 'presence, participation and achievement of pupils in local neighbourhood schools' (M. Ainscow, 2003:15). With this in mind, schools showed serious efforts to create integrative settings within the cultural values available, and their commitment showed an interest in those inclusive values such as social justice, equity and democracy. Despite the financial constraints, social pressures, bureaucratic regulations, curricular limitations, the schools promoted projects, extra-curricular activities and community initiatives that could potentially support inclusion. For example, by participating in the network of the primary school *Arcobaleno*, they attempted to promote a collaboration that could re-create a sense of community, solve contingent problems and promote relations with parents. Not to mention that many schools together may be more powerful than an individual school in the struggle for resources and better schooling.

Drawing on Apple (Apple, 2000, 2006; Apple & Beane, 1999) this book wants to disentangle some key issues from a reductionist and conservative description of *integrazione scolastica* which focuses mainly on exemplars of 'good practice'. In doing so, the schools under investigation, were not portrayed as exemplars of success-ful schools, but as real schools struggling with difficulties. These schools were seeking to find their own way out of an obsolete education system and out of the boundaries of bureaucratized regulations, although often reproducing the same inequality they wished to confront. Clearly, any effort to change practice, is parti-cularly difficult in a country that has often been criticised for being immobile and rigid (Aiello, et al., 2002; Giddens, 2007; Polesel, 2006). Nevertheless, there is enough evidence to identify some integrative features that potentially could facilitate the deve-lopment of inclusive education. My data showed that the schools investigated engaged with a series of initiatives that could be conducive to inclusion in the long term:

The collaboration with other schools within the network of the primary school *Arcobaleno* and the signature of local agreements (*accordi di programma*). These collaboration tools are central as they could potentially transform the schools into community active centres enabling them to increase mutual support. More specifically, research about collaboration between schools shows that schools know more than what they use (Ainscow, 1999; Ainscow, Muijs, & West, 2006) and that many difficulties could be addressed by making a better use of existing resources (Ainscow, Howes, Farrell, & Frankham, 2003; Ianes, 2005).

- The introduction of teaching flexibility, capable of responding to all students learning styles through in-service training for all teachers (in particular through the Arcobaleno primary school).
- The involvement of parents, including those belonging to ethnic minorities (for example afternoon events to promote the integration of parents from ethnic minorities with parents from the local area of *Adriazzurra*).
- The carrying out of extra-curricular projects designed by students (such as the project carried out to know the local area of *Adriazzurra*).
- The use of peer-tutoring among students, in particular to support the learning of those classmates experiencing difficulties.
- A strong leadership that created a common ethos and connective supportive structures (Canevaro, 1986; Corbett, 2001).
- The attempts to increase the collaboration between mainstream and support teachers in order to tackle the practice of delegation.

The participation of disabled students in the process of self-assessment (for example the participation of Emanuele in the school *Fellini* in the writing of his IEP – in particular in relation to his behavioural targets).

Moreover, from my interviews with the teachers and head teachers, it emerged that both schools seemed to be willing to engage with the limits and the contradictions they faced. For example, the very presence of a researcher allowed the educators of a classroom in the *Fellini* School, to reconsider their work and their interactions with some pupils. Thus, as indicated in Chapter Five, they struggled with the possibility of modifying the curriculum to promote the participation of a Chinese student in the classroom and they questioned the head teacher for not having provided them with extra-time to organise themselves. Under these circumstances, teachers and educators became more aware of the lack of time for self-enquiry and reflection to improve their teaching, but also of their capacities to intervene and to promote change if put in the conditions where it is possible. It is important therefore, that space for dialogues and reflection on practice are created within the schools in order to facilitate debate that may lead to more inclusive thinking.

Consequently, the schools investigated proved to be good exemplars of integrative schools, as they attempted to promote the participation of all students in the process of learning within the cultural and political principles available. Yet, the problem arises, as Ainscow, Booth and Dyson (2006) also argue, when schools refuse to engage in a fundamental rethinking of the standpoints in which their social functions are located. As discussed in Chapter Six, the discourse of change remains constrained within struggles, contradictions and reductionist views of *integrazione scolastica*. Barriers were mostly identified around management factors, such as lack of support and resources from local and national bodies, collaboration and cooperation with the latter, rather than with the interrogation of the principles supporting teaching and learning routines. Evidently, the schools under investigation did not seem to consider the possibility of re-examining educational goals and structures.

RECOMMENDATIONS FOR THE SCHOOLS IN ADRIAZZURRA

Achieving inclusive education, as Barton (2001a; 2003; 2001b) repeatedly argues is not an easy task, rather it is a struggle. Drawing on Allan, inclusive education 'starts with ourselves' (2005:282), and it requires the re-examination of taken-for-granted assumptions and self-evident ideas that are perceived as natural. At the same time, I am aware that to criticise and speculate about change without providing possible trajectories for those who operate within the education system is unsatisfactory. By doing this, one risks adding to the critique of inclusive education as being too idealistic. Moreover, without context-related suggestions one risks being constrained in the field of intellectual reasoning and loose allies in the struggle for a just and equal society. Instead, a paradigmatic change, like the one that inclusive education should support, requires the identification of possibilities and spaces for action, however provisional, contingent and contextual they might seem. As Slee (2003) also argues, critiquing policies is a much easier task than attempting to reconstruct them and/or to contribute in the process of building local practices of inclusion. With this in mind, in the contexts in which my research took place, I have identified possible areas of intervention that could move the debate for inclusive education forward. Placing Foucault and Gramsci's views in context, linking the normalisation process and the interplay of power relations, with the reproduction of social system and the acquiescence to hegemonic system beliefs, I have identified some possible areas of struggle at a micro-level. These points are only tentative and seek to open a space for reflection and debate within the schools investigated:

- To provide formalised - and not resulting from teachers' good will - space and time for teachers to reflect upon their practices. In this way, schools may be able to develop their own practices that could be conducive to inclusion within their own contexts. One possible way could be to promote reciprocal observations of lessons that elicit further discussions.
- To make effective use of teaching assistants. They are often used for marginal activities, while they seem to be sufficiently qualified to support teaching and learning. More adult resources in the schools represent a strength that the schools should not underestimate.
- To make effective use of support teachers as partners. It is necessary not to derogate activities concerning a statemented pupil to the support teacher. In particular, to experiment possibilities of swapping roles and planning class lessons together.
- To listen to students' voices. Their suggestions should be considered as possible ways of organising teaching and learning, and concretely encapsulate those suggestions into teaching routines.
- To draw on the experiences held by the primary school Arcobaleno. Serious efforts should be made to render the Arcobaleno network into a resource for implementing change not only from a practical perspective (for example the curriculum) but also from a theoretical perspective (for example principles). In this concern, to attempt taking risks by experimenting with some practices as developed in the primary school (for example the use of circle time, pupil and learning-friendly organisation of space and time, absence of marks, getting rid of text books).
- To reconsider the role of special units and how to learn from what is done within the special units in order to improve ordinary teaching.
- To develop strong leadership that is supportive of teachers' initiatives, even when they may seem unconventional.
- To engage with difficulties and contradictions in order to identify the structural barriers impacting upon teachers' work.

NEW AREAS OF DEBATE: HOW TO DEVELOP INCLUSIVE THINKING

The contextually situated recommendations are examples of actions that could identify possible barriers and lead to suggestions about how to start implementing changes at a micro-level. At the same time, the possibility of promoting inclusive practice should be supported by the development of inclusive thinking at a macro-level. This aim is to be achieved by promoting the development of a counter-hegemonic

inclusive thinking that challenges existing assumptions about disability and schooling. In order to achieve this I have identified some broader areas of intervention to promote the development of an inclusive culture at a macro-level:
- Reformulating teacher education.
- Investigating issues about self-advocacy, empowerment and voice in policy making process.
- Going beyond the old confrontation between integration and segregation to develop inclusion.
- Moving from a positive discrimination to a human rights approach.

Reformulating Teacher Education

Reiterating the importance of language in fighting against oppression and culturally dominant ideologies, I have chosen to talk about teacher education rather than teacher training. Whilst teacher education seems to be inscribed within an inclusive vision which fosters the formation of teachers as critical educators and actors for change, by contrast, teacher training seems to remain embedded within a traditional construction of teachers as clerical agents and bureaucratic professionals of school accountability. Teacher education is a key aspect in the quest for inclusion and needs to be addressed with careful attention in the making of educational policies and in the redefinition of programmes (M. Ainscow, 1993; Len Barton, 2003; Booth, Nes, & Stromstad, 2003; Slee, 1993). As my research has shown, teacher education becomes central to face the contradictions and tensions that emerge during the practical implementation of the policy. Examples of contradictions include: the practice of delegation, the unequal relation between mainstream and support teachers and the reproduction of special education within regular classrooms.

In Italy, initial teacher training for primary school class teachers became compulsory in 1998 (Law n. 341/1990 and Law n. 315/1998). It now consists of a four-year university degree and it focuses on both the study of disciplines and on training in schools. In contrast, secondary school teachers training was not available and the qualification was granted through a public state exam. It was only in 1998 (Decree n. 460 26/11/1998) that teacher training for secondary school teacher became optional thanks to the creation of higher education courses (such as the *Scuola di Specializzazione all'Insegnamento Secondario* – or *SSIS*). At the moment, a new plan for secondary school initial teacher training is currently under scrutiny. It envisions that, in a few years, teacher qualification will be obtained by attending specialised university courses (five years of university courses) plus one year (475 hours) of practicum (this should be applied to support teacher as well).

Support teachers, both primary and secondary, have always been trained. In 1975, support teachers were required to specialize by attending the so-called *corsi biennali* (two-year master courses), held by private associations or institutions, mostly with a medical orientation, although under the aegis of the Ministry of Public Instruction. Subsequently, two different courses became available for support teachers: one type of training for those teachers who had already qualified as class teachers (standard *SSIS* course with additional 400 hours) and a second type of training for those teachers qualifying as support teachers only (full *SSIS* course, 800 hours). The training for support teachers focused on subjects such as neuropsychiatry, psychology, infant pathologies, learning disorders, behavioural disorders, special legislation, special didactics and special pedagogy. Consequently, not only mainstream and support teachers were trained under different training institutions (universities versus private institutions), but also following different curricula (subject-oriented courses versus specialized courses concerning students' deficiencies). Clearly, this institutional division between the two careers contributes to the perpetuation of a separation between support and mainstream teachers within the classrooms and to the reproduction of the practice of delegation observed in the schools investigated in this study.

Currently, the Ministry of Public Instruction is passing a new decree (known as the Gelmini's decree 2010), which envisages university education for all class teachers and the insertion of specialised courses, such as special pedagogy and didactics to promote the integration of disabled pupils in regular classrooms. Policy makers claim that by doing so disabled children will not be considered as an 'issue to be dealt with' by the support/ specialised teacher only. Nevertheless, these special courses are mostly focused on specific types of pathologies, such as autism and Down syndrome. They do not address more general teaching skills, such as managing diversity within the classroom, which could really lead to the development of integration-related abilities. Consequently, there seems to be a very limited understanding that a mandatory course which is still largely medically oriented, and focussed on students' deficiencies, will only exacerbate existing special needs education discourses. These medical courses not only reproduce the clinical mind-set that the social model of disability is trying to counteract, but they also perpetuate the division between special and mainstream education within ordinary settings (D'Alessio, 2009b).

Conversely, teacher education should not be focused on how to manage children's deficits but to prepare class teachers and school practitioners to revolutionise, to radically reform their practice and their ideas of schooling (Allen, 2005; Len Barton, 2003; Booth, et al., 2003; Giroux, 2001). Given these considerations, it would be advisable that teacher training pay particular attention to the way in which pedagogy, assessment and curricula can be oppressive forms of marginalization and exclusion (Slee, 2001a). Inclusive teacher education should engage not only with new educational approaches and teaching methods, but with a reconsideration of the role of education and its purposes and what is the role of the teacher for the twenty first century (D'Alessio, 2009). As Ballard argues (2003), teacher education should give teachers 'theoretical tools of analysis that will help them to see injustice and understand its institutional and structural origin' (2003:68) and to challenge forms of oppression and cultural ideology that create poverty and exclusion, often enshrined within discourses of which they may be part. Finally, teacher education should focus on how to train teacher trainers as we should not forget that most people teach the way they were taught, regardless of the amount of training they are provided with:

> If the new intellectuals see themselves as a direct continuation of the preceding 'intelligentsia' they are not in fact 'new', that is, they are not tied to the new social group which represent organically the new historical situation, but are

rather a conservative and fossilised residue of the historically superseded social group. (Gramsci, 1970:113)

What emerges is that there is still a dominant idea of how an 'ideal teacher' should be like. This ideal is still ingrained in narrow forms of ablement that, for example, do not include, teachers and teacher trainers with impairments.

Moreover, there seems to remain a strong division between support and class teachers training, with the former attending completely different education pathways. This division, I believe is one of the most difficult challenges that Italian scholars will have to tackle in order to develop inclusive teacher training (D'Alessio, 2009b).

Supporting Empowerment and Self-Advocacy

The social model of disability and inclusive education, as theorised in this book, are intertwined with notions of empowerment, self-advocacy and voice. These issues are potential tools in the struggle for breaking up the oppression of the individual/ medical model of disability that constructs disability as a human pathology and focuses on students' adjustment skills rather than on educational and societal change. At the same time, empowerment, self-advocacy and voice are problematic concepts as they may reproduce the same reality they are seeking to confront, unless they are fully valued and correctly understood. In this regard, the international catchphrase of 'nothing about us without us' (Charlton, 1998) risks becoming a rhetorical discourse of justice, unless current power relations systems are seriously unhinged. Critical examination and further research is required to unpack the rhetoric of pursuing democratic schools and societies by means of empowerment, advocacy and voice, whilst reproducing traditional school pedagogies and disabling systems.

Given the above considerations the concept of empowerment has been used to foster the independence and autonomy of disabled people, especially those living within the care and service providers systems. However, as Goodley (2005) states, 'when professionals seek to "empower" people with learning difficulties, there is a danger of reinforcing the victim status of people with learning disability' (2005:334). Such a perspective is not only 'disempowering', as you cannot empower somebody; but it also maintains power relations in place, disguised under the egalitarian principle of recognising previously marginalised groups of the population. Disability studies scholars (L. Barton, 2005; Clough & Barton, 2000; Morris, 1997) argue that empowerment runs counter to dependence and care, and that in order to achieve this state of independence and self-determination disabled people must be in the condition to empower themselves and to contribute actively to the making of society. These considerations raise issues about what kinds of voices are heard within the different arenas and about issues of self-advocacy as a tool to exert power within the decision-making process.

The issue of self-advocacy is central to articulate the effects of a disabling society. It allows the identification of those structures and factors that are disabling from the perspectives of those people who are still oppressed (Goodley, 1997). Self-advocacy is concerned with the process of self-representation, self-determination and 'public recognition' (Goodley, 2005) of previously marginalised sections of the population through consulting processes. In particular, disabled peoples organisations have chosen to refer to self-advocacy as a means to empower themselves by transferring power from experts, tutors, carers or parents to disabled people (Aspis, 1997). However, self-advocacy is a complex issue. Crucial to the endeavour of supporting self-advocacy, is the removal of those assumptions that underestimate the contribution of disabled people (for example medical/individual model) and deny identity recognition. In the Italian context, an attempt to face the issue of self-advocacy has been made with the creation of the National Observatory for the Integration of Disabled People at the Ministry of Public Instruction. Disabled peoples organisations are considered as advisors to ministerial policy makers on issues concerning education. Yet questions arise concerning the actual power that disabled people have to place items onto the policy makers' agenda and thus initiate impacts upon institutions. As Aspis (1997) argues, disabled people often discuss about what is already available, with limited alternative choices among what is being offered. Moreover, it is not possible to assume that because disabled people are being consulted, they are actually exercising self-determination and self-advocacy. This situation is particularly true when self-advocacy is exercised within existing constructions and assumptions of disability.

Voice can offer an insight into the power relations of educational sites, especially the voice of those students who have been silenced for long periods (Arnot & Reay, 2007). By doing so, teachers may discover what discourses are dominant within their classrooms and how they could change their pedagogy to facilitate learning (Arnot & Reay, 2007). Central to this endeavour is to promote the voices of pupils and fight against the 'culture of silence' (Freire, 1985). Children should not be merely consulted, but listened to in the process of change. Policy makers should be reminded that students' views matter, not only to comply with policy requirements but offering real potentials for improvement. An attempt to do so has been made by the European Agency for Development in Special Needs Education that organised a European Hearing for young people with special educational needs to take place in Lisbon in September 2007 (Soriano, Kyriazopoulou, Weber, & Grunberger, 2008). In this occasion, young representatives from 29 countries were able to speak to policy makers and discuss their educational priorities with them.

Nevertheless, as Fielding (2001) repeatedly argues, student voices should not be disregarded, misunderstood and most importantly, managed, for other purposes than those of the students. What often happens is that schools and educational bodies involve students in the consulting process as a result of a 'vogue' (ibid. 2001), which does not challenge the existing status quo of power relations and does not bring about educational change. This practice is stifling rather than liberating, as students' interests are only marginally taken on board and their decisions are made to reinforce current assumptions (ibid. 2001). Evidence of this could be found, for example, when in plenary sessions in conferences or meetings with students with impairments there are no speakers and policy makers who are also disabled.

In the schools investigated student voices were often heard as opinions, since their impact upon the regular unfolding of schooling was almost nonexistent. In the Italian context student consultation is safeguarded by law (Decree n. 249, 1998). Yet, students perceive their participation in decision-making procedures as additional bureaucratic measures and prefer to desert meetings: 'teachers do listen to what you say, but then they do as they like, so why bother about going to these meetings?' (Focus group interview 01, *Fellini* School, June 2005). Similarly, in the writing of the IEP, disabled students cannot participate 'on the grounds of safety (when inclusion in decision-making processes could harm the child) or 'competency' (when the child is not thought capable of understanding the process)' (Davis & Watson, 2000:212). Conversely, the children interviewed suggested many possible alternatives according to which schooling could be conducted (for example more laboratories, new pedagogies, additional and alternative syllabi content, flexible use of time, the organisation of school breaks, and the incorporation of new space):

R: so if you were the Ministry of Public Instruction how would you change school?

S1) I would do less technology and design and I would do more swimming pool and less Italian, 13 hours per week is too much! You cannot spend 13 hours with the same teacher.

S2) I would give less homework. We have too much homework to do;

S3) I just would like to do nothing;

S4) I would not make changes at the level of the structure, but I will create more labs, I would create places where we can socialise with our classmates and schoolmates. Moreover, I would do more tests throughout the school year and not only at the end of the school year when everybody is under pressure. On the contrary I would reduce testing when we are at the end of the school year because we are more tired!

S5) I would like to work in groups, we could laugh a bit more and we would enjoy staying in the classroom. (Focus group interview 01, *Fellini* School, June 2005)

R: If you were the Minister of Public Instruction what would you change?

S1) I would close schools on Saturday.

S2) I would have a later start in the morning.

S3) I would keep Saturdays but I would not give homework for the weekend, you should not be studying on Sundays.

S4) I would have each day one single teacher and subject.

S5) We have got too much homework to do, it is too heavy for me.

S6) I would like to have more holidays…and… I do not know …

S1) I would like longer breaks during the morning.

(Focus group interview 03, *Don Milani* School, June 2005)

These ideas should be taken on board as further areas of intervention to implement school change. This study seems to suggest that voices, and personal accounts, can be powerful tools to deconstruct existing knowledge and practice of taken-for-granted grand narratives. Furthermore, these voices could provide room for dissent (D. Armstrong, 2003), and by drawing on Gramsci (1970, 1971) identify spaces for counter-hegemonic actions. Thus, inclusive education is also about recognition of different voices, not as another policy caveat of 'user participation' (Goodley, 1997), or as a means to reproduce teachers' pedagogies (Arnot & Reay, 2007) but as a way of identifying potential trajectories to challenge official assumptions. Put simply, the issue of voice is central to sociological study as the inequality of voices mirrors the relations of power inherent in society. It is only by giving voice to previously silenced groups that the reproduction of relations of subordination and domination begins to be broken.

Rearticulating the Debate Over Inclusion

An important area to promote inclusive education is to disentangle research studies from the old debate that conceives integration in opposition to segregation, and most importantly, that identifies segregation as the only common enemy to confront in order to struggle against exclusion. Clearly, this traditional division assumes that integration and segregation represent opposing conceptual frameworks, which stem from different theoretical paradigms and conceptualisation of modern societies. Conversely, Foucault's (2003) insights concerning modern societies and Western apparatuses of correction and of control over disruptive individuals are illuminating to show that what appears to be in opposition, may instead, be embedded in the same mechanism of social control:

> It seems to me that essentially there have been only two major models in the West: one is the exclusion of the lepers and the other is the model of the inclusion of plague victims. And I think that the replacement of the exclusion of lepers by the inclusion of plague victims as the model of control was a major phenomenon of the 18th century. (Foucault, 2003:44)

With the birth of modern societies, therefore, Foucault indicates that the main aim was not to exclude potential deviant individuals, but rather to assimilate them. Interestingly enough, it was in the eighteenth century that special needs education became to be conceptualised as a separate branch of knowledge. Thus Foucault adds:

> It is not a question of driving out individuals but rather of establishing and fixing them, of giving them their own place, of assigning places and of defining presences and subdivided presences. Not rejection but inclusion. You can see that there is no longer a kind of global division between two types of population, one that is pure and the other impure ... rather there is a series of fine and constantly observed differences between individuals who are ill and those who are not. It is a question of individualization. (Foucault, 2003:44)

From these extracts, it seems that what distinguishes Western countries, therefore, is not the adoption of opposite models, but rather the implementation of different tactics of control and management enshrined within the same mind-set. Clearly, although some countries have chosen to exert their control over problematic individuals through a model of exclusion, other countries might have chosen to adopt a model of inclusion. Thus, the adoption of apparently contrasting models does not necessarily imply different intellectual schemata, purposes and consequences. Whilst, the model of inclusion, identified by Foucault with that of the plague, can be considered as the 'invention of positive technologies of power which fashions, observes, knows and multiplies itself' (2003:48), the model of exclusion, identified by Foucault with that of leprosy, is a 'negative reaction' that 'drives out, excludes, banishes, marginalises and represses' (2003:48). Although one alternative may be for a country less attractive than the other, they both make use of mechanisms of power that stem from the same driving force of normalisation. Thus, they share a common commitment, which is one of social cohesion 'within a cohesive but highly differentiated and hierarchical ordering of place, values and norms (Armstrong, D., 2003:19). What becomes central is not the exclusion of the deviant ones, but rather their incorporation according to rationalising policies embedded with the 'realm of reason' (Armstrong, D., 2003:76).

Given these considerations, then, the inclusive debate should not concern the differences between integration and segregation models, but rather the similarities of two apparently diverging models. With this in mind, it is necessary to engage with reasons that lie behind the adoption of a model, rather than on the seeming diversity of the tactics adopted. It can be argued that although Italy was an exception to the proliferation of segregated education and institutions (Canevaro, 2006; Stiker, 1999) it developed similar tactics of control and management of diversity as those countries that chose to adopt a model of segregation.

As already discussed in Chapter Two with a description of the history of special education in Italy and the myth of the young boy Victor, I argue that to assume that *integrazione scolastica* is conducive to inclusive education because there are very few special schools still available, is the wrong issue to raise. In contrast, the policy of *integrazione scolastica* should be considered not only as antithetical to segregation – such as special education - but, possibly, as another strategy of power and control that still stems from the same branch of knowledge that rationalises, individualises and normalises disability. This position is also evident when segregation and integration have the same 'starting point' (Foucault, 1988:116), such as pupils deficiencies. Not only does a debate which opposes integration with segregation deflects attention from the tactics of control and management of disability and diversity, but it also leads, as Slee pertinently writes (2001b) 'to accept current school organisation and policy precepts as the point of commencement for a discussion about the practice of inclusion' (2001b:114). This position is 'conceptually limiting; it denies us the possibility to 'think otherwise' about educational studies and the world in which schools are located' (Ball, 1998 in Slee, 2001b:114). Conversely, I argue that it is only by engaging in a debate which attempts to challenge traditional schooling, teaching routines and assessment procedures that the policy of *integrazione scolastica* may lead to inclusion.

Keeping in mind the centrality of the issue of change in relation to the implementation of an inclusive agenda an approach to disability and inclusion should encompass a paradigmatic shift of perspective, in particular in relation to traditional ways of conceiving mainstream education and education systems (Ainscow & Booth, 1998; Armstrong, Armstrong, & Barton, 2000; Corbett, 2001; Morin, 2000; Oliver, 2000; Slee & Allan, 2001). Indeed, modifying and exiting current frameworks in which one belongs is very demanding, and there is evidence that it needs to undergo a radical shift of perspective. Whilst a non radical type of change consists of the process of adaptation, adjustments to surroundings and modification of current structures and systems within current frameworks of reference, more radical change requires a paradigmatic transformation (Morin, 2001; Sclavi, 2000) hence an overthrowing of the premises from which one looks at and understands things. Inclusion, from an educational perspective in particular, requires a change of the second type. From an educational perspective this shift requires the abandonment of special education stances which focus on compensatory approaches to individual 'needs', to embrace a pedagogy of inclusion and a commitment to the rights of all to belong (Ainscow & Booth, 1998; Slee & Allan, 2001).

Addressing the Issue of Positive Discrimination

Positive discrimination, a conceptual underpinning of the policy of *integrazione scolastica*, is concerned with the enactment of state legislative measures to favour particular 'categories' of people (for example women, disabled people, ethnic minorities), who are at risk of being excluded from active participation in different social domains. While most academics and policy makers never directly discuss the policy of *integrazione scolastica* in terms of positive discrimination or re-distribution, they clearly state that many anti-discrimination and welfare policies are fundamental and inevitable steps towards the construction of a more inclusive society (Canevaro, 2007). Italy promoted the passing of anti-discrimination legislation known as Law n. 67/2006. This law is in line with the European anti-discrimination policy, which allows disabled people to claim compensation if the State, or any other third sector organisation, is in breach of any anti-discrimination law. Although this policy is an indication of how different countries in Europe are currently addressing issues around disability, it fails to directly challenge the social construction of the notion of disability as an individual pathology. This policy does not address the causes of discrimination and seems to confine its role to one of reporting how the phenomenon of discrimination is still present within Europe.

To put it simply, positive discrimination ratifies rights, such as the right to education and the right to employment, for those social groups that were historically deprived of them. Although such measures may be well intentioned and may help to confront current discriminatory policies and practices, yet they need to mark some individuals as 'other' in order to ensure they enjoy the same rights as the majority of the population. Consequently, whereas some social groups are naturally entitled to these rights, other people's rights need to be ratified by means of affirmative action. It seems that positive discrimination fails to question the reasons why for some people, these rights are conceived as natural, while for others these same rights are conceived as 'privileges' that must be acquired through legislative entitlement. Positive discrimination, although often considered as necessary, is enshrined in a compensatory rationale which aims to redistribute resources without investigating the origin of inequality.

For instance, in the schools under investigation, a positive discrimination approach was prioritised in the discussion about resources. The main issue that participants remarked was the lack of funding and resources, to the detriment of inquiring how resources were provided, how they could be better used and under which priorities.

Supporting a Human Rights Approach to Education

Although I acknowledge that solutions to promote inclusive education are many and local, and should promote issues of advocacy and marginalised people's voice, I also argue for the need for a shared approach that limits the possibilities of misinterpretation and promotes the removal of structural and systemic barriers. In this concern, in order to go beyond the controversies around the issue of the social model of disability, some scholars (F. Armstrong & Barton, 1999) have argued that it is necessary to envisage a human rights approach to disability. This approach concerns all human beings without focusing on a particular 'category' and, as Armstrong and Barton (1999) also argue, it is in opposition with a 'needs' discourse. It is concerned with issues of change and engages with barriers at the social, economic and political levels by challenging issues of power relations.

For this reason, a possible way in which the social model could be used and interpreted is the human rights approach. This position has been supported by many international organisations such as the United Nation (UN Human Rights Report 2003) and Disability Peoples International. A human rights approach is concerned with:

1) The empowerment of disabled people in order to ensure their participation in all aspects of social life
2) The active pursuit of equal rights
3) The participation of disabled people in all decision-making processes (United Nations, 2003).

Despite the large number of international recommendations, the DPI often reported the deaths of disabled people as a result of human rights abuse – for example, from the use of caged beds in institutions for intellectually impaired people, in particular in Eastern European countries. Such events suggest that a human rights approach cannot be considered only in abstract terms, but on the contrary, it needs a concrete political dimension made up of specific safeguarding procedures. It is necessary to articulate these through commonly agreed standards, procedures and actions so that each country must take active measures as appropriate.

Indeed, a human rights approach remains a very contested and unstable terrain, as it may run the risk of reproducing the limits embedded within positive discrimination legislative measures. This is why a human right approach requires that disabled people should not be categorised as a particular group of people in order to benefit from the same rights that other people obtain without the need of being identified or classified by means of legislative action. As pointed out by Žižek (2005) it is crucial to problematize human rights and their supposed universality, as they are usually associated to those individuals who have been deprived of any other socio-political identity and left only with their 'bare life' (Žižek, 2005). To put simply, it is important that the human rights issue is not transformed into a new politically correct ideology supporting other ends that those related to justice and equality.

Another important issue is that although human rights principles may appear to be widely shared, they are continuously violated. For this reason the role of the monitoring bodies and of the non governmental organisations is fundamental, in protecting and implementing those rights, even in countries that have officially ratified them. Furthermore, human rights are not intrinsically fundamental, as they are not eternal and homogenous. On the contrary, their meaning is modified according to time and contexts. The need for enforceable human rights in relation to disability has also been underlined by Bickenback (2001), who stresses the link between individual and social environmental barriers to participation. In alignment with this, legislation is not enough if nothing is done to apply it. For example, the International Convention on the Rights of People with Disabilities (United Nations, 2006) is a declaration which becomes enforceable only if signatory countries ratify its content. The Convention which was ratified in 2007 identifies disability as a concept that changes with time (Griffo, 2007). A possible recommendation to promote inclusive education across countries could be to contribute to the ratification of this declaration. Although the Convention does not produce new rights, it enforces those already existing, as countries are obliged to eliminate institutional barriers that hamper disabled peoples participation in all sectors of society. Moreover, such measures are developed from the perspective of the disabled people who will have a tool to refer to whenever rights have been breached. Based on the application of the principle of 'nothing about us without us' (Charlton, 1998), it aims to guarantee the social inclusion of disabled people in all aspects of modern life. Finally, the UN Convention does not address issues about 'inclusive education' specifically. Thus, it limits the possibility of misinterpreting the notion of inclusion and the risk of appropriating a terminology and of changing definitions – for example from special education or *integrazione scolastica* to inclusive education - without modifying the ways of thinking in which these theories are enshrined.

The notion of inclusive education as a human rights issue is now celebrated by national and international organizations, and governments alike, and often referred to as the principle to fight discrimination against disabled people in education (UNESCO 2009). Despite this concept has become widely accepted, it may, however, run the risk of being used as mere rhetoric and/or discussed in terms of humanitarian affairs only. For example, there is still a growing confusion about what are the concrete implications of human rights statements for schooling. Although education is now addressed as an issue of participation, equality and quality, there do not seem to exist clear indications that discuss how participation can take place beyond placement, what are the origins of inequality beyond re-distribution of wealth and what do we exactly mean with school quality. I therefore argue for the need to explore the relationships between education and human rights beyond a theoretical approach, taking into account different social, political and geographical contexts. Human rights approach in education, I believe, require a thorough understanding of its implications for policy-making and schooling rather than abstract ideas of human development and full potential.

CONCLUSION

In this chapter I have shown that the schools investigated may be considered good exemplars of *integrazione scolastica*. Although they presented some potentially inclusive features, they could not be identified as inclusive schools. Nevertheless, I have attempted to provide some recommendations for construction of inclusive education both at the levels of schooling and cultural ways of thinking. These recommendations suggest that powerful areas of development can be envisaged if a paradigm shift, which breaks with the theoretical framework of special needs education. The human rights approach can be conducive to such an end, but only if it is addressed not as a positive discrimination approach but as a way of doing without the need to categorise and label some people in order to provide them with the same rights of other individuals.

CHAPTER 8

CONCLUDING COMMENTS

A Critical Analysis of the Policy of Integrazione Scolastica

This book is not intended to undermine or offset the significant work done in more than thirty years of *integrazione scolastica* nor to ignore what has been achieved - most notably, that no child is denied the right to education in his/her local school. Rather it seeks to provide an alternative way of critically analysing the policy of *integrazione scolastica* and its inclusive potential in Italy. Indeed, much could be learnt from the struggles that Italian educationalists and others have fought to achieve a mainstreaming policy which rejects complicity with the rationale of segregated education, even if only via a transitional modality. Therefore, it is crucial to acknowledge the inheritance of this policy, and its potential 'instrumental values' (Gramsci, 1971) that could be reappraised (for example the transformative agenda inscribed within the notion of hegemony, the commitment for democracy of the post-war years) for new projects, such as those concerned with the development of inclusion.

Through a discussion and an application of the social model of disability, I made a case for *integrazione scolastica* as being a problematic policy, which requires the analysis of the theoretical framework in which this legislative initiative is enshrined, in particular in relation to the construction of the notion of disability. By drawing on the social model of disability, I attempted to draw on the insights of disabled people's movements whose perspectives and voices have been silenced for many years in the history of education and in the struggles for civil rights. As a result of this sociological approach, the research focus shifted from investigating students' deficiencies and compensatory responses to these, to one which was concerned with identifying contextual constraints and systemic barriers that hinder the participation of all learners, including disabled students, in regular school settings.

Attention was drawn to the complex and contradictory nature of the process of policy-making, both at the levels of formulation and implementation. Taking into account that my enquiry drew on empirical data collected in two schools and the theoretical efforts of one single researcher, I do not intend to generalise from my findings. Conversely, I wish to draw attention to a reading of the policy of *integrazione scolastica* from a perspective that questions why reductionist interpretations of the policy of *integrazione* began to be deployed as dominant discourses. By exploring historical accounts, discursive formations and practices, my research has shown that this potentially inclusive policy initiative has been transformed into a hegemonic discourse of normalisation that aims to construct, manage and control disability in educational sites. As emerging from the contradictions rose within the historical analysis and the discourses articulated within the school contexts, this policy fails to be an inclusive policy, rather it shares continuity with the theoretical framework of special needs education.

Although the two case studies proved to be effective exemplars of integrative schools, yet they could not be identified as inclusive schools. Despite having made some progress in terms of widening the participation of disabled pupils, *integrazione scolastica* is primarily focused on questions relating to compensation for individual deficiencies. It does not question, challenge or explore the nature of education systems and pedagogical routines and tools, as inclusive education policies should do. On the contrary, current Italian research regarding the policy of *integrazione scolastica* continues to focus on a technical investigation of how this legislation has been applied within the school setting (such as allocation of financial, material and human resources), and on underlining the increase in the number of disabled students enrolled in regular classrooms, thus restricting the opportunities for improvement for mainstream settings.

FINAL REFLECTIONS

From an historical perspective, the policy of *integrazione scolastica* was not the end of the process of integration, but rather a means to an end - that of constructing a better school capable of welcoming all students and contributing to the creation of a more just and equitable society. By conducting a historical, policy and empirical analysis of this policy, the book has shown that reductionist interpretations of this policy still dominate educational settings and policy documents today, thus limiting the inclusive potential of what was once a liberating policy initiative. Although policy documents, participants' interviews and relevant literature articulate discourses concerning school change and a celebration of diversity, examples of actual modifications of school practices, which are meant to value difference, are difficult to find. The policy of *integrazione scolastica* therefore has failed to challenge the structures and the practice of mainstream school and has continued to operate within mechanisms of adaptations and adjustments of already existing education systems. In contrast, the development of inclusive education involves a deconstruction of current notions of schooling, learning and education in order to establish the pre-conditions of learning for all. Consequently, I argue that policy makers, practitioners and researchers alike have mistaken the *means* of *integrazione* - mainstreaming disabled students into regular classrooms - for the *end* of it - the transformation of the education system and schools – thus denying what was conceived as being the original purpose of *integrazione scolastica*.

Fundamentally, what emerges from this book is that the policy of *integrazione scolastica* has a contradictory and contentious nature. As is inherent in the notion of hegemony, this policy is both a liberating and an oppressive initiative. It is a liberating policy as it managed to break with the rigidity of the Fascist school, and it triggered the dismantling of segregated education and the participation of disabled people in regular schools. But it is also, an oppressive policy because the participation of disabled people occurs within an uncritical conceptualisation of the notion of disability, which stems from a special needs education paradigm. The analysis shows that the policy under investigation, and the practice that derives from it, seem to legitimate mechanisms, such as individualisation, categorisation, standardised assessment, the allocation of resources and specialised teachers, based on the severity of impairment and other special arrangements that undermine inclusion. All these mechanisms may be 'well intended' in terms of confronting previously discriminatory policies and practices, yet, paradoxically, they persist in constructing some individuals as 'other'. By investigating these contradictions, I showed how it is possible to deconstruct the policy of *integrazione scolastica* and, construct inclusive education.

Bearing in mind the complexity and, at the same time, the rigidity of the Italian education system, this book looks with a critical eye at those mechanisms, devices and tools originating in the individual/medical model of disability which, crystallised with time, have gone unnoticed and have perpetuated disguised forms of exclusion within the mainstream settings (such as special units, individualised education plans). Unless educationalists and policy makers are aware of policies, discourses and language which are still embedded in a special education rationale, and unless they re-consider the policy of *integrazione scolastica* and the notion of disability in the light of new theories and perspectives (such as the social model of disability), this policy, and the schools implementing it, will continue to reproduce the very reality they seek to challenge.

Inclusive education is about all of us, the nature of the education we want, the type of society we wish to live in, and the management of relations of power within it. The process of deconstructing the policy of *integrazione scolastica* aligns with the process of research as a self-reflexive journey that starts with a deconstruction of one's own positions and knowledge. Although such a process can be a disturbing one, as agents of change we need to promote inclusion, 'to accept our responsibility and do our work which starts with oneself' (Allan, 2005:293).

In summary, this book suggests that the quest for inclusive education requires radical changes. A type of change that envisions a cultural revolution, which sets aside past hegemonic discourse of *integrazione scolastica* and substitutes it with a new one, as resulting from new ways of thinking developed by organic intellectuals. In particular, and here Gramsci is crucial, I would like to underline the central role played by disabled activists, students and teachers. We need to bring forward new social movements that are capable of reshuffling traditional regimes of truth and power hierarchies. Deconstructing the policy of *integrazione scolastica* also means to identify spaces (for example teacher education, human rights approach to education) for counter-hegemonic actions necessary to subvert existing knowledge and to break the continuity with old structures and prejudices that are embedded in a special needs education framework.

This book reflects only my personal position and it aims to present the analysis of *integrazione scolastica* from a different angle and at the point in time when I am writing. It is not intended to 'convince', or to deplore the policy of *integrazione scolastica* and its supporters. In contrast, in the light of research integrity, any further development could lead me to reject or, alternatively, reinforce my beliefs and doubts. The discourses and the debate over *integrazione scolastica* and inclusive education are a contentious space for engaging in dialogues and equal confrontation. This book is an attempt to shake the conscience from the lethargy of rhetoric and to open up dialogues and possibilities concerning different types of research that presuppose critical engagement and envision radical thinking. Hopefully, such dialogues and possibilities will inspire and generate alternative approaches that will contribute to the development of an inclusive society.

REFERENCES

Adams, F. (1990). *Special education in the 1990s*. Harlow: Longman.

Aiello, A. D., Di Cori, P., Marchetti, L., Pontecorvo, C., & Rossi Doria, M. (2002). *La scuola deve cambiare*. Napoli: L'Ancora.

Ainscow, M. (1993). Teacher education as a strategy for developing inclusive schools. In R. Slee (Ed.), *Is there a desk with my name on it? The politics of integration*. London, Washington, DC: The Falmer Press.

Ainscow, M. (1994). *Special needs in the classroom: A teacher education guide*. London: Jessica Kingsley/UNESCO.

Ainscow, M. (1997). Towards inclusive schooling. *British Journal of Special Education, 24*, 3–6.

Ainscow, M. (1999). *Understanding the development of inclusive schools*. London: Falmer.

Ainscow, M. (2000). The next step for special education. Supporting the development of inclusive practices. *British Journal of Special Education, 27*, 76–80.

Ainscow, M. (2003). Using teacher development to foster inclusive classroom practices. In T. Booth, K. Nes, & M. Stromstad (Eds.), *Developing inclusive teacher education*. London and New York: RoutledgeFalmer.

Ainscow, M. (2005). Developing inclusive education systems: What are the levers for change? *Journal of Educational Change, 6*, 109–124.

Ainscow, M. (2007). Taking an inclusive turn. *Journal of Research in Special Educational Needs, 7*, 3–7.

Ainscow, M., & Booth, T. (Eds.). (1998). *From them to us: An international study of inclusion in education*. London: Routledge.

Ainscow, M., Booth, T., & Dyson, A. (2006). *Improving schools, developing inclusion*. London, New York: Routledge.

Ainscow, M., Howes, A., Farrell, P., & Frankham, J. (2003). Making sense of the development of inclusive practices. *European Journal of Special Needs Education, 18*, 227–242.

Ainscow, M., Muijs, D., & West, M. (2006). Collaboration as a strategy for improving schools in challenging circumstances. *Improving Schools, 9*, 192–202.

Allan, J. (1996). Foucault and special educational needs: A 'box of tools' for analysing children's experiences of mainstreaming. *Disability and Society, 11*, 219–233.

Allan, J. (1999). *Actively seeking inclusion. Pupils with special needs in mainstream schools*. London: Falmer Press.

Allan, J. (Ed.). (2003). *Inclusion, participation and democracy: What is the purpose?* Dordrecht, Boston, London: Kluwer Academic Publishers.

Allan, J. (2005). Inclusion as an ethical project. In S. Tremain (Ed.), *Foucault and the government of disability*. United States of America: University of Michigan.

Allen, B. (2005). Foucault's nominalism. In S. Tremain (Ed.), *Foucault and the government of disability*. United States of America: University of Michigan.

Althusser, L. (1971). Ideology and the ideological state apparatuses. In *Lenin and philosophy and other essays*. New York: Monthly Review Press.

Altman, M. B. (2001). Disability, definitions, models, classification schemes, and applications. In L. Albrecht, G. K. D. Seelman, & M. Bury (Eds.), *Handbook of disability studies*. Thousand Oaks, London, New Delhi: Sage Publications.

Apple, M. (1990). *Ideology and curriculum*. New York - London: Routledge.

Apple, M. (2000). *Official knowledge. Democratic education in a conservative age*. New York, London: Routledge.

Apple, M. (2006). *Educating the 'Right way: Markets, standards, god, and inequality*. New York and London: Routledge.

Apple, M. (2008). The tasks of the critical scholar/activist in education. In R. Winkle-Wagner, D. Orloff Henterliter, & C. Hunter (Eds.), *Methods at the margins*. New York: Palgrave (in press).

REFERENCES

Apple, M., & Beane, A. J. (Eds.). (1999). *Democratic schools. Lessons from the chalk face.* Buckingham: Open University Press.
Aprea, V. (2002). *Inserimento e integrazione delle persone handicappate nella scuola.* Roma: Commissione Bicamerale Infanzia.
Arksey, H., & Knight, P. (1999). *Interviewing for social scientists.* London, Thousand Oaks, New Delhi: Sage Publications.
Armstrong, D. (1998). Changing faces, changing places: Policy routes to inclusion. In P. Clough (Ed.), *Managing inclusive education. From policy to experience* (pp. 31–47). London: Paul Chapman Publishing.
Armstrong, D. (1999). Histories of inclusion: Perspectives on the history of special education. In L. Barton & F. Armstrong (Eds.), *Difference and difficulty: Insights, issues and dilemmas.* Sheffield: University of Sheffield.
Armstrong, D. (2003). *Experiences of special education. Re-evaluating policy and practice through life stories.* London: Routledge.
Armstrong, D. (2005). Reinventing 'inclusion'. New labour and the cultural politics of special education. *Oxford Review of Education, 31,* 135–151.
Armstrong, F. (1998a). Curricula, 'Management' and special and inclusive education. In P. Clough (Ed.), *Managing inclusive education. From policy to experience* (pp. 48–63). London: Paul Chapman Publishing.
Armstrong, F. (1998b). The curriculum as alchemy: School and the struggle for cultural space. *Curriculum Studies, 6,* 145–160.
Armstrong, F. (1999). Comparative perspectives on difference and difficulty: A cross-cultural approach. In L. Barton & F. Armstrong (Eds.), *Difference and difficulty: Insights, issues and dilemmas.* Sheffield: University of Sheffield.
Armstrong, F. (2002a). The historical development of special education: Humanitarian rationality or 'wild profusion of entangled events'? *History of Education, 31,* 437–456.
Armstrong, F. (2002b). Managing difference: Inclusion, performance and power. *Critical Quarterly, 44,* 51–56.
Armstrong, F. (2003a). Difference, discourse and democracy: The making and breaking of policy in the market place. *International Journal of Inclusive Education, 7,* 241–257.
Armstrong, F. (2003b). *Spaced out: Policy, difference and the challenge of inclusive education.* Dordrecht-Boston-London: Kluwer Academic Publishers.
Armstrong, F. (2007). Disability, education and social change since 1960. *History of Education, 36,* 551–568.
Armstrong, F., Armstrong, D., & Barton, L. (Eds.). (2000). *Inclusive education. Policy, contexts and comparative perspectives.* London: David Fulton Publisher.
Armstrong, F., & Barton, L. (Eds.). (1999). *Disability, human rights and education. Cross-cultural perspectives.* Buckingham: Open University Press.
Armstrong, F., & Barton, L. (2001). Disability, education and inclusion. In L. Albrecht, G. D. Seelman, K. & M. Bury (Eds.), *Handbook of disability studies* (pp. 693–710). Thousand Oaks, London, New Delhi: Sage Publications.
Armstrong, F., & Moore, M. (Eds.). (2004). *Action research for inclusive education: Changing places, changing practices, changing minds.* London: Routledge Falmer.
Arnot, M., & Reay, D. (2007). A sociology of pedagogic voice: Power, inequality and pupil consultation. *Discourse: studies in the cultural politics of education, 28,* 311–325.
Aspis, S. (1997). Self-advocacy for people with learning difficulties: Does it have a future? *Disability and Society, 12,* 647–654.
Ball, S. J. (1987). *The micro-politics of the school. Towards a theory of school organisation.* London: Methuen.
Ball, S. J. (1990). *Politics and policy making in education. Explorations in policy sociology.* London: Routledge.
Ball, S. J. (1993). What is policy? Texts, trajectories and toolboxes. *Discourse, 132,* 10–17.

Ball, S. J. (1994). Some reflections on policy theory: A brief response to Hatcher and Troyna. *Journal of Education Policy, 9*, 171–182.

Ball, S. J. (1998). Educational studies, policy entrepreneurship and social theory. In R. Slee, G. Weiner, & S. Tomlinson (Eds.), *School effectiveness for whom?* London: Falmer Press.

Ballard, K. (2003). The analysis of context. Some thoughts on teacher education, culture, colonisation and inequality. In T. Booth, K. Nes, & M. Stromstad (Eds.), *Developing inclusive teacher education*. London and New York: RoutledgeFalmer.

Barbieri, P. (2007). *Welfare e democrazia: tra partecipazione ed esclusione*. Paper presented at the Stati Generali della Disabilità, Rome.

Barnes, C. (1991). *Disabled people in Britain and Discrimination: A case for anti-discrimination legislation*. London: Hurst.

Barnes, C. (1997). A legacy of oppression: A history of disability in western culture. In L. Barton & M. Oliver (Eds.), *Disability studies: Past, present and future*. Leeds: The Disability Press.

Barnes, C. (2003a). Rehabilitation for disabled people: A 'Sick' Joke? *Scandinavian Journal of Research, 5*, 7–24.

Barnes, C. (2003b). What a difference a decade makes: Reflections on doing 'emancipatory' disability research. *Disability and Society, 18*, 3–17.

Barnes, C., & Mercer, G. (Eds.). (2005). *The social model of disability: Europe and the majority world*. Leeds: The Disability Press.

Barnes, C., Mercer, G., & Shakespeare, T. (1999). *Exploring disability. A sociological introduction*. Cambridge: Polity Press.

Barnes, C., Oliver, M., & Barton, L. (Eds.). (2002). *Disability studies today*. Cambridge: Polity Press.

Barthes, R. (1993). *Mythologies* (A. Lavers, Trans.). London: Vintage Books.

Barton, L. (1986). The politics of special educational needs. *Disability, Handicap & Society, 1*, 273–290.

Barton, L. (1998). Markets, managerialism and inclusive education. In P. Clough (Ed.), *Managing inclusive education. From policy to experience* (pp. 78–91). London: Paul Chapman Publishing.

Barton, L. (Ed.). (2001a). *Disability, politics and the struggle for change*. London: David Fulton.

Barton, L. (2001b). Disability, struggle and the politics of hope. In L. Barton (Ed.), *Disability, politics and the struggle for change*. London: David Fulton.

Barton, L. (2003). *Inclusive education and teacher education: A basis of hope or a discourse of delusion*. London: Institute of Education, University of London.

Barton, L. (2005a). Emancipatory research and disabled people: Some observations and questions'. *Educational Review, 57*, 317–327.

Barton, L. (2005b). *Special educational needs: An alternative look*. Centre for Disability Studies, Leeds University. Retrieved May 1, 2008, from http://www.leeds.ac.uk/disability-studies/archiveuk/barton/Warnock.pdf

Barton, L. (2008). Social justice, human rights and inclusive education. In G. Richards & F. Armstrong (Eds.), *Key issues for teaching assistants. Working in diverse and inclusive classrooms*. London and New York: Routledge.

Barton, L., & Armstrong, F. (Eds.). (2007). *Policy, experience and change: Cross-cultural reflections on inclusive education*. Dordrecht: Springer.

Barton, L., & Oliver, M. (1992). Special needs: A personal trouble or public issue? In M. Arnot & L. Barton (Eds.), *Voicing concerns: Sociological perspectives on contemporary education reforms*. Oxford: Triangle Books.

Barton, L., & Oliver, M. (Eds.). (1997). *Disability studies: Past, present and future*. Leeds: Disability Press.

Barton, L., & Slee, R. (1999). Competition, selection and inclusive education: Some observations. *International Journal of Inclusive Education, 3*, 3–12.

Barton, L., & Tomlinson, S. (Eds.). (1981). *Special education: Policy, practices and social issues*. London: Harper and Row Publishers.

Bassey, M. (1999). *Case study research in educational settings*. Maidenhead - Philadelphia: Open University Press.

Begum, N. (1992). Disabled women and the feminist agenda. *Feminist Review, 40*, 70–84.

REFERENCES

Benadusi, L., & Consoli, F. (Eds.). (2004). *La governance della scuola. Istruzioni e soggetti alla prova dell'autonomia*. Bologna: Il Mulino.

Benjamin, S. (2001). *Student identity work and the micro/politics of 'Special educational needs' in a girls' comprehensive school*. Unpublished Ph.D Thesis, Institute of Education, University of London, London.

Benjamin, S. (2003). *The micropolitics of inclusive education. An ethnography*. Buckingham, Philadelphia: Open University Press.

Bickenback, J., Chatterji, S., Bradley, E. M., & Ustun, T. B. (1999). Models of disablement, universalism and the international classification of impairments, disabilities and handicaps. *Social Science and Medicine, 48*, 1173–1187.

Bickenback, J. E. (2001). Disability human rights, law, and policy. In L. Albrecht, D. Seelman, & M. Bury (Eds.), *Handbook of disability studies* (pp. 565–583). Thousand Oaks, London, New Delhi: Sage Publications.

Bobbio, N. (1990). *L'età dei diritti*. Torino: Einaudi.

Boggs, C. (1976). *Gramsci's marxism*. London: Pluto Press.

Booth, T. (1982). Integration Italian style. In C. Gravell & J. Pettit (Eds.), *National perspectives. Unit 10*. Milton Keynes: The Open University.

Booth, T. (1995). Mapping inclusion and exclusion: Concept for all? In C. Clark, A. Dyson, & A. Millward (Eds.), *Towards inclusive schools?* London: David Fulton Publishers.

Booth, T. (1996). Stories of exclusion. Natural and unnatural selection. In E. Blyth & R. J. Milner (Eds.), *Exclusion from school. Inter-professional issues for policy and practice* (pp. 21–36). London, New York: Routledge.

Booth, T. (2000). Inclusion and exclusion policy in England: Who controls the agenda? In D. Armstrong, F. Armstrong, & L. Barton (Eds.), *Inclusive education policy, contexts and comparative perspectives*. London: David Fulton Publisher.

Booth, T., & Ainscow, M. (2000). *Index for inclusion. Developing learning and participation in schools*. Bristol: Centre for Studies on Inclusive Education (CSIE).

Booth, T., & Ainscow, M. (2002). *Index for inclusion. Developing learning and participation in schools* (Rev. ed.). Bristol: Centre for Studies on Inclusive Education (CSIE).

Booth, T., Nes, K., & Stromstad, M. (Eds.). (2003). *Developing inclusive teacher education*. London, New York: RoutledgeFalmer.

Borg, C., Buttigieg, J., & Mayo, P. (Eds.). (2002). *Gramsci and education*. Lanham, Boulder, New York, Oxford: Rowman & Littlefield Publishers.

Borghi, L. (Ed.). (1984). *L'educazione attiva oggi: un bilancio critico*. Firenze: La Nuova Italia.

Brown, A., & Dowling, P. (1998). *Doing research/reading research: A mode of interrogation for education*. London, Washington, DC: The Falmer Press.

Brown, S. C. (2003). Vers une taxonomie du handicap et des droits de l'homme. *Handicap. Revue de sciences humaines et sociales, 100*, 1–17.

Bruner, J. (1996). *The culture of education*. Cambridge, MA: Harvard University Press.

Bruner, J. S. (1972). *The relevance of education*. London: Allen, Unwin.

Burgio, A. (2007). *Per Gramsci. Crisi e potenza del moderno*. Roma: DeriveApprodi.

Burke, B. (1999). *Antonio Gramsci and informal education*. The Encyclopedia of Informal Education (online). Retrieved May 5, 2008, from http://www.infed.org/thinkers/et-gram.htm

Burman, E. (2006). Emotions and reflexivity in feminised education action research. *Educational Action Research, 14*, 315–332.

Bury, M. (2000). A comment on the ICIDH2. *Disability and Society, 15*, 1073–1077.

Buzzi, M. I. (1993). Handicap e Europa: verso paradigmi comuni di integrazione. *Valore Scuola, 188*, 3–7.

Caldin, R. (2004). Abitare la complessità: insegnanti e processi inclusivi. *L'integrazione scolastica e sociale, 3*, 114–123.

Cambi, F. (2005). *Le pedagogie del novecento*. Roma, Bari: Laterza.

Campbell, C. (Ed.). (2002). *Developing inclusive schooling: Perspectives, policies and practices*. London: Institute of Education.

Campbell, C., Gillborn, D., Lunt, I., Sammons, P., Vincent, C., Warren, S., et al. (2001). Developments in inclusive schooling: Scottish executive education department.

Canevaro, A. (Ed.). (1983). *Handicap e scuola. Manuale per l'integrazione scolastica.* Urbino: Nuova Italia Scientifica.

Canevaro, A. (1986). Introduzione. In P. Zanelli (Ed.), *Uno sfondo per integrare. Progettazione didattica, integrazione e strategie di apprendimento* (pp. 9–16). Bologna: Cappelli editore.

Canevaro, A. (1997). Le prospettive dell'integrazione. *HP - Accaparlante, 59,* 2–5.

Canevaro, A. (1999a). Alla ricerca degli indicatori della qualità dell'integrazione. In D. Ianes & M. Tortello (Eds.), *La qualità dell'integrazione scolastica* (pp. 21–29). Trento: Erickson.

Canevaro, A. (1999b). *Pedagogia speciale. La riduzione dell'handicap.* Milano: Bruno Mondadori.

Canevaro, A. (2001). L'Integrazione in Italia. In S. Nocera (Ed.), *Il diritto all'integrazione nella scuola dell'autonomia. Gli alunni in situazione di handicap nella normativa italiana* (pp. 209–223). Trento: Erickson.

Canevaro, A. (2002). Il progetto Moratti per la riforma: scuola superiore e formazione professionale. *L'integrazione scolastica e sociale, 1,* 229–234.

Canevaro, A. (2002). *Pedagogical, psychological and sociological aspects of the Italian model. A methodological preamble.* Paper presented at the Mainstreaming in Education, Rome.

Canevaro, A. (2004). Handicappati. Davvero non abbiamo fatto niente? In A. Canevaro & M. Mandato (Eds.), *L'Integrazione e la prospettiva 'inclusiva'.* Roma: Monolite Editrice.

Canevaro, A. (2006a). Integrazione scolastica: aspetti pedagogici, psicologici e sociologici del modello italiano. In G. Solidarietà (Ed.), *Disabilità dalla Scuola al Lavoro.* Jesi (Ancona): Gruppo Solidarietà.

Canevaro, A. (2006b). *Le logiche del confine e del sentiero. Una pedagogia dell'inclusione (per tutti, disabili inclusi).* Trento: Erickson.

Canevaro, A. (2006c). *L'inclusione competente.* Pedagogia Speciale (online). Retrieved May 5, 2008, from http://www.pedagogiaspeciale.it/Materiali-inclusionecompetente.htm

Canevaro, A. (Ed.). (2007). *L'integrazione scolastica degli alunni con disabilità.* Trento: Erickson.

Canevaro, A. (2008). La diagnosi come indicatore di modello sociale. *Integrazione scolastica e sociale, 7,* 15–18.

Canevaro, A., Cocever, E., & Weis, P. (1996). *Le ragioni dell'integrazione.* Torino: UTET.

Canevaro, A., & Gaudreau, J. (1993). *L'educazione degli handicappati. Dai primi tentativi alla pedagogia moderna.* Roma: NIS.

Canevaro, A., & Ianes, D. (Eds.). (2001). *Buone prassi di integrazione scolastica. 20 realizzazioni efficaci.* Trento: Erickson.

Canevaro, A., & Ianes, D. (2003). *Diversabilità. Storie di dialoghi nell'anno europeo delle persone disabili.* Trento: Erickson.

Canevaro, A. & Ianes, D. (2008). *L'integrazione scolastica. Tendenze, strategie operative e 100 buone prassi.* Trento: Erickson

Canevaro, A., & Malaguti, E. (2002). A proposito di ICF: quali prospettive e scenari? Dialogo tra Andrea ed Elena. *Integrazione scolastica e sociale, 1,* 434–440.

Canevaro, A., & Mandato, M. (2004). *L'integrazione e la prospettiva 'inclusiva'.* Rome: Monolite Editrice.

Carabine, J. (2001). Unmarried motherhood 1830–1990: A genealogical analysis. In M. Wetherell, S. Taylor, & J. Simeon (Eds.), *Discourse as data. A guide for analysis.* London: The Open University.

CDH Bologna & CDH Modena. (Eds.). (2003). *Bambini, imparate a fare le cose difficili. Alunni disabili e integrazione scolastica di qualità.* Trento: Erickson.

Charlton, I. J. (1998). *Nothing about us without us: Disability oppression and empowerment.* Berkeley, Los Angeles, London: University of California Press.

Cigman, R. (Ed.). (2007). *Included or excluded? The challenge of the mainstream for some SEN children.* London and New York: Routledge.

Clough, P. (Ed.). (1998). *Managing inclusive education: From policy to experience.* London: Paul Chapman Publishing.

Clough, P., & Barton, L. (2000). *Articulating with difficulties. Research voices in inclusive education.* London: Paul Chapman Publishing.

REFERENCES

Clough, P., & Corbett, J. (2000). *Theories of inclusive education. A student's guide*. London: Paul Chapman Publishing.

Clough, P. T. (1992). *The end(s) of ethnography: From realism to social criticism*. Newbury Park, CA: Sage.

Codd, J. A. (1999). The construction and deconstruction of educational policy documents. In J. Marshall & M. Peters (Eds.), *Education policy*. Cheltenham, UK - Northampton, MA, USA: The Elgar Reference Collection.

Coffey, A. (1999). *The ethnographic self. Fieldwork and the representation of identity*. London, Thousand Oaks, New Delhi: Sage Publications.

Coffey, A. (2001). *Education and social change*. Buckingham: Open University Press.

Coffey, A., & Atkinson, P. (1996). *Making sense of qualitative data*. Thousand Oaks, London, New Delhi: SAGE.

Cohen, L., Manion, L., & Morrison, K. (2000). *Research methods in education* (5th ed.). London: Routledge.

Colic-Peisker, V. (2004). Doing ethnography in 'One's own ethnic community. In L. Hume & J. Mulcock (Eds.), *Anthropologists in the field: Cases in participant observation*. New York: Columbia University Press.

Corbett, J. (1996). *Bad mouthing*. London: Falmer Press.

Corbett, J. (2001). *Supporting inclusive education: A connective pedagogy*. London: RoutledgeFalmer.

Corbett, J., & Norwich, B. (1999). Learners with special educational needs. In P. Mortimore (Ed.), *Understanding pedagogy and its impact on learning*. London: Paul Chapman Publishing Ltd.

Corbett, J., & Slee, R. (2000). An international conversation on inclusive education. In D. Armstrong, F. Armstrong, & L. Barton (Eds.), *Inclusive education. Policy, contexts and comparative perspectives*. London: David Fulton.

Corker, M. (2000). The U.K. disability discrimination act. Disabling language, justifying inequitable social participation. In L. P. Francis & A. Silvers (Eds.), *Americans with disabilities. Exploring implications of the law for individuals and institutions*. New York, London: Routledge.

Corker, M., & French, S. (Eds.). (1999). *Disability discourse*. Buckingham, Philadelphia: Open University Press.

Cornoldi, C., & Vianello, R. (1989). *Handicap, memoria e apprendimento*. Bergamo: Juvenilia.

Cornoldi, C., & Vianello, R. (1990). *Handicap, autonomia e socializzazione*. Bergamo: Juvenilia.

Cornoldi, C., & Vianello, R. (1995). *Handicap e apprendimento*. Bergamo: Junior.

Crow, L. (1996). Including all of our lives: Renewing the social model of disability. In C. Barnes & G. Mercer (Eds.), *Exploring the divide* (pp. 55–72). Leeds: The Disability Press.

Cummins, J. (2003). Challenging the construction of difference as deficit: Where are identity, intellect, imagination, and power in the new tegime of truth? In P. Trifonas (Ed.), *Pedagogies of difference*. New York, London: RoutledgeFalmer.

D'Alessio, S. (2002). Osservazioni sull'utilizzo dell'ICF nei Paesi intervenuti al seminario della Commissione Europea. *L'integrazione scolastica e sociale, 1*, 452–455.

D'Alessio, S. (2004). L'Europa e la sfida dell'inclusione scolastica. *No Limits - Il mensile senza barriere, 11*, 39–40.

D'Alessio, S. (2005). Inclusive education ed integrazione scolastica: alcune riflessioni. *Innovazione Educativa, 3*, 12–16.

D'Alessio, S. (2006). Disabilità e certificazione: una nuova prospettiva. *Innovazione Educativa, 5–6*, 22–28.

D'Alessio, S. (2007a). Made in Italy: Integrazione scolastica and the new vision of inclusive education. In L. Barton & F. Armstrong (Eds.), *Policy, experience and change: Cross cultural reflections on inclusive education*. Dordrecht, Boston, London: Springer.

D'Alessio, S. (2007b). Prospettive di cambiamento: dall'integrazione scolastica all'inclusive education. *L'integrazione scolastica e sociale, 6*, 342–365.

D'Alessio, S. (2009). L'integration scolaire en Italie. Quelques réflexions pour le développement de l'éducation inclusive in La nouvelle revue de l'adaptation et de la scolarisation (IN SHEA Revue). Hors Série n. 5, 35–50.

D'Alessio, S. (2009b). La formazione iniziale degli insegnanti da una prospettiva inclusiva. Recenti sviluppi in ambito europeo. *RicercAzione*, 2, 193–208

D'Alessio, S., & Watkins, A. (2009). International comparisons of inclusive policy and practice: Are we talking about the same thing? *Research in Comparative and International Education Journal*, 4(3), 233–249.

D'Alessio, S., Watkins, A. and Donnelly, V. (in press) Inclusive education across Europe: the move in thinking from integration to inclusion in *Revista de Psicología y Educación* Madrid. Universidad Complutense Madrid

D'Alonso, L., & Ianes, D. (2007). L'integrazione scolastica dal 1977 al 2007: i primi risultati di una ricerca attraverso lo sguardo delle famiglie. In A. Canevaro (Ed.), *L'integrazione scolastica degli alunni con disabilità*. Trento: Erickson.

Daniels, H. (2006). The dangers of corruption in special needs education. *British Journal of Special Education*, 33, 4–9.

Davies, A. C. (1999). *Reflexive ethnography*. London and New York: Routledge.

Davis, J., & Watson, N. (2000). Disabled children's rights in every day life: Problematising notions of competency and promoting self-empowerment. *The International Journal of Children's Rights*, 8, 211–228.

de Anna, L. (1983). *Aspetti normativi dell'inserimento sociale degli handicappati in Italia e all'estero*. Roma: Tempinuovi.

de Anna, L. (1997). Pedagogical, curricular and classroom organisation in Italy'. In OECD (Ed.), *Implementing inclusive education* (pp. 91–95). Paris: OECD.

de Anna, L. (1998). *Pedagogia speciale. I bisogni educativi speciali*. Milano: Guerino.

de Anna, L. (2000). Généalogie de l'intégration scolaire en Italie. In M. Chauviére & E. Plaisance (Eds.), *L'école face aux handicaps* (pp. 133–147). Paris: Presses Universitaires de France.

de Anna, L. (2002a). Educazione, ineguaglianza ed esclusione sociale: qual è attualmente la conoscenza dell'ICF in Europa? *Integrazione scolastica e sociale*, 1, 449–455.

de Anna, L. (2002b). La riforma Moratti e l'integrazione scolastica degli alunni in situazione di handicap. *L'integrazione scolastica e sociale*, 1, 11–14.

de Anna, L. (2003). Un enfant gravement handicapé à l'école. In B. Belmont & A. Vérillon (Eds.), *Diversité et handicap à l'école. Quelles pratiques éducatives pour tous?* (pp. 37–59). Paris: CTNERHI - INRP.

de Anna, L. (2007). Le politiche di inclusione in Europa e in Italia, dalla scuola di base all'università. In A. Canevaro (Ed.), *L'integrazione scolastica degli alunni con disabilità* (pp. 75–84). Trento: Erickson.

Denzin, K. N. (1997). *Interpretive ethnography. Ethnographic practices for the 21st century*. Thousand Oaks, London, New Delhi: Sage Publications.

Department for Education and Employment. (1997). *Excellence for all children. Meeting special educational needs*. London: DfEE.

Department for Education and Skills. (2001). *Special educational needs: Code of practice*. London: DfES.

Department for Education and Skills. (2004a). *Every child matters: Change for children in schools*. London: DfES.

Department for Education and Skills. (2004b). *Removing barriers to achievement: The government's strategy for SEN*. London: DfES.

Dessent, T. (1987). *Making the ordinary school special*. London, New York, Philadelphia: The Falmer Press.

DPI. (2005a). *DPI position paper on inclusive education*. New York: DPI.

DPI. (2005b). *DPI position paper on the definition of disability*. New York: DPI.

Drake, F. R. (1999). *Understanding disability policies*. Houndsmills, Bakinstoke: Macmillan.

Dyson, A. (1999). Inclusion and inclusions': Theories and discourses in inclusive education. In H. Daniels & P. Garner (Eds.), *Inclusive education*. London: Kogan Page.

Dyson, A. (2003). Making space in the standards Agenda: Developing inclusive practices in schools. *European Educational Research Journal*, 2, 228–244.

Dyson, A., & Millward, A. (2000). *Schools and special needs. Issues of innovation and inclusion*. London: Paul Chapman Publishing Ltd.

REFERENCES

EDF. (2004). *In review: 2003 the European year of people with disabilities* (Bulletin ed.). Brussels: European Disability Forum.

Ellis, C., & Bochner, A. P. (2000). Autoethnography, personal narrative, reflexivity. Researcher as subject. In K. Denzin, N., & S. Lincoln (Eds.), *Handbook of qualitative research*. Thousand Oaks, London, New Delhi: Sage Publications.

Evans, J., & Lunt, I. (2002). Inclusive education: are there limits? *European Journal of Special Needs Education, 17*, 1–14.

Farrell, P. (2000). The impact of research on developments in inclusive education. *International Journal of Inclusive Education, 4*, 153–162.

Fendler, L. (1998). What is it impossible to think? A genealogy of the educated subject. In S. Popkewitz, T., & M. Brennan (Eds.), *Foucault's challenge. Discourse, knowledge, and power in education*. New York, London: Teachers College Press.

Fielding, M. (2001). Students as radical agents of change. *Journal of Educational Change, 2*, 123–141.

Fiorin, I. (2007). La scuola luogo di relazioni e apprendimenti significativi. In A. Canevaro (Ed.), *L'integrazione scolastica degli alunni con disabilità* (pp. 129–157). Trento: Erickson.

Fioroni, G. (2006). *Audizione del Ministro dell'Istruzione Giuseppe Fioroni VII Commissione Cultura, Scienza e Istruzione*. Camera dei Deputati, Rome: Ministero per la Pubblica Istruzione.

Flood, T. (2005). 'Food' or 'Thought'? The social model and the majority world. In C. Barnes & G. Mercer (Eds.), *The social model of disability: Europe and the majority world* (pp. 180–192). Leeds: The Disability Press.

Fornasa, W., & Medeghini, R. (2003). *Abilità differenti. Processi educativi, co-educazione e percorsi delle differenze*. Milano: FrancoAngeli.

Foucault, M. (1970). *The order of things: An archeology of the human sciences*. London: Tavistock Publications.

Foucault, M. (1972). *The archeology of knowledge*. New York: Pantheon.

Foucault, M. (1977). *Discipline and punish* (A. Lane, Trans.). London: Penguin.

Foucault, M. (1978). *The history of sexuality. An introduction* (R. Hurley, Trans., Vol. 1). London: Penguin.

Foucault, M. (1980). 'Two lectures'. In C. Gordon (Ed.), *Power-knowledge: Selected interviews and other writings 1972–1977* (pp. 78–108). Brighton: The Harvester Press.

Foucault, M. (1982). The subject and power. In L. Dreyfus & P. Rabinow (Eds.), *Michel Foucault: Beyond structuralism and hermeneutics. With an afterword by Michel Foucault*. Brighton: The Harvester Press.

Foucault, M. (1988a). On power. In D. Kritzman, Lawrence (Ed.), *Michel Foucault. Politics, philosophy, culture. Interviews and other writings, 1977–1984*. London: Routledge.

Foucault, M. (1988b). Politics and reason. In D. Kritzman, Lawrence (Ed.), *Michel Foucault. Politics, philosophy, culture. Interviews and other writings, 1977–1984* (pp. 57–85). New York, London: Routledge.

Foucault, M. (2003). *Abnormal. Lectures at the Collège de France, 1974–1975* (G. Burchell, Trans.). London, New York: Verso.

Fraser, N. (1996). *Social justice in the age of identity politics: Redistribution, recognition and participation*. Stanford University: The Tanner Lectures on Human Values.

Freire, P. (1985). *The politics of education: Culture power and liberation*. London: Macmillan.

Freire, P. (1996). *Pedagogy of the oppressed* (B. M. Ramos, Trans., New Revised 20th Anniversary ed.). New York: Continuum.

French, S. (1993). Disability, impairment or something in-between. In J. Swain, V. Finkelstein, S. French, & M. Oliver (Eds.), *Disabling barriers - Enabling environments*. London: Sage (in association with The Open University).

Fulcher, G. (1989). *Disabling policies? A comparative approach to education policy and disability*. London, New York, Philadelphia: The Falmer Press.

Galloway, D., Armstrong, D., & Tomlinson, S. (1994). *The assessment of special educational needs: Whose problem?* London and New York: Longman.

Gaspari, P. (1999). L'identikit della Pedagogia Speciale. In D. Ianes & M. Tortello (Eds.), *Handicap e risorse per l'integrazione. Nuovi elementi di Qualità per una scuola inclusiva* (pp. 90–93). Trento: Erickson.

Gelati, M. (2004). *Pedagogia speciale e integrazione. Dal pregiudizio agli interventi educativi*. Roma: Carocci.

Giacobini, C. (2005). Sopra la panca. *Mobilità, 41*, 1.

Gibson, S. (2006). Beyond a 'culture of silence': Inclusive education and the liberation of 'voice'. *Disability and Society, 21*, 315–329.

Giddens, A. (1997). *Oltre la destra e la sinistra* (P. Palminiello, Trans.). Bologna: Il Mulino.

Giddens, A. (2007). *L'Europa nell'età globale* (F. Galimberti, Trans.). Roma, Bari: Laterza.

Giovanni Paolo II. (2000). *Giubileo della comunità con i disabili*. Vatican speeches: (online). Retrieved May 25, 2008, from http://www.vatican.va/holy_father/john_paul_ii/speeches/documents/hf_jp-ii_spe_20001203_jubildisabled_it.html

Giroux, H. A. (2001). *Theory and resistance in education: Towards a pedagogy for the opposition*. Westport, CT, London: Bergin & Garvey.

GLAD. (2000). *Reclaiming the social model of disability*. London: Great London Action on Disability (GLAD).

Glaser, B. G., & Strauss, A. L. (1967). *The discovery of grounded theory: Strategies for qualitative research*. Chicago: Aldine.

Goodley, B., & Moore, M. (2000), Doing disability research: Activist lives and the academy. *Disability and Society, 15*, 861–882.

Goodley, D. (1997). Locating self-advocacy in models of disability: Understanding disability in the support of self-advocates with learning difficulties. *Disability and Society, 12*, 367–379.

Goodley, D. (2005). Empowerment, self-advocacy and resilience. *Journal of Intellectual Disabilities, 9*, 333–343.

Gramsci, A. (1952). *Gli intellettuali e l'organizzazione della cultura*. Torino: Einaudi.

Gramsci, A. (1970). *The modern prince and other writings* (L. Marks, Trans.). New York: International Publishers.

Gramsci, A. (1971). *Selections from the Prison Notebooks* (Q. Hoare & N. G. Smith, Trans.). London and New York: Lawrence & Wishart.

Hamilton, D. (1999). The pedagogic paradox (or Why No Didactics in England?). *Pedagogy, Culture and Society, 7*, 135–152.

Hanau, C. (2002). Complementarietà dell'ICD e dell'ICF. *Integrazione scolastica e sociale, 1*, 443–448.

Hegarty, S. (1987). *Special needs in ordinary schools: Meeting special needs in ordinary schools*. London: Cassell.

HMSO. (1995). *Disability discrimination act*. London: HMSO.

HMSO. (2001). *Special educational needs and disability act 2001*. London: HMSO.

hooks, b. (1994). *Teaching to transgress. Education as the practice of freedom*. New York, London: Routledge.

House of Commons. (2006). *Education and inspection bill*. London: The Stationery Office Limited.

Hughes, B. (2005). What can a foucauldian analysis contribute to disability theory? In S. Tremain (Ed.), *Foucault and the government of disability*. United States of America: University of Michigan.

Hunt, P. (1966). A critical condition. In P. Hunt (Ed.), *Stigma: The experience of disability* (pp. 145–149). London: Geoffrey Chapman.

Ianes, D. (2001). Il bisogno di una "speciale normalità per l'integrazione". *Difficoltà di Apprendimento, 7*, 157–164.

Ianes, D. (2003). Integrazione scolastica: un intreccio tra speciale e normale. *Rassegna, XI*, Periodico dell'Istituto Pedagogico Provinciale di Bolzano (online). Retrieved May 5, 2008, from http://www.darioianes.it/slide/speciale_normale.pdf

Ianes, D. (2004). *La diagnosi funzionale secondo l'ICF: il modello OMS, le aree e gli strumenti*. Trento: Erickson.

REFERENCES

Ianes, D. (2005). *Bisogni Educativi Speciali e inclusione. Valutare le reali necessità e attivare le risorse.* Trento: Erickson.

Ianes, D. (2006). *La speciale normalità.* Trento: Erickson.

Ianes, D. (2007). *The Italian model for the inclusion and integration of students with special needs; some issues.* Dario Ianes (online). Retrieved May 5, 2008, from http://www.darioianes.it/focus4a.htm

Ianes, D. (2008). Due prospettive strategiche sul tema della Diagnosi Funzionale e della lettura dei bisogni. *Integrazione scolastica e sociale, 7,* 9–15.

Ianes, D., & Banal, S. (2002). Descrizione dello strumento. *Integrazione scolastica e sociale, 1,* 422–433.

Ianes, D., & Biasoli, U. (2005). L'ICF come strumento di identificazione, descrizione e comprensione delle competenze. Un'esperienza in un percorso di alternanza scuola-lavoro. *Integrazione scolastica e sociale, 4,* 391–422.

Ianes, D., & Canevaro, A., (2008), *L'integrazione scolastica. Tendenze, strategie operative e 100 buone prassi. Collana Facciamo il punto su ....* Trento: Erickson

Ianes, D., & Cramerotti, S. (Eds.). (2007). *Il Piano Educativo Individualizzato - Progetto di vita.* Trento: Erickson.

Ianes, D., & Tortello, M. (Eds.). (1999). *Handicap e risorse per l'integrazione. Nuovi elementi di Qualità per una scuola inclusiva.* Trento: Erickson.

Imrie, R. (2004). Demystifying disability: A review of the international classification of functioning, disability and health. *Sociology of Health & Illness, 26,* 287–305.

Iosa, R. (2000). *Relazione al Parlamento sullo Stato di Attuazione della Legge Quadro dei Diritti delle Persone in Situazione di Handicap. Legge 5.2.1992, n. 104, art. 41, comma 2.* Rome: Ministero Pubblica Istruzione.

Iosa, R. (2008). Fenomenologia e patologia della certificazione di handicap. *Integrazione scolastica e sociale, 7,* 28–33.

Jordan, L., & Goodey, C. (1996). *Human rights and school change. The Newham story.* Bristol: Centre for Studies on Inclusive Education (CSIE).

Kenway, J. (1990). Education and the right's discursive politics. Private versus state schooling. In S. Ball, J., (Ed.), *Foucault and education. Disciplines and knowledge.* London, New York: Routledge.

Kuhn, T. S. (1970). *The structure of scientific revolutions.* Chicago: University of Chicago Press.

Larocca, F. (2007). Integrazione/inclusione in Italia. In A. Canevaro (Ed.), *L'integrazione scolastica degli alunni con disabilità* (pp. 39–57). Trento: Erickson.

Liggett, H. (1988). Stars not born: An interpretive approach to the politics of disability. *Disability, Handicap & Society, 3,* 263–275.

Lindsay, G. (2003). Inclusive education: A critical perspective. *British Journal of Special Education, 30,* 3–12.

Llewellyn, A., & Hogan, K. (2000). The use and abuse of models of disability. *Disability and Society, 15,* 157–165.

Lloyd, C. (2000). Excellence for all children - false promises. The failure of current policy for inclusive education and implications for schooling in the 21st century. *International Journal of Inclusive Education, 4,* 133–151.

Lunt, I. (2002). The challenge of inclusive schooling for pupils with special educational needs. In C. Campbell (Ed.), *Developing inclusive schooling: Perspectives, policies and practices.* London: Institute of Education.

Lunt, I., & Norwich, B. (1999). *Can effective schools be inclusive schools?* London: Institute of Education.

Malaguti Rossi, E. (2004). *Handicap e rinnovamento della didattica. Esperienze e riflessioni dell' Autonomia.* Roma: Anicia.

Marcus, E. G. (1994). What comes (Just) after 'Post'? The case of ethnography. In K. Denzin, N., & S. Lincoln, Y., (Eds.), *Handbook of qualitative research.* Thousand Oaks, London, New Delhi: Sage Publicatioins.

Marx, K., & Engels, F. (1970). *The German ideology.* London: Lawrence and Wishart.

Matshedisho, R. K. (2005). *Access to higher education for students with sisabilities in South Africa: A tensive intersection of benevolence, rights, and the impasse of the social model of disability.* Unpublished Ph.D Thesis, University of Cape Town, Cape Town.

Maviglia, M. (2008). Vedi alla voce: Integrazione. In G. Onger (Ed.), *Trent'anni di integrazione. Ieri, oggi, domani* (pp. 15–38). Brescia: Vannini Editrice.

McCulloch, G., & Richardson, W. (2000). *Historical research in educational settings.* Buckingham, Philadelphia: Open University Press.

Mckenzie, J.A., (2009*). Constructing the Intellectually Disabled Person as a Subject of Education: a Discourse Analysis Using Q-Methodoloy.* Unpublished PhD Thesis, Rhodes University

Medeghini, R. (2006). *Dalla qualità dell'integrazione all'inclusione. Analisi degli indicatori di qualità per l'inclusione.* Brescia: Vannini Editrice.

Medeghini, R. (2007). *Idee di differenze. Rappresentazioni e prassi per le disabilità nella formazione professionale di Bergamo e provincia.* Brescia: Vannini Editrice.

Medeghini, R. (2008). 'Dall'integrazione all 'inclusione'. In G. Onger (Ed.), *Trent'anni di integrazione. Ieri, oggi, domani.* Brescia: Vannini Editrice.

Medeghini, R., & Valtellina, E. (2006). *Quale disabilità? Culture, modelli e processi di inclusione.* Milano: FrancoAngeli.

Meijer, C., Soriano, V., & Watkins, A. (Eds.). (2003a). *Special needs education in Europe. Provision in post-primary education. Thematic publication.* Middelfart: European Agency for Development in Special Needs Education.

Meijer, C., Soriano, V., & Watkins, A. (Eds.). (2003b). *Special needs education in Europe. Thematic publication.* Middelfart: European Agency for Development in Special Needs Education.

Meijer, C. J. W. (Ed.). (1999). *Financing of special needs education: A seventeen-country study of the relationship between financing of special needs education and inclusion.* Middelfart: European Agency for Development in Special Needs Education.

Meijer, C. J. W. (2003). *Inclusive education and classroom practices. Summary Report.* Middelfart: European Agency for Development in Special Needs Education. Electronic source. Retrieved May 5, 2008, from http://www.european-agency.org/site/info/publications/agency/ereports/04.html

Meijer, C. J. W., & Abbring, I. (1994). Italy. In C. J. W. Meijer, J. S. Pijil, & S. Hegarty (Eds.), *New perspectives in special education. A six-country study of integration.* London, New York: Routledge.

Mercer, G. (2002). Emancipatory disability research. In C. Barnes, M. Oliver, & L. Barton (Eds.), *Disability studies today.* Cambridge: Polity Press.

Ministero della Pubblica Istruzione. (1975). *Relazione conclusiva della Commissione Falcucci concernente i problemi scolastici degli alunni handicappati.* Roma: Ministero della Pubblica Istruzione.

Ministero della Pubblica Istruzione. (2007a). *Indicazioni per il curricolo.* Roma: MPI.

Ministero della Pubblica Istruzione. (2007b). *Piano nazionale di formazione per l'integrazione degli alunni disabili 'I care': Imparare, Comunicare, Agire in una Rete Educativa - anni scolastici 2007/2008 e 2008/2009.* Roma: Ministero della Pubblica Istruzione. Retrieved May 5, 2008, from http://www.pubblica.istruzione.it/normativa/2007/prot1536_07.shtml

Ministero dell'Istruzione Università e Ricerca. (2003). *2003: l'handicap e l'integrazione nella scuola* (Report). Rome: MIUR.

Ministero dell'Istruzione Università e Ricerca. (2005). *La Scuola Statale: Sintesi dei Dati. Anno scolastico 2004–2005.* Rome: Direzione Generale per i Sistemi Informativi.

Ministero Pubblica Istruzione. (2006). *La scuola in cifre. I dati dell'anno scolastico 2005–2006.* Roma: Ministero Pubblica Istruzione.

Ministero dell'Istruzioine, Università e Ricerca (2009). Linee guida per l'integrazione degli alunni con disabilità. MIUR: Roma

Mittler, P. (2000). *Working towards inclusive education.* London: David Fulton.

Montessori, M. (1991). *The advanced Montessori Method - I* (F. Simmonds & L. Hutchinson, Trans.). Oxford: Clio Press.

Moore, A. (2004). *The good teacher. Dominant discourses in teaching and teacher education.* London, New York: RoutledgeFalmer.

REFERENCES

Morgan, J. (2000). Critical pedagogy: The spaces that make the difference. *Pedagogy, Culture and Society, 8*, 273–289.

Morin, E. (2000). *La testa ben fatta. Riforma dell'insegnamento e riforma del pensiero* (S. Lazzari, Trans.). Milano: Raffaello Cortina Editore.

Morin, E. (2001). *I sette saperi necessari all'educazione del futuro.* Milano: Raffaello Cortina Editore.

Morris, J. (1991). *Pride against prejudice. A personal politics of disability.* London: The Women's Press.

Morris, J. (1993). Gender and disability. In J. Swain, V. Finkelstein, S. French, & M. Oliver (Eds.), *Disabling Barriers - Enabling environments.* London: Sage (in association with The Open University).

Morris, J. (1997). Care or empowerment? A disability rights perspective. *Social Policy and Administration, 31*, 54–60.

Mouffe, C. (1979). Hegemony and ideology in Gramsci. In C. Mouffe (Ed.), *Gramsci and Marxist theory.* London, Boston, Henley: Routledge and Kegan Paul.

Mura, A. (2007). Tra welfare state e welfare society: il contributo culturale e sociale dell'associazionismo al processo di integrazione delle persone disabili. In A. Canevaro (Ed.), *L'integrazione scolastica degli alunni con disabilità* (pp. 413–430). Trento: Erickson.

Neri, S. (1999). L'integrazione: una scelta irreversibile della scuola e dell'intera società. In D. Ianes & M. Tortello (Ed.), *Handicap e risorse per l'integrazione. Nuovi elementi di qualità per una scuola inclusiva* (pp. 97–103). Trento: Erickson.

Nicholl, K., & Edwards, R. (2004). Lifelong learning and the sultans of spin: Policy as persuasion? *Journal of Education Policy, 19*, 43–55.

Nind, M., Benjamin, S., Sheehy, K., Collins, J., & Hall, K. (2005). Methodological challenges in researching inclusive school cultures. In K. Sheehy, M. Nind, J. Rix, & K. Simmons (Eds.), *Ethics and research in inclusive education. Values into practice.* London, New York: RoutledgeFalmer.

Nind, M., Rix, J., Sheehy, K., & Simmons, K. (Eds.). (2005). *Curriculum and pedagogy in inclusive education. Values into practice.* London, New York: Routledge, The Open University Press.

Nocera, S. (1988). Sono ancora presenti le scuole speciali? *Problemi di pedagogia, 34*, 55–67.

Nocera, S. (Ed.). (2001). *Il diritto all'integrazione nella scuola dell'autonomia. Gli alunni in situazione di handicap nella normativa scolastica italiana.* Trento: Erickson.

Nocera, S. (2008). La diagnosi, i diritti della persona e l'inclusione. *Integrazione scolastica e sociale, 7*, 33–40.

Nocera, S., & Gherardini, P. (2000). *L'integrazione scolastica delle persone Down. Una ricerca sugli indicatori di qualità in Italia.* Trento: Erickson.

Nussbaum, M. C. (1995). *Women, culture and development: A study of human capabilities.* Oxford: Clarendon.

Nussbaum, M. C. (2000). *Women and human development: The capabilities approach.* Cambridge: Cambridge University Press.

Oakley, A. (1981). Interviewing women: A contradiction in terms. In H. Roberts (Ed.), *Doing feminist research.* London, Boston, Henley: Routledge and Kegan Paul.

OECD. (1994). *The integration of disabled children into mainstream education: Ambitions, theories and practices.* Paris: OECD.

OECD. (1997). *Implementing inclusive education.* Paris: OECD.

OECD. (1999). *Inclusive education at work. Students with disabilities in mainstream schools.* Paris: OECD.

OECD. (2004). *Equity in education. Students with disabilities, learning difficulties and disadvantages. Statistics and indicators.* Paris: OECD.

OECD. (2005). *Students with disabilities, learning difficulties and disadvantages. Statistics and indicators.* Paris: OECD.

O'Hanlon, C. (Ed.). (1995). *Inclusive education in Europe.* London: David Fulton Publishers.

Oliver, M. (1985). The integration-segregation debate: Some sociological considerations. *British Journal of Sociology of Education, 6*, 75–92.

Oliver, M. (1990). *The politics of disablement.* Basingstoke: Macmillan.

Oliver, M. (1992). Changing the social relations of research production. *Disability, Handicap & Society, 7*, 101–114.

Oliver, M. (1996a). A sociology of disability or a disablist sociology? In L. Barton (Ed.), *Disability and society: Emerging issues and insights* (pp. 18–42). Harlow, Essex: Longman.

Oliver, M. (1996b). *Understanding disability: From theory to practice*. Houndsmills, Basingstoke, New York: Palgrave.

Oliver, M. (1997). Emancipatory research: Realistic goal or impossible dream? In C. Barnes & G. Mercer (Eds.), *Doing disability research*. Leeds: The Disability Press.

Oliver, M. (2000). *Decoupling education policy from the economy in the late capitalist societies. Some implications for special education*. Paper presented at the ISEC 2000 'Including the excluded', Manchester.

Oliver, M., & Barnes, C. (1998). *Disabled people and social policy*. Essex & New York: Addison Wesley Longman.

Oliver, M., & Zarb, G. (1989). The politics of disability: A new approach. In L. Barton & M. Oliver (Eds.), *Disability studies: Past, present and future*. Leeds: The Disability Press.

Olssen, M. (2006). *Michel Foucault. Materialism in education*.

Olssen, M., Codd, M., & O'Neill, A. M. (2004). *Education policy: Globalisation, citizenship and democracy*. London, Thousand Oaks, New Delhi: Sage Publications.

OMS. (2002). *Classificazione Internazionale del Funzionamento, della Disabilità e della Salute* (G. Lo Iacono, D. Facchinelli, F. Cretti, F. Banal, Trans.). Trento: Erickson.

OMS. (2007). *ICF-CY/Classificazione Internazionale del Funzionamento, della Disabilità e della Salute - Versione per bambini e adolescenti*. Trento: Erickson.

Onger, G. (Ed.). (2008). *Trent'anni di integrazione scolastica. Ieri, oggi e domani*. Brescia: Vannini Editrice.

Onger, G., & Robazzi, C. (2008). Conoscere l'altro. In G. Onger (Ed.), *Trent'anni di integrazione scolastica. Ieri, oggi e domani*. Brescia: Vannini Editrice.

Oury, F., & Vasquez, A. (1982). *Vers une pédagogie institutionnelle?* Paris: Librairie Francois Maspero.

Ozga, J. (1990). Educational policy analysis and the politics of interpretation. In J. Marshall & M. Peters (Ed.), *Education policy* (pp. 137–153). Cheltenham, UK - Northampton, MA, USA: An Elgar Reference Collection.

Pavone, M. (2002), Le nuove prospettive aperte dall'ICF. *Integrazione scolastica e sociale, 1*, 455–460.

Pavone, M. (2007). La via italiana all'integrazione scolastica degli allievi disabili. Dati quantitativi e qualitativi. In A. Canevaro (Ed.), *L'integrazione scolastica degli alunni con disabilità*. Trento: Erickson.

Pfeiffer, D. (1998). The ICIDH and the need for its revision. *Disability and Society, 13*, 503–523.

Pfeiffer, D. (2000). The devils are in the details: The ICIDH2 and the disability movement. *Disability and Society, 15*, 1079–1082.

Pillow, S. W. (2003). Confession, catharsis, or cure? Rethinking the uses of reflexivity as methodological power in qualitative research. *International Journal of Qualitative Studies in Education, 16*, 175–196.

Polesel, J. (2006). Reform and reaction: Creating new education and training structures in Italy. *Comparative Education, 42*, 549–562.

Popkewitz, S. T., & Brennan, M. (Eds.). (1998). *Foucault's challenge. Discourse, knowledge, and power in education*. New York, London: Teachers College Press.

Popkewitz, S. T., & Brennan, M. (1998). Restructuring of social and political theory in education: Foucault and a social epistemology of school practices. In S. T. Popkewitz & M. Brennan (Eds.), *Foucault's challenge. Discourse, knowledge, and power in education*. New York, London: Teachers College Press.

Prior, L. (1997). Following in Foucault's footsteps. Text and context in qualitative research. In D. Silverman (Ed.), *Qualitative research. Theory, method and practice*. London, Thousand Oaks, New Delhi: Sage Publications.

Putnam, R. D. (1993). *Making democracy work. Civic traditions in modern Italy*. Princeton, NJ: Princeton University Press.

Reiser, R. (2001). The struggle for inclusion: The growth of a movement. In L. Barton (Ed.), *Disability, politics and the struggle for change* (pp. 132–148). London: David Fulton.

REFERENCES

Reiser, R., & Mason, M. (1990). *Disability equality in the classroom: A human rights issue*. London: Inner London Education Authority.

Ricci, C. (1999). L'integrazione della persona in situazione di handicap grave nella prospettiva della psicologia della salute. In D. Ianes & M. Tortello (Eds.), *Handicap e risorse per l'integrazione. Nuovi elementi di Qualità per una scuola inclusiva* (pp. 207–209). Trento: Erickson.

Ricci, C. (2002). L'ICF: quali ricadute? *Integrazione scolastica e sociale, 1*, 440–443.

Ritchie, J., & Spencer, L. (2002). Qualitataive data analysis for applied policy research. In M. A. Huberman & B. M. Miles (Eds.), *The qualitative researcher's companion*. Thousands Oaks, London, New Delhi: Sage Publications.

Rix, J., Simmons, K., Nind, M., & Sheehy, K. (Eds.). (2005). *Policy and power in inclusive education*. London and New York: Routledge Falmer.

Robson, C. (2002). *Real world research* (2nd ed.). Oxford: Blackwells.

Rodger, J. J. (2004). *Il nuovo welfare societario* (F. Folgheraiter & M. Raineri, Trans.). Trento: Erickson.

Rose, R. (2001). Special educational needs. In D. Hill & M. Cole (Eds.), *Schooling and equality. Fact, concept and policy* (pp. 231–248). London: Kogan Page.

Rossignol, C. (2002). La "Classification" dite CIF proposée par l'OMS peut-elle avoir une portée scientifique? *Handicap. Revue de sciences humaines et sociales, 94–95*, 51–93.

Rugiu, S. A. (1979). *Storia sociale dell'educazione*. Milano: Principato Editore.

Rustemier, S., & Booth, T. (2005). *Learning about the index in use: A study of the use the index for inclusion in schools and LEAs in England*. Bristol: CSIE.

Ryan, W. G., & Bernard, H. R. (2003). Data management and analysis methods. In K. N. Denzin & S. Y. Lincoln (Eds.), *Collecting and interpreting qualitative materials*. Thousand Oaks, London, New Delhi: Sage Publications.

Sbarbati, L. (Ed.). (1998). *Handicap e integrazione scolastica. Venti anni di esperienze*. Roma: Armando Editore.

Sclavi, M. (2000). *Arte di ascoltare e mondi possibili: come si esce dalle cornici di cui siamo parte*. Milano: Le Vespe.

Scull, A. T. (1979). *Museums of madness. The social organisation of insanity in 19th century England*. London: Penguin Books Ltd.

Scuola di Barbiana. (1996). *Lettera a una professoressa*. Firenze: Libreria Editrice Fiorentina.

Sebba, J., & Sachdev, D. (1997). *What works in inclusive education?* Barkingside: Barnados.

Segal, P., Maigne, M., & Gautier, M. (2003). *La compensation du handicap en Italie*. Paris: CTNERHI.

Selleri, G. (1987). Trent'anni per la cultura dell'handicap e l'integrazione: dalla beneficenza pubblica alla crisi dello stato sociale. *Orizzonti Aperti, 4/5/6*. Retrieved May 24, 2008, from http://www.handybo.it/news_crh/culturadell%27handicap.rtf

Sen, A. (1992). *Inequality Re-examined*. New York, Oxford: Russell Sage Foundation and Clarendon Press.

Shakespeare, T. (1996). Disability, identity and difference. In C. Barnes & G. Mercer (Eds.), *Exploring the divide* (pp. chapter 6). Leeds: The Disability Press.

Shakespeare, T., & Watson, N. (1997). Defending the social model. *Disability and Society, 12*, 297–300.

Shakespeare, T., & Watson, N. (2002). The social model of disability: An outdated ideology? *Research in Social Science and Disability, 2*, 9–28.

Simon, B. (1999). Why no pedagogy in England? In J. Leach & B. Moon (Eds.), *Learners and pedagogy* (pp. 34–45). London: Paul Chapman Publishing Ltd.

Skeggs, B. (1995). Situating the production of feminist ethnography. In M. Maynard & J. Purvis (Eds.), *Researching women's lives from a feminist perspective*. London: Taylor and Francis.

Slee, R. (1993a). Inclusive learning initiatives: Educational policy lessons from the field. In R. Slee (Ed.), *Is there a desk with my name on it? The politics of integration* (pp. 185–200). London, Washington, DC: The Falmer Press.

Slee, R. (1993b). The politics of integration - new sites for old practices? *Disability, Handicap & Society, 8*, 351–360.

Slee, R. (1996). Clauses of conditionality: The 'reasonable' accommodation of language. In L. Barton (Ed.), *Disability and society. Emerging issues and insights* (pp. 107–122). Harlow, Essex: Longman.

Slee, R. (1998). High reliability organisations and liability students. The politics of recognition. In R. Slee, G. Weiner, & S. Tomlinson (Eds.), *School effectiveness for whom? Challenges to the school effectiveness and school improvement movements* (pp. 101–114). London: The Falmer Press.

Slee, R. (2001a). Driven to the margins: Disabled students, inclusive schooling and the politics of possibility. *Cambridge Journal of Education, 31*, 385–397.

Slee, R. (2001b). Inclusion in practice: Does practice make perfect? *Educational Review, 53*, 113–123.

Slee, R. (2003). Teacher education, government and inclusive schooling: The politics of the Faustian Waltz. In J. Allan (Ed.), *Inclusion, participation and democracy: What is the purpose?* Dordrecht, Boston, London: Kluwer Academic Publishers.

Slee, R. (2007). It's a Fit-up! Inclusive education, higher education, policy and the discordant voice. In L. Barton & F. Armstrong (Eds.), *Policy, experience and change: Cross cultural reflections on inclusive education.* Dordrecht: Springer.

Slee, R., & Allan, J. (2001). Excluding the included: A reconsideration of inclusive education. *International Studies in Sociology of Education, 11*, 173–192.

Smith, A. J., Jarman, M., & Osborn, M. (1999). Doing interpretative phenomenological analysis. In M. Murray & K. Chamberlain (Eds), *Qualitative health psychology. Theories and methods.* London: Sage Publications.

Stellacci, L. (2003). *Una scuola a misura di tutti e di tutte, in una regione accogliente.* Rimini: CSA.

Stiker, H.-J. (1999). *A history of disability* (W. Sayers, Trans.). Michigan Press.

Stone, A. D. (1984). *The disabled state.* Houndsmills, Basingstore, Hampshire, London: Macmillan.

Strauss, A. L. (1987). *Qualitative analysis for social scientists.* Cambridge, UK: Cambridge University Press.

Taylor, S. (1997). Critical policy analysis: Exploring contexts, texts and consequences. *Discourse: Studies in the Cultural Politics of Education, 18*, 23–35.

Taylor, S. (2001). Locating and conducting discourse analytic research. In M. Wetherell, S. Taylor, & J. Simeon, Y. (Eds.), *Discourse as data: A guide for analysis.* London: The Open University.

Terzi, L. (2005a). Beyond the Dilemma of difference: The capability approach to disability and special educational needs. *Journal of Philosophy of Education, 39*, 443–458.

Terzi, L. (2005b). *Equality, capability and social justice in education: Re-examining disability and special educational needs.* Unpublished Ph.D Thesis, Institute of Education, London.

Terzi, L. (2007). Beyond the dilemma of difference. In R. Cigman (Ed.), *Included or excluded? The challenge of the mainstream for some SEN children.* London, New York: Routledge.

Terzi, L. (2008). *Justice and equality in education.* London, New York: Continuum.

Tescari, B. (2004). *Ghetto per sani. Fame di liberta.* Roma: Azienda Grafica Meschini.

Thomas, C. (1999). *Female forms. Experiencing and understanding disability.* Buckingham, Philadelphia: Open University Press.

Thomas, C. (2001). Feminism and disability: The theoretical and political significance of the personal and the experiential. In L. Barton (Ed.), *Disability, politics and the struggle for change.* London: David Fulton Publishers.

Thomas, C. (2002). Disability theory: Key ideas, issues and thinkers. In C. Barnes, M. Oliver, & L. Barton (Eds.), *Disability studies today* (pp. 38–57). Cambridge: Polity Press.

Thomas, G., & Glenny, G. (2005). Thinking about inclusion. Whose reasons? What evidence? In K. Sheehy, M. Nind, J. Rix, & K. Simmons (Eds.), *Ethics and research in inclusive education. Values into practice.* London and New York: Routledge Falmer - Open University Press.

Thomas, G., & Loxley, A. (2001). *Deconstructing special education and constructing inclusion.* Buckingham, Philadelphia: Open University Press.

Tinagli, P. (2003). *Iniziative Istituzionali del Ministero Istruzione Università e Ricerca a favore degli alunni in situazione di handicap nella prospettiva europea.* Rome: Ministero Istruzione Università Ricerca.

Tomlinson, S. (1982). *A sociology of special education.* London, Boston, Henley: Routledge & Kegan Paul.

REFERENCES

Tremain, S. (Ed.). (2005). *Foucault and the government of disability*. United States of America: University of Michigan.

UNESCO. (1990). *Education for all: Meeting basic learning needs*. Jomtien: UNESCO.

UNESCO. (1994). *The Salamanca statement and framework for action on special needs education*. Salamanca: UNESCO.

UNESCO. (2000). *The dakar framework for action. Education for all: Meeting our collective commitments*. Dakar: UNESCO.

UNESCO. (2003a). *Open file on inclusive education. Support materials for managers and administrators*. Paris.

UNESCO. (2003b). *Overcoming exclusion through inclusive approaches in education. A challenge and a vision. Conceptual paper*. Paris: Early Childhood and Inclusive Education Basic Education Division - UNESCO. Retrieved May 5, 2008, from http://unesdoc.unesco.org/images/0013/001347/134785e.pdf

UNESCO (2009). *Policy Guidelines on Inclusion in Education*. UNESCO: Paris

United Nations. (1989). *Convention on the rights of the child*. New York: UN.

United Nations. (1993). *Standard rules on the equalization of opportunities for persons with disabilities*. New York: UN.

United Nations. (2003). *Report of the United Nations high commissioner for human rights on progress in the implementation of the recommendations contained in the study on the human rights of persons with disabilities*. New York and Geneva: Economic and Social Council.

United Nations. (2006). *Convention on the rights of persons with Disabilities*. New York. Retrieved 5, 2008, from http://www.un.org/esa/socdev/enable/documents/tccconve.pdf

UPIAS. (1976). *Fundamental principles of disability*. London: Union of the Physically Impaired Against Segregation and the Disability Alliance. Retrieved May 5, 2008, from http://www.leeds.ac.uk/disability-studies/archiveuk/UPIAS/fundamental%20principles.pdf

Vaughn, S., & Schumm, S. J. (1995). Responsible inclusion for students with learning disabilities. *Journal of Learning Disabilities, 28*, 264–270.

Vianello, R. (1990). *L'adolescente con handicap mentale e la sua integrazione scolastica*. Padova: Liviana.

Vianello, R. (1999). Integrazione in Italia: esperienze, documentazione e ricerca. In D. Ianes & M. Tortello (Eds.), *Handicap e risorse per l'integrazione. Nuovi elementi di qualità per una scuola inclusiva* (pp. 65–68). Trento: Erickson.

Vianello, R. (2008). *Diversamente abile? Inclusione? Disabilità intellettive? A proposito della terminologia: Disabilità Intellettive* (online). Retrieved May 4, 2008, from http://www.disabilitaintellettive.it/index.php?option=com_content&task=view&id=398&Itemid=165

Vianello, R,, & Lanfranchi, S. (2009). Genetic Syndromes Causing Mental Retardation: deficit and surplus in school performance and social adaptability compared to cognitive capacity. Life Span and Disability, XII, 1, 41-52

Vlachou, A. (1997). *Struggles for inclusive education*. Buckingham: Open University Press.

Vlachou, A. (2004). Education and inclusive policy-making: Implications for research and practice. *International Journal of Inclusive Education, 8*, 3–21.

Vygotskij, L. S. (1987). *Il processo cognitivo* (C. Ranchetti, Trans.). Milano: Bollati Boringhieri.

Walford, G. (2001). *Doing qualitative educational research. A personal guide to the research process*. London, New York: Continuum.

Warnock, M. (2005). *Special educational needs: A new look*. London: Philosophy of Education Society of Great Britain.

Warnock, M. (2007). Foreword. In R. Cigman (Ed.), *Included or excluded? The challenge of the mainstream for some SEN children*. London, New York: Routledge.

Watkins, A. (Ed.). (2007). *Assessment in inclusive settings. Key issues for policy and practice*. Odense: European Agency for Development in Special Needs Education.

Wedell, K. (2005). Dilemmas in the quest for inclusion. *British Journal of Special Education, 32*, 1–11.

Wellington, J. (2000). *Educational research. Contemporary issues and practical approaches*. London, New York: Continuum.

WHO. (1980). *International classification of impairment, disability and handicap*. Geneva: WHO.

WHO. (2001). *International classification of functioning, disability and health.* Geneva: WHO.

Whyte, W. F. (1943). *Street corner society: The social structure of an Italian slum.* Chicago: University of Chicago Press.

Wiliam, D. (2007). *Assessment for learning: Why, what and how.* London: Institute of Education, University of London.

Wolfensberger, W. (1989). Human service policies: The rhetoric versus the reality. In L. Barton (Ed.), *Disability and dependency.* London, New York, Philadelphia: The Falmer Press.

Yin, K. R. (2003). *Case study research. Design and methods.* Thousand Oaks, London, New Delhi: Sage Publications.

Zappaterra, T. (2003). *Braille e gli altri. Percorsi storici di didattica speciale.* Milano: Unicopli.

Zarb, G. (1992). On the road to Damascus: First steps towards changing the relations of disability research production. *Disability, Handicap & Society, 7,* 125–138.

Žižek, S. (2005, July-August). Against human rights. *New Left Review, 34,* 115–131. Retrieved March 15, 2010, from http://www.reifiedrecords.com/drew/dl/zizekRights.pdf

CPSIA information can be obtained at www.ICGtesting.com
Printed in the USA
LVOW100806220712

291022LV00001B/43/P

9 789460 913402